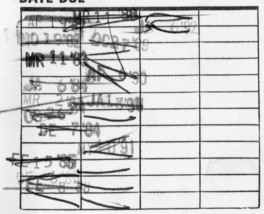

THE BEST SHORT PLAYS 1981

THE BEST SHORT PLAYS *1981*

selected and edited by
STANLEY RICHARDS

with introductions by
RAMON DELGADO

Best Short Plays Series

Chilton Book Company
Radnor, Pennsylvania

e are fully protected under the
America, the British Empire,
other countries of the Interna-
pyright Convention. Permission
10d, must be obtained from the
ION notices at the beginning of

1 2 3 4 5 6 7 8 9 0   0 9 8 7 6 5 4 3 2 1

In Memoriam:
STANLEY RICHARDS
1918–1980

BOOKS AND PLAYS BY STANLEY RICHARDS

BOOKS:

The Best Short Plays, issued annually, 1968–81
Great Musicals of the American Theatre: Volume One
Great Musicals of the American Theatre: Volume Two
Best Plays of the Seventies
America on Stage: Ten Great Plays of American History
The Tony Winners
Best Plays of the Sixties
Twenty One-Act Plays
Best Mystery and Suspense Plays of the Modern Theatre
10 Classic Mystery and Suspense Plays of the Modern Theatre
The Most Popular Plays of the American Theatre
Great Rock Musicals
Modern Short Comedies from Broadway and London
Best Short Plays of the World Theatre: 1968–1973
Best Short Plays of the World Theatre: 1958–1967
Canada on Stage

PLAYS:

Through a Glass, Darkly
August Heat
Sun Deck
Tunnel of Love
Journey to Bahia
O Distant Land
Mood Piece
Mr. Bell's Creation

The Proud Age
Once to Every Boy
Half-Hour, Please
Know Your Neighbor
Gin and Bitterness
The Hills of Bataan
District of Columbia

PLAYS BY RAMON DELGADO:

The Youngest Child of Pablo Peco
Waiting for the Bus
The Little Toy Dog
Once Below A Lighthouse
Sparrows of the Field
The Knight-Mare's Nest

Omega's Ninth
Listen, My Children
A Little Holy Water
The Fabulous Jeromes
The Jerusalem Thorn

CONTENTS

INTRODUCTION

Thousands of play readers and scores of playwrights lost one of their most cherished friends when Stanley Richards died on July 26, 1980.

A man of wide dramatic taste and extensive practical theatre experience, Mr. Richards was the most prolific and widely praised play anthologist of the last thirteen years. His twenty-nine collections won universal raves. *The Writers Guild of America News* called him ". . . easily the best anthologist of plays in America."

Starting with *The Best Short Plays 1968*—a resumption of Margaret Mayorga's series suspended with her retirement in 1962—Mr. Richards reaffirmed a policy of including in each annual volume of the series established playwrights, emerging playwrights and those new voices that evidenced signs of significant developing talent. The production statistics bear out his judgment. With Stanley Richards as editor, *The Best Short Plays* series (including this volume) published 176 plays Of the new dramatists represented, more than a dozen have gone on to national or international recognition. Nearly fifty percent of the plays published were presented in New York —still the nation's theatrical capital—in productions on Broadway, Off- or Off-Off-Broadway. Of the others, a majority were produced in schools, colleges, community and commercial theatres throughout this country and abroad.

Dozens of playwrights have testified to the encouragement and practical suggestions Mr. Richards made, helping them to develop their submissions to a level of excellence meriting publication or production. Playwright Benjamin Bradford (whose *Where Are You Going, Hollis Jay?* appeared in the 1970 volume of this series) once remarked that he had learned more about playwriting from a two hour conversation with Stanley Richards than in several years of study and writing.

When I learned of Stanley's death, I was concerned about the future of this series, for during the past decade many of my directing students had selected their first projects from the varied offerings in Stanley's collections, and my students in playwriting and play analysis had studied the contents and techniques of many of the selections.

I also was interested in helping to preserve the tradition begun in 1919 by Margaret Mayorga with *Representative One-Act Plays by American Authors,* the forerunner of *The Best Short Plays* series. The standards of this tradition were crystalized by Mr. Richards in his introduction to the 1968 volume: "I hope to include plays that are both entertaining and dramatically stimulating. Plays that restore a sense of reality, immediacy, dramatic excitement and personal involvement to the theatre. Plays that convey the author's sense of life to us, for a work of art is a direct extension of the personality of the artist. Plays that offer pertinent commentary and dramatically striking ideas, spoken in original and articulate voices. . . . A play in its highest estate must reveal man's deepest insight and dramatically explore and express those values by which he lives. Without these basic elements of truth and humanity, the theatre is left with nothing more than shallow contrivances."

All of the plays in this volume had been selected by Mr. Richards, and most of the editing on them had been completed before he died. Some of the material for the introductions had been collected but not yet written. My task in bringing this volume to print was to compile the material, write the introductions, and present the volume for publication. This I have done, hopeful of fulfilling Mr. Richards' intentions as closely as possible.

My deep gratitude for his confidence in my ability goes to Warren Bayless, Stanley's agent and friend during the years of Mr. Richards' anthology work. I also extend my thanks to Philip Minges III of Curtis Brown, Ltd. and to the Chilton Book Company for their assistance in contractual and editorial details.

The tradition of *The Best Short Plays* will continue, and my hope is that the present decade will bring to these pages as many exciting new plays and new playwrights as have the last thirteen years under the editorship of Stanley Richards.

RAMON DELGADO
Montclair, New Jersey

Murray Schisgal

THE PUSHCART
PEDDLERS

Murray Schisgal

The whimsical and seemingly random events in the plays of Murray Schisgal are glittering reflections of his multifarious background. Before his writing supported him, he supported it with such odd jobs as setting pins in a bowling alley, playing saxophone and clarinet in a small band, pushing a hand truck in New York's garment district and working as a dress hanger-upper in Klein's Department Store. He was a high school dropout, earning his diploma later in the U.S. Navy, where he became radioman, third class. He attended the Brooklyn Conservatory of Music and Long Island University, received a law degree from Brooklyn Law School, a B.A. from the New School for Social Research, taught English at the James Fenimore Cooper Junior High School in East Harlem, and wrote sixty short stories and three and a half novels—all before the age of thirty-five.

The first productions of his plays suggest the luck of the enchanted. Having written five one-act plays while still employed as a teacher, he confidently quit the security of educating American youth and took off for Spain to continue his playwriting. On his way he left the five short plays with The British Drama League in London, which immediately offered to produce *The Typists* and *The Tiger* in 1960, three years before any of the plays were presented in New York. When the plays were finally staged in the author's home town, they received both the Vernon Rice Award and the Outer Circle Award. His first commercial success, *Luv*, was also first produced in London in 1963, a year before the play opened at the Booth Theatre in New York with Eli Wallach, Anne Jackson, and Alan Arkin, directed by Mike Nichols. Walter Kerr was delighted: ". . . I like Murray Schisgal because he is one step ahead of the avant-garde. . . . If the avant-garde, up to now, has successfully exploded the bright balloons of cheap optimism, Mr. Schisgal is ready to put a pin to the soapy bubbles of cheap pessimism . . . [He] doesn't necessarily deny that things are tough all over; he just sees how preposterous it is that we should take such *pleasure* in painting clouds black."

A steady flow of plays have come bubbling from Mr. Schisgal's artesian well: a collection of one-acts, *Fragments, Windows and Other Plays* (published in 1965); *Jimmy Shine* (published in 1968); *Ducks and Lovers* (published in 1972); *The Chinese and Dr. Fish* (published in 1973); *All American Million-*

aire (published in 1974) and *All Over Town* (published in 1975).

Like much of Schisgal's work, *The Pushcart Peddlers* has a cartoon-like quality. Schisgal sets a familiar American scene and probes the phoniness of our unquestioned shibboleths. In *The Pushcart Peddlers* his satiric pen pricks the gaudy optimism of the newly-arrived immigrant with his dreams of instant capitalistic success and that of a flower girl with stardom's rags-to-riches in her eyes. The play was first produced in November, 1979, at Curt Dempster's Ensemble Studio Theatre with the following cast:

CORNELIUS J. HOLLINGSWORTH III   Fred Kareman
SHIMMEL SHITZMAN   Bernie Mantell
MAGGIE CUTWELL   Mary Catherine Wright

Director: Peter Maloney

Characters:

CORNELIUS J. HOLLINGSWORTH III
SHIMMEL SHITZMAN
MAGGIE CUTWELL

Scene:

Waterfront, New York City.

Time:

Many years ago.

At Rise:

A backdrop on which there is painted almost photographic, a symmetrically designed, Customs House, side and front view: smaller buildings nearby.
Several kegs and wooden crates at both sides of backdrop. Lidded trashcan, downstage.
Sound: waterfront noises, steamship whistle.
Music: in the style of the Ragtime section of Zukerman/Bolling "Suite for Violin and Jazz Piano."
Cornelius, in vest, collarless shirt, baggy pants and a soiled derby, is seated on a wooden box beside his banana-filled pushcart; his legs are crossed and a newspaper is spread in front of his face.
Shimmel enters, looks about, and proceeds across stage. He carries a battered suitcase, wears a threadbare suit, open-necked shirt and wilted tie, a soft cap on his head.
Music out.

CORNELIUS: (As Shimmel passes, peeks out from behind newspaper) Bananas. (Shimmel stops, turns to Cornelius, waits in vain for him to speak further, then moves on. Cornelius, peeking out from behind newspaper) Bananas.

SHIMMEL: (*Stops again*) Excuse me.

CORNELIUS: (*Rises; folds and puts newspaper on pushcart; expansively*) What a day! What a beautiful day. When I got up this morning I said to myself, "This is going to be one rotten day." But look at it. Look for yourself. It's a beautiful day. Absolutely beautiful. It just goes to show you. You can't be too smart in this world. (*Snaps open paper bag*) How many?

SHIMMEL: How many what?

CORNELIUS: How many bananas do you want?

SHIMMEL: I don't want any bananas.

CORNELIUS: You don't want any bananas?

SHIMMEL: (*Shakes his head*) No.

CORNELIUS: Then why did you disturb me?

SHIMMEL: I thought you were talking to me.

CORNELIUS: You thought . . . ? Why should I talk to you? Are you a millionaire? (*Shimmel shakes his head*) Are you a politician? (*Shimmel shakes his head*) Are you a celebrity? (*Shimmel shakes his head*) Then why should I talk to you?

SHIMMEL: I . . . I'm sorry. I made a mistake. It is a beautiful day. A wonderful day. Excuse me. (*He starts off*)

CORNELIUS: (*Returns paper bag*) The nerve of some people. Coming over and making a spectacle of themselves. Hey, you!

SHIMMEL: (*Runs to him*) Yes?

CORNELIUS: Who are you, anyway?

SHIMMEL: (*Removes cap, pushes it into jacket pocket*) Shitzman. Shimmel Shitzman.

CORNELIUS: (*Amazed*) You're Shimmel Shitzman?

SHIMMEL: Do you know me?

CORNELIUS: Why should I know you? Are you a millionaire? (*Shimmel shakes his head*) Are you a politician? (*Shimmel shakes his head*) Are you a celebrity? (*Shimmel shakes his head*) Then why should I know you?

SHIMMEL: I thought you . . .

CORNELIUS: Where are you from, Shimmel Shitzman?

SHIMMEL: From the vicinity of Kovno-Vilna.

CORNELIUS: (*Amazed*) You're from the vicinity of Kovno-Vilna?

SHIMMEL: Are you from the vicinity of Kovno-Vilna?

CORNELIUS: (*Dusts bananas with feather mop*) As a matter of fact, I'm not. I'm from the vicinity of Minsk-Pinsk.

SHIMMEL: (*Enthusiastically*) Minsk-Pinsk! Why, that's practically walking distance from the vicinity of Kovno-Vilna. We're practically neighbors!

CORNELIUS: Does that surprise you?

SHIMMEL: In all honesty, it does. You're the first person I talked to since I got off the boat. And to talk to someone who was practically my neighbor in the old country, that's what I call a stroke of good luck. Can I ask you a few impersonal questions, neighbor?

CORNELIUS: (*Sits*) So long as you don't take up too much of my time, neighbor. You happen to have caught me during my rush hour.

SHIMMEL: Business is good?

CORNELIUS: Business is excellent. Couldn't be better.

SHIMMEL: When did you arrive from Minsk-Pinsk?

CORNELIUS: Is today Tuesday or Wednesday?

SHIMMEL: Wednesday.

CORNELIUS: Then I arrived yesterday.

SHIMMEL: (*Puts suitcase down*) You arrived yesterday from Minsk-Pinsk?

CORNELIUS: That's correct.

SHIMMEL: And you're in business for yourself already?

CORNELIUS: That's correct. (*He lights a cigar butt*)

SHIMMEL: Why, that's wonderful, marvelous!

CORNELIUS: You think that's wonderful, marvelous? I heard of a man from the vicinity of Ozrokow-Pruszkow who arrived here in the morning and owned two factories, three warehouses and a hotel in the Catskill Mountains before he sat down for lunch!

SHIMMEL: Fantastic! What a country this is! What a great country. I can't wait to get started myself, but . .

CORNELIUS: But what?

SHIMMEL: I don't know where to begin.

CORNELIUS: Well, since we're practically from the same vicinity . . . maybe I can give you a hint or two.

SHIMMEL: (*Sits on suitcase*) I would appreciate that more than anything in the world.

CORNELIUS: (*With emphasis*) Are you listening?

SHIMMEL: I'm listening.

CORNELIUS: Are you paying attention?

SHIMMEL: I'm paying attention.

CORNELIUS: First thing you have to do . . .

SHIMMEL: Yes?

CORNELIUS: Is buy yourself an American name.

SHIMMEL: Buy myself an American name?

CORNELIUS: That's absolutely essential, (*Steps on cigar butt; takes slips of papers from vest pocket*) And I'll tell you something else, neighbor: this is your lucky day. It so happens I have several American names that are up for sale.

SHIMMEL: But what's wrong with Shimmel Shitzman?

CORNELIUS: Shimmel Shitzman? They'll laugh you out of the country with a name like that. Do you know what my name was when I got off the boat? (*Shimmel shakes his head*) Elias Crapavarnishkes.

SHIMMEL: Crapavarnishkes. That's not a bad name. There was a judge from the vicinity of Lvov who had the name Crapavarnishkes. He was a very respected man.

CORNELIUS: Your Judge Crapavarnishkes couldn't get a job as a street cleaner here. The first thing I did when I got off the boat was to buy myself a brand new legitimate name. And since then I've been prospering beyond my wildest dreams.

SHIMMEL: That's fantastic. What is your American name?

CORNELIUS: (*Slight English accent*) Cornelius J. Hollingsworth.

SHIMMEL.   Wow!

CORNELIUS: The Third.

SHIMMEL: The Third?

CORNELIUS: That's correct. It cost me fifteen dollars with the middle initial and the Third thrown in. It was the only one like it they had. I could have gotten John Smith for fifty cents, but I wouldn't have any part of it. Well, what do you say, Mr. Shitzman? (*Reading from slips of paper*) I have Andrew Hamilton for five dollars, Sylvester Peterson for six-fifty, Thomas Hathaway, six dollars and fifteen cents, Roger Williams Carnegie, five seventy-five, Samuel P. Stone, five dollars without the tax . . .

SHIMMEL: I'm sorry, Mr. Hollingsworth. I couldn't change my name. It's been in my family for generations. I was born a Shitzman and I guess I'll have to die a Shitzman.

CORNELIUS: (*Returning slips of paper to vest pocket*) Have it your own way. But don't say I didn't try to help you. It just goes to show: mind your own business and you're better off. (*Indignantly, he spreads newspaper in front of his face*)

SHIMMEL: (*Rises; lifts suitcase*) Mr. Hollingsworth?

CORNELIUS: (*Behind newspaper*) What is it now?

SHIMMEL: Can I ask you one more question?

CORNELIUS: (*Behind newspaper*) I told you I was busy! I don't have all day to sit here and chat with you!

SHIMMEL: One more question and I won't bother you any more, I promise.

CORNELIUS: (*Puts newspaper aside*) Go on. What is it? What is it?

SHIMMEL: (*Puts suitcase down*) Where do you think I should look for a job?

CORNELIUS: A job? Why do you want to look for a job?

SHIMMEL: To work. To earn money . . .

CORNELIUS: Ridiculous. Nobody comes to this country to look for a job. There's no future in it. You have to go into business for yourself. It's the only decent way to make a living here.

SHIMMEL: (*Sits on suitcase*) But I don't know anything about going into business. I'm a worker. I have experience as a tinsmith, a carpenter, a . . .

CORNELIUS: You people from the vicinity of Kovno-Vilna are all a bunch of blockheads! What did I know about going into business when I got off the boat? Nothing. Absolutely nothing. I was a shoemaker, a leather-stitcher. But did I let that stop me? Not on your life. I used my head and here I am: in business for myself!

SHIMMEL: But what kind of business could I get into? I don't have much capital . . .

CORNELIUS: Ohhh, there are plenty of good profitable businesses you can go into. Why don't you open your eyes and look around and see what's available? (*As Shimmel rises and "looks around," Cornelius plants a FOR SALE on his pushcart*) If I were you, Mr. Shitzman, I'd grab the first business up for sale and get right to work. I wouldn't waste any time. Things happen fast in this country. Very fast. You have to stay up on your toes and use your old noodle! (*He spreads newspaper in front of his face*)

SHIMMEL: (*Turns to see sign on pushcart*) Mr. Hollingsworth?

CORNELIUS: (*Behind newspaper*) Yes?

SHIMMEL: Is your . . . business up for sale?

CORNELIUS: (*Folds newspaper; stares at FOR SALE sign*) Hmmmmm. As a matter of fact, it is.

SHIMMEL: Do you think I could make a go of it?

CORNELIUS: (*Puts newspaper aside; rises*) You?

SHIMMEL: (*Nods*) Me.

CORNELIUS: Hmmmmm. That's a *tough* question. Let me hear you say: bananas.

SHIMMEL: Bananas.

CORNELIUS: Hmmmmm. You're not without talent. Let me hear you say: bananas, bananas, get your fresh ripe bananas!

SHIMMEL: Bananas, bananas, get your fresh ripe bananas!

CORNELIUS: Try it a little louder and try to speak out of the side of your mouth so your voice has a distinctive quality: bananas, bananas, get your fresh ripe bananas!

SHIMMEL: (*Imitating him: from the side of his mouth, jerking his head*) Bananas, bananas, get your fresh ripe bananas!

CORNELIUS: No, no, your arms have to swing out, from the side, as if you own the whole street. And kick your leg up a little. Like this. (*Demonstrating: throws arms out, kicks up one leg, tips derby on last word*) Bananas, bananas, get your fresh ripe bananas! (*To Shimmel*) Try it. (*He puts derby on Shimmel's head; sits on trash can*)

SHIMMEL: (*Imitating him*) Bananas, bananas, get your fresh ripe bananas! (*Tips derby*)

CORNELIUS: Excellent. Excellent. How did it feel?

SHIMMEL: Fine. It felt fine.

CORNELIUS: Were you relaxed? Were you comfortable?

SHIMMEL: I was very relaxed and comfortable.

CORNELIUS: (*Rises*) I'm going to tell you something now, Mr. Shitzman: between the two of us and the pushcart, you'll make a fortune in this business.

SHIMMEL: (*Excitedly*) You think so?

CORNELIUS: (*Takes derby from Shimmel's head; puts it on*) I know so. It's a definite positive.

SHIMMEL: How much would it cost me?

CORNELIUS: (*Moves to pushcart; arms outspread*) The whooole business?

SHIMMEL: (*Nods*) The whole business.

CORNELIUS: Hmmmmm. I could . . . no, no, I couldn't do that. We're practically from the same vicinity. Let me ask you this, Mr. Shitzman. How much do you have?

SHIMMEL: I have exactly . . . (*Takes out change purse*) Forty-three dollars and twenty-five cents.

CORNELIUS: Could you raise another six dollars and seventy-five cents by five o'clock?

SHIMMEL: (*Sits on trash can*) How? I don't know anyone here.

CORNELIUS: (*Sits on box*) What a shame! I couldn't possibly sell for under fifty dollars unless . . . (*Rises*)

SHIMMEL: (*Rises*) Unless what?

CORNELIUS: Unless I took a bunch of bananas to make up the difference.

SHIMMEL: A bunch of bananas is worth six dollars and seventy-five cents?

CORNELIUS: (*He picks up a bunch of bananas*) Are you serious? Do you know what they call a bunch of bananas in this country? (*Shimmel shakes his head. Cornelius holds out bananas, pointed upwards*) Goldfingers.

SHIMMEL: That's fantastic! Here you are, Mr. Hollingsworth. (*Gives him money*) I'm anxious to get right to work. Do I need any papers to prove ownership?

CORNELIUS: (*Bananas under arm*) You'll find them under the fifth banana in the fourth row from the left. (*Shakes his hand*) Congratulations Mr. Shitzman. And the best of everything to you.

SHIMMEL: Thank you. Thank you, Mr. Hollingsworth.

CORNELIUS: (*Moving off*) I have to be off now. If you sell out, go to Pier 26 and ask for Pete. He'll give you a fair shake.

SHIMMEL: (*Shouts after him*) Thanks again, Mr. Hollingsworth. And drop around and say hello once in a while! (*Music. Shimmel puts on cap, carries suitcase behind pushcart, places FOR SALE sign on top of it; he then examines pushcart, proudly, with proprietary air; he dusts off bananas with feather mop, dusts off his jacket, looks about as if he owns the whole street. He suddenly shouts, swinging his arms, kicks up a leg, in imitation of Cornelius*) Bananas, bananas, get your fresh ripe bananas! (*He runs to pushcart, snaps open a paper bag, as if expecting an avalanche of customers. Undismayed he returns paper bag, sits on box, crossing his legs, and spreads the newspaper in front of his face. Offstage, Cornelius shouts, "Bananas, bananas, get your fresh ripe bananas!" Shimmel lowers his newspaper and gapes in astonishment as Cornelius rolls in a second pushcart, an exact replica of the one he sold to him, shouting, two or three times more, "Bananas, bananas, get your fresh ripe bananas!" Cornelius stops his pushcart parallel to Shim-*

mel's, removes a wooden box from it, sits down and unfolds a newspaper in front of his face. Music out. Shimmel removes his cap, speaks softly, uncertainly) Mr. Hollingsworth?

CORNELIUS: *(Behind newspaper)* Yes?

SHIMMEL: You're not staying here, are you?

CORNELIUS: *(Behind newspaper)* Of course I'm staying here. *(Reads aloud)* Hmmmmm. This is interesting. "Bride hurls wedding cake at groom for criticizing her dress. Brawl ensues." *(He hawks a laugh)*

SHIMMEL: But . . .

CORNELIUS: But what?

SHIMMEL: But can we both make a living selling the same merchandise at the same location?

CORNELIUS: *(Puts newspaper aside; rises)* Unfortunately we can't. The competition will force us to lower the price and we'll probably have to begin bankruptcy proceedings in a matter of days. *(Shouts)* Bananas, bananas!

SHIMMEL: *(Rises; desperately)* Mr. Hollingsworth!

CORNELIUS: What is it now?

SHIMMEL: I don't want to sound rude, but if we both can't make a living here, why don't you be considerate and go somewhere else?

CORNELIUS: Why don't I . . . ? *(Sharply)* Why don't you be considerate and go somewhere else?

SHIMMEL: It was my understanding when you sold me this business that I would be the only one at this location. Otherwise I can assure you, I would have thought twice about buying it!

CORNELIUS: Ohhh, it was your understanding! But I didn't say anything to that effect, did I?

SHIMMEL: You didn't have to . . .

CORNELIUS: This is a free country, Mr. Shitzman, and I have as much right to sell at this location as you have! *(Shouts)* Bananas, bananas!

SHIMMEL: Can't we talk about it? *(Shouts in a panic)* Bananas, bananas!

CORNELIUS: Talk, who's stopping you? *(Shouts)* Bananas, bananas!

SHIMMEL: I'm new here, Mr. Hollingsworth. I don't know this city! *(Shouts)* Bananas, bananas!

CORNELIUS: Mr. Shitzman, I have to make a living, too. My

customers expect to find me here and I'm not disappointing them! Not for you or the King of Siam! (*Shouts*) Bananas, bananas!

SHIMMEL: Mr. Hollingsworth, I gave you my last penny! I trusted you! (*Shouts*) Bananas, bananas!

CORNELIUS: I can't help you more than I did, Mr. Shitzman! (*Shouts*) Bananas! Bana . . . (*Suddenly turns to Shimmel*) Unless . . .

SHIMMEL: (*Eagerly*) Unless what?

CORNELIUS: Unless we went into partnership.

SHIMMEL: Partnership?

CORNELIUS: (*Nods*) The two of us.

SHIMMEL: Why, that would be wonderful, Mr. . . .

CORNELIUS: (*Grins*) Call me Cornelius.

SHIMMEL: Cornelius. Cornelius, that would be wonderful! It would solve all our problems! We could work together, cooperate . . .

CORNELIUS: There's only one thing that stands in the way.

SHIMMEL: What's that?

CORNELIUS: (*Sits on trash can*) Money.

SHIMMEL: Money?

CORNELIUS: That's correct. Money. You don't expect us to become full and equal partners with all my experience, do you?

SHIMMEL: But I don't have any money left, Mr. . . . Cornelius. I gave you my last penny, word of honor. (*He raises his hand*)

CORNELIUS: Can't you borrow some from friends or relatives or a philanthropic organization?

SHIMMEL: (*Sits on box*) Impossible I told you, I don't know anyone here.

CORNELIUS: (*Rises*) Then there's only one thing for us to do.

SHIMMEL: (*Rises*) What's that?

CORNELIUS: Negotiate.

SHIMMEL: Can we negotiate without money?

CORNELIUS: Of course.

SHIMMEL: How do we do it?

CORNELIUS: (*Using his hands*) It's simple. You make an offer. I refuse your offer and make a counter-offer. You refuse my counter-offer and make a counter-counter-offer of your own. I refuse your counter-counter-offer and I make what is called a proposal which leads you to make a counter-proposal and so on and so forth and so on and so forth until we whittle the difference to nil and come to equitable terms.

SHIMMEL: But I still don't have any money.

CORNELIUS: Who's talking about money! Jesus Christ, you are a dumb-dumb. We negotiate percentages! (*Throws arms out at one pushcart, then the other*) How much of the business do you own in contradistinction to how much of the business do I own! (*He sits on box, crosses legs, puts newspaper in front of his face*) Make me an offer.

SHIMMEL: On a percentage of the business?

CORNELIUS: (*Behind newspaper*) That's correct. Do it formally.

SHIMMEL: Yes, sir. (*Puts on cap, brushes jacket; clears throat*) Excuse me, Mr. Hollingsworth.

CORNELIUS: (*Newspaper on lap; innocently*) Did you wish to speak to me, sir?

SHIMMEL: Yes, sir. About the possibility of our going into partnership, sir. I make an offer that you receive fifty percent of the business and I receive fifty percent of the business . . . sir.

CORNELIUS: What about my superior experience, sir?

SHIMMEL: I can learn the business very quickly and if I work twice as hard that will offset the difference, sir.

CORNELIUS: No deal, sir. I respectfully decline your offer. (*Newspaper in front of his face*)

SHIMMEL: (*Clears throat; whispers*) You make your counter-offer now. (*No response*) I make my offer, fifty-fifty, you're supposed to make a counter-offer. (*No response; loudly*) Aren't you going to make me a counter-offer, sir? Did I do anything improper, sir? (*Desperately*) Mr. Hollingsworth, we have to reach an agreement! You yourself said we both can't make a living here! For God's sake, make me a counter-offer!

CORNELIUS: (*Lowers newspaper*) Bananas, ripe lovely bananas here! (*Newspaper in front of his face*)

SHIMMEL: This is crazy! You're being unfair, unreasonable! I . . . (*Resigned to it*) All right, sixty-forty! Sixty for you, forty for me. Is it a deal, sir?

CORNELIUS: (*Puts newspaper aside: shouts*) Bananas, get your ripe lovely bananas here! (*Without looking at him; coaching him*) Get down on your knees. Beg me. Tell me how hard up you are. Tell me your family depends on you for support. Get to me emotionally. (*Shouts*) Bananas, bananas here! Get your ripe bananas!

SHIMMEL: (*On his knees*) Mr. Hollingsworth, I beg you to consider my offer. I think it's very equitable. Besides, I'm broke. I don't have a penny. I don't have money to buy dinner tonight . . . I don't have a roof over my head . . . (*Cornelius rises, paces. Shimmel is emotional indeed, on the verge of tears, building his lines to a crescendo*) Mr. Hollingsworth, my family is still in the old country. They're depending on me to send them something each week. I have an elderly father who's confined to his bed. My mother suffers from arthritis and bursitis. My two little sisters don't have clothes to wear to school. My baby brother, my little baby brother . . . (*He breaks into sobs*)

CORNELIUS: (*Tears streaming down his cheeks*) What a terrible story. What a tragedy. How old is your little baby brother?

SHIMMEL: (*Weeping*) Who knows? Who knows?

CORNELIUS: (*Weeping*) What dis-ease, what afflic-tion does he have?

SHIMMEL: (*Weeping; louder*) Who knows? Who knows?

CORNELIUS: (*Weeping*) Your two little sisters . . .

SHIMMEL: (*Weeping; still louder*) My two little sisters . . . without clothes!

CORNELIUS: (*Weeping*) Don't say another word, Shimmel. Please, please don't! Not another word! I'll help you. I'll do whatever you want.

SHIMMEL: (*Rises*) Does that mean we're partners?

CORNELIUS: Sixty-forty?

SHIMMEL: (*Nods*) Sixty-forty!

CORNELIUS: (*Embracing him*) Partner!

SHIMMEL: Thank you, Cornelius; thank you.

CORNELIUS: (*Breaks away, takes out handkerchief, blows his nose*) Oh, boy, that was a good cry. Oh, boy. I have to admit . . . I enjoyed it thoroughly.

SHIMMEL: (*Wiping his eyes*) I did, too. I didn't know that negotiations could be so emotional.

CORNELIUS: There's a lot you have to learn, partner. But don't worry. I'll teach you every aspect of this business. From now on your gain becomes under contract my profit. Okay, now let's get to work. No more horsing around.

(*Music. Cornelius sits down on box, crosses legs, spreads newspaper in front of his face. Shimmel, imitating him, does likewise.*

Cornelius soon rises, yawns, stretches his arms over his head, shakes out one leg, then the other, looks about, then flaps handkerchief over top of wooden box before sitting down, spreading newspaper in front of his face. Shimmel does likewise, but before spreading newspaper in front of his face, speaks. Music out)

SHIMMEL: Cornelius?

CORNELIUS: *(Behind newspaper)* Yes?

SHIMMEL: How's business?

CORNELIUS: *(Newspaper on lap)* Excellent. Excellent. If it keeps up at this rate, I think we should buy another pushcart.

SHIMMEL: Can we afford it?

CORNELIUS: What a question.

SHIMMEL: I didn't know we were that successful.

CORNELIUS: If I told you how successful we were, Shimmel, you'd get a swollen head, so let's not discuss it and just keep working.

SHIMMEL: I will. I promise. You'll get nothing but hard work from me.

CORNELIUS: That's what I expect from you. Now let's get to work.

(They both spread their newspapers in front of their faces. Romantic, lyrical music. Maggie Cutwell, a young, very pretty girl, in a shapeless black frock, enters, carrying a tray of small bunches of colorful flowers strapped around her neck. She walks with her hand held slightly in front of her)

MAGGIE: *(In a sweet, angelic voice)* Flowers. Flowers. Pretty flowers for sale. Fresh, pretty flowers. *(She doesn't turn to the men but stands at the side of Shimmel's pushcart, staring forward. She wipes her perspiring face with a rag. Music out)*

SHIMMEL: *(Whispers; puts newspaper aside)* Cornelius? Do you see that?

CORNELIUS: *(Puts newspaper aside)* Oh, yes.

SHIMMEL: She's beautiful, isn't she?

CORNELIUS: I've seen better heads on cabbages. But it's a pity, just the same.

SHIMMEL: What's a pity?

CORNELIUS: She's blind.

SHIMMEL: Is she?

CORNELIUS: All the flower girls are blind in this country.

SHIMMEL: That is a pity. She looks destitute. She looks like she hasn't had a piece of food in her mouth all day. Cornelius, can I get a credit for one banana?

CORNELIUS: (*Makes an entry in notebook*) If you want to be extravagant . . .

SHIMMEL: Thank you. (*He takes banana from pushcart and moves to Maggie. She doesn't turn to look at him. Gently he places the banana on her flower tray; returns to his seat*)

MAGGIE: (*Looks down at banana; shouts*) Get your fucking banana off my fucking flowers!

SHIMMEL: (*Jumps up, retrieves banana*) Forgive me. I . . . I thought you were blind.

MAGGIE: I'll give you blind in a minute. I'll poke out both your eyes and feed 'em to the cats!

SHIMMEL: But I . . .

MAGGIE: I know what you're after, Buster! If I wanted to be a whore, I wouldn't be selling these fucking flowers!

SHIMMEL: You're mistaken, believe me. I only wanted to help you.

MAGGIE: Yeah, and how the hell were you gonna do that? By slipping me a banana?

SHIMMEL: I thought you were hungry.

MAGGIE: I don't need your lousy banana. If I'm hungry, I know where to eat. I've been taking care of myself since I'm six years old and I haven't starved to death yet!

SHIMMEL: You're an orphan?

MAGGIE: You bet your sweet ass!

SHIMMEL: I'm sorry. Life must have been difficult for you.

MAGGIE: I got no complaints. How about buying a bunch of these stinkweeds for your girl friend?

SHIMMEL: I'm afraid I have no money. (*Laughs self-consciously*) I have no girl friend either,

MAGGIE: That figures, you crumb-bum, you creep! Wasting a girl's time for nothing. I oughta call the police. I oughta bop you in the nose. (*Shouts as she forces him back so that he sits on trash can*) Get away from me! I hate your lousy guts! (*Suddenly in a sweet, angelic voice*) Flowers. Pretty flowers for sale. Fresh pretty flowers. (*Cornelius rises, derby in hand; he moves to Maggie, speaks with great formality*)

CORNELIUS: Allow me to apologize for my partner, ma'am. He's new here. He has no sense of propriety.

MAGGIE: They should send him back where he came from, the creep! Doesn't he have the decency to introduce himself like a gentleman? Did his parents name him before they dumped him into a garbage can?

CORNELIUS: His name is Shitzman. Shimmel Shitzman.
(Shimmel stands as if expecting an introduction)
MAGGIE: Shitzman! Shimmel Shitzman! *(She breaks out into laughter)* It fits him. It fits him perfectly! *(To Shimmel)* Shitzman. Mr. Shitzman! *(And she laughs again)*
(Shimmel sits down on trashcan, dejectedly)
CORNELIUS: *(Bows)* Perhaps you'd be good enough to permit me to introduce myself to you, ma'am. I am Cornelius J. Hollingsworth, the Third.
MAGGIE: *(Curtsies a bit)* Pleased to make your acquaintance, Mr. Hollingsworth. I am Maggie Cutwell and although I find it necessary to sell flowers in order to sustain myself, I am by profession an actress, a thespian, a tap dancer, a toe dancer, and a highly regarded chanteuse.
CORNELIUS: All good fortune to you, Miss Cutwell. I am myself in the banana business at present, but it is merely transitional. My one true and genuine ambition is to gain a seat on the Stock Exchange and invest substantial sums of money in musical comedy productions. *(Puts on derby)*
MAGGIE: Am I to believe that it is your intention to become a theatrical producer?
CORNELIUS: Precisely, Miss Cutwell, *(Picks up a banana)* May I offer you a banana?
MAGGIE: *(Takes it from him)* I will be happy to take your banana. Mr. Hollingsworth, but I will never take his banana. *(To Shimmel)* Never! Not even if it was covered with diamonds!
CORNELIUS: I am doing all I can for him, Miss Cutwell, but it's a sad, a terribly sad and tragic story.
MAGGIE: I'm sure it is.
CORNELIUS: How much are your flowers, Miss Cutwell?
MAGGIE: These are ten cents a bunch, and those wilted ones on the side are three cents a bunch.
CORNELIUS: I would like to purchase two ten cent bunches, please. *(She hands them to him; he gives her the coins)* Thank you. Here's your money and these . . . these are for you. *(Gallantly he hands her back the flowers. He then passes Shimmel, extending his arms as if to say, "See how easy it is?")*
MAGGIE: You are a very kind person, I can see that right away. Mr. Hollingsworth, it may be premature of me to suggest, but in the event you actually become a theatrical producer in the foreseeable future, could you possibly keep me in mind for a part in one of your musical productions?

CORNELIUS: To be frank with you, Miss Cutwell, I don't know whether you're talented or not.

MAGGIE: Can't I show you? Won't you at least give me the opportunity to show you what I can do?

CORNELIUS: Ordinarily I would say yes immediately, without reservation, but you've caught me during my busiest day of the week. It's impossible. I can't. I have obligations. (*He puts foot on box, ties his shoelace*)

MAGGIE: Please, Mr. Hollingsworth! This is extremely important to me. If I don't succeed in my chosen profession, I'll have to go on selling flowers for the rest of my life, or marry some beer-bellied creep who'd beat me every night just for the exercise. I'll be forced to kill myself, Mr. Hollingsworth! (*Cornelius turns to her as she gets down on her knees*) I couldn't go on living like that, I couldn't, I couldn't . . . (*She weeps*)

CORNELIUS: (*Tears streaming down his cheeks*) What a tragedy. What a terrible, terrible story. How long have you been selling flowers?

MAGGIE: (*Weeping*) Ever since I was six years old.

CORNELIUS: (*Weeping*) Tragic. Tragic. Have you experienced no pleasure, no happiness, no joy in all your young years?

MAGGIE: (*Weeping*) No. Nothing but pain and heartache.

CORNELIUS: (*Weeping*) Ohhhhh, pain and heartache. And you would take your own life?

MAGGIE: (*Weeping*) Yes, yes, I have the pills at home and today there was a sale at Woolworth's and I bought . . . I bought six bottles of iodine!

CORNELIUS: (*Moves away; she follows him on her knees*) No more, Miss Cutwell. No more. I can't take it. I can't. It's too much for a human being to bear. If you'd like to perform for me, go home, change, rearrange your appearance, prepare yourself, and come back when you're ready. But, please, hurry. I don't have the time! I have a business to run here!

MAGGIE: Thank you. Thank you. You're my light in the darkness. You're my savior. (*Rises*) Two minutes, Mr. Hollingsworth. (*Turns to Shimmel*) Two minutes . . . Sh-Sh-Sh-Sh-Shitzman? Shitzman? That's a riot. Shitzman. (*And she exits*)

CORNELIUS: (*Sits on box*) Well, what do you think?

SHIMMEL: (*Rises; looks after Maggie*) I . . . I think she's beautiful.

CORNELIUS: Good. I'm glad you feel that way because I'd like you to get her off my hands.

SHIMMEL: But I thought . . .

CORNELIUS: (*Rises; moves to him*) Don't think, Shimmel. You can be arrested for it. Feel, feel, start feeling and start expressing your feelings, your fantasies, your dreams! Use your imagination! You're a very repressed person. If I had known that before, I would never have gone into partnership with you!

SHIMMEL: But why do you want me to take Miss Cutwell off your hands? Aren't you attracted to her?

CORNELIUS: Attracted, retracted, contracted, who has time for those shennanigans. It so happens, be it as it may, willy-nilly, hocus-pocus, I'm a married man, (*Moves toward his box; stops*) I also have three brats. (*Moves; stops*) And a gypsy girl friend, (*Moves*) It's unprofessional for me to get further involved. (*Sits on box*)

SHIMMEL: I'd be very glad to take her off your hands.

CORNELIUS: Excellent. Excellent. (*Rises*) Unfortunately one problem remains.

SHIMMEL: What's that?

CORNELIUS: Our partnership name. Hollingsworth and Shitzman. It's out of the question. Didn't you hear how Miss Cutwell laughed at it? We'll get the same treatment from everyone who hears it. We'll be the laughing stock of the banana business.

SHIMMEL: But I told you . . .

CORNELIUS: (*Shouts*) I know what you told me! I know what you said! But don't I count for anything? Shimmel, please! Consider someone else for a change? There's no limit to how far we could go together, but you're destroying everything we created with your ridiculous name! It's like a cancer preventing our full growth and prosperity!

SHIMMEL: Even if I wanted to . . . I don't have the money . . .

CORNELIUS: (*Sits on box*) We'll negotiate. I'll take an I.O.U. I'll place a lien on your forty percent. Don't worry about it. (*Pulls out slips of paper*) Now what will it be? Thomas Hathaway. Roger Williams Carnegie. Samuel P. Stone . . .

SHIMMEL: (*Pleading*) Cornelius, my family name . . . (*Sits on box*)

CORNELIUS: Which one, Shimmel? Which one? (*Shimmel doesn't reply. Cornelius rises; hands him slip of paper*) Samuel P. Stone it is! Five dollars even. Hollingsworth and Stone. Perfect. It couldn't be better. Congratulations, partner. (*Sits; makes entry in notebook*) Well, do you feel any differently, Sam? (*Shimmel shakes his head*) You have to feel differently. A Crapavarnishkes isn't a Hollingsworth and a Shitzman isn't a Stone.

SHIMMEL: Samuel P. Stone. I am Samuel P. Stone.

CORNELIUS: Sam Stone!

SHIMMEL: (*Rises*) I am Sam Stone. (*He faces upstage*)

CORNELIUS: That's it. Feel Stone. Feel rock. Feel hard. Feel firm. Feel strong. Feel . . .

(Maggie rushes back in, wearing a Shirley Temple dress and tap shoes)

MAGGIE: (*Panting*) I'm here, Mr. Hollingsworth! I'm ready to perform for you.

CORNELIUS: (*Rises*) Yes, yes, but before you begin, I'd like to introduce you to my partner, Sam Stone.

MAGGIE: But that's Mr. Shitzman. I met him . . .

CORNELIUS: I beg to differ with you, Miss Cutwell. That *was* Mr. Shitzman. But he has changed considerably since you last saw him.

(Shimmel turns downstage, posture straight, hand in pocket; speaks with pronounced certainty and sophistication)

SHIMMEL: That's correct, Miss Cutwell. And if you've come to perform for us, please begin. We don't have all day to dilly-dally.

(Both men nod to each other, curtly, and return to sit on their boxes. Maggie looks about to make sure no one is about, then breaks into a bright song and tap dance, something in the style of "I Don't Care." She sings intro without moving, merely bouncing up and down, hands clenched as if riding a horse. She tap dances as she sings the chorus, moving around the peddlers, posing beside them—a nightclub performance of sorts. This is followed by a tap dance as she da-da's tune of chorus. She ends by whirling around several times, almost stumbling. Her talent is not noteworthy. When she is done, she turns to them, waits breathlessly for their verdict)

CORNELIUS: Sam?

SHIMMEL: Yes, Cornelius?

CORNELIUS: What do you think of her performance?

SHIMMEL: (*Rises; fervently*) What do I think? Do you have to ask? Are you blind? Are you deaf? Do you not have a heart to feel with? I have just witnessed a performance of such precision, of such exquisiteness and beauty, that if I were in the producing business today, this young lady would be a star tomorrow!

MAGGIE: (*Embracing him*) Oh, Mr. Stone! You don't know how much I needed to hear that! You made me so happy!

SHIMMEL: (*Circling around her*) Enough of this, enough! You have a lot of work to do, Maggie. I am not now in the producing business, but I have every hope of being in the producing business in the very near future. Go home and practice! Practice! Practice! Day and night! Twenty-four hours around the clock! I'm going to be relentless with you, I give you fair warning. I'll pay the bills; I'll see to it that you have the necessities . . . (*Stops circling; holds her chin in his hand*) But I want you to be the best there is, the absolute best!

MAGGIE: I will be! I will! (*Starts off*)

SHIMMEL: And Maggie . . .

MAGGIE: (*Returns*) Yes, Mr. Stone?

SHIMMEL: No intimacy. No personal relationship. This is strictly a professional deal, is that clear?

MAGGIE: Yes, Mr. Stone. (*Starts off*)

SHIMMEL: Where did you say you lived?

MAGGIE: (*Returns*) Number eleven Perry Street.

SHIMMEL: I'll be up this evening to formalize our contractual arrangement.

MAGGIE: I'll be home. I'll be practicing.

SHIMMEL: Have a bite for me to eat. I'll be hungry and tired.

MAGGIE: I'll put a tuna fish casserole in the oven. Thank you. Thank you, Mr. Stone. I have hope. You gave me hope. God bless you! (*She kisses him on cheek, runs off, singing a line or two of song ending with "2, 3, 4!"*)

SHIMMEL: (*Staring after her*) What a girl! What an incredible girl!

CORNELIUS: So you've become fond of her.

SHIMMEL: Fond of her? I'm in love with her! I'm head-over-heels in love with her! Cornelius, Cornelius, I never felt this way before. I never thought I could feel this way. My heart is in my mouth. I have a temperature of over a hundred. My legs are shaking. My stomach is bubbling. It's too much. I can't breathe. Is all this happening to me or am I dreaming? Did I meet someone named Maggie Cutwell or did I make it up? Pinch me, Cornelius, pinch me! I have to know the truth!

CORNELIUS: (*Rises*) Hold it, Sam, just hold it a minute! I have to ask you: are you rich enough to support yourself and her, too? After all, you just started in business, this is your first day here . . . I don't understand. How can you . . .

SHIMMEL: You don't understand! Of course you don't understand! You don't look, you don't listen, you don't pay attention! I met a woman I love, Cornelius. I'm going to marry her. She is going to appear in a musical that I am going to produce . . . (*Points*) with you! Now I have the inspiration, the dedication to succeed in a big way. Nothing can stop me. Nothing! Now, come, no more horsing around. This is a matter of life and death to me. Let's get to work. (*He sits on box, crosses legs, puts newspaper in front of his face*)

CORNELIUS: (*Stares at him, incredulously; then sits on box, takes newspaper*) How's business, Sam?

SHIMMEL: (*Behind newspaper*) Good, Cornelius. Excellent.

CORNELIUS: You know, I think it's time we started a corporation. What do you think?

SHIMMEL: (*Newspaper down*) I don't know why we waited so long.

CORNELIUS: If I have one fault, it's being too conservative. (*Shimmel puts newspaper in front of his face*)

CORNELIUS: Sam?

SHIMMEL: (*Newspaper down*) Yes, Cornelius?

CORNELIUS: (*Simply*) Welcome to America. (*Music as they both lift newspapers in front of their faces, simultaneously uncross and cross their legs—left over right, then right over left—with music punctuating their actions and ending abruptly. Blackout*)

David Mamet

REUNION

David Mamet

Sometimes controversial, frequently penetrating, and always provocative, Chicago-based playwright David Mamet has achieved an impressive reputation since his first productions in 1974. Recognition came early in Mr. Mamet's writing career with a 1976 Obie Award for *Sexual Perversity in Chicago* and *American Buffalo*. This was followed immediately by a CBS Fellowship in Creative Writing at Yale School of Drama, the New York Drama Critics Circle Award for best American play in 1977 for *American Buffalo*, and The Outer Critics Circle Award in 1978 for contributions to the American theatre.

In his native Chicago, Mr. Mamet was artistic director of the St. Nicholas Theatre Company from 1973 to 1976 and is presently associate artistic director of the Goodman Theatre.

With an undergraduate education from Goddard College in Vermont, Mamet broadened his background by working at a variety of jobs—in a canning plant, at a truck factory, in a real estate agency, and as a window washer, an office cleaner, and a taxi driver. His fine ear for dialogue undoubtedly was tuned by these experiences.

Yet his dialogue goes far beneath the surface. Commenting on Mamet's remarkable dialogue, critic Richard Eder wrote: "His is no ear, but a stethoscope. His characters' words are heartbeats—evidence of their state of life and its constant fibrillating transformations . . . For Mr. Mamet, speech can testify in its awkwardnesses and silences to the opposite of what it seems to say. The gun flash is precisely not where the bullet lodges. Mr. Mamet's extraordinary talent is to report the flash and show us where the wound really is."

Reunion vibrates with such inner lacerations. After separation for twenty years, a father and his daughter are drawn together out of loneliness, each searching for a relationship to fill his empty life. Mel Gussow describes this attempt: "Circling each other, they try to communicate . . . They almost touch . . . [the effect] is wistful, enveloping us in the isolation of two lonesome people. Their mutual need is almost as strong as their inability to make contact."

First produced at the St. Nicholas Theatre Company in Chicago on January 9, 1976, *Reunion* had the following cast:

BERNIE CARY   Don Marston
CAROL MINDLER   Linda Kimbrough
Director: Cecil O'Neal

A year later, Yale Repertory Theatre in New Haven, Connecticut, produced the play on October 14, 1977, with the following cast:

BERNIE CARY   Michael Higgins
CAROL MINDLER   Lindsay Crouse

Director: Walt Jones

The same cast directed by Mr. Mamet opened two years later at the Circle Repertory Company in October of 1979.

Reunion is the second Mamet play to appear in this series. The first, *The Duck Variations*, is contained in *The Best Short Plays 1977*. Other published plays by Mr. Mamet include: *Sexual Perversity in Chicago, American Buffalo, The Water Engine, A Life in The Theatre, The Woods, Dark Pony*, and *The Revenge of the Space Pandas, or Binky Rudich and the Two-Speed Clock*, the last a one-act play for children.

Characters:

CAROL MINDLER, *twenty-four years old*
BERNIE CARY, *her father*

Scene:

Bernie's apartment.

Time:

Sunday afternoon in early March.

Scene One:

BERNIE: I would of recognized you anywhere.
It is you. Isn't it?
Carol. Is that you?
You haven't changed a bit.
I would of recognized you anywhere . . .
This is a very important moment.
But there's no reason why we should have it in the hall so let
me take your coat . . .
I feel like a racehorse. You ever go to the track?
Well, that's what I feel like.
If I was still drinking, I'd offer you a drink.
If I was still drinking, you probably wouldn't be here.
That's all right.
   CAROL: Bernie . . .
   BERNIE: You're not going to call me Dad, or like that? . .
Thank God.
So here we are.
   CAROL: Yes.
   BERNIE: So how you been?
   CAROL: Fine.
   BERNIE: Great.
   CAROL: You?

BERNIE: Since the last time you saw me, mainly bad, lately good. You look wonderful.

CAROL: You don't look so bad yourself. For an old man. You take good care of yourself.

BERNIE: Well, I better. Who else is going to take care of me? . . .

The VA, of course. They take pretty good care of me, I'm forced to admit.

I still go to see them about three times a year for my back.

They take good care of you in the hospital.

The guys at A.A., I don't see them much anymore.

Thank God. They took pretty good care of me.

I hated those sonofabitches . . .

Frank over at the place. He took care of me for a while.

Five there, ten here . . . he gave me a job.

Knows the restaurant business like the back of his hand.

I've been a very lucky guy.

CAROL: You've got a lot of friends, Bernie.

BERNIE: Always have.

For some reason.

You take pretty good care of yourself.

CAROL: Got to.

BERNIE: Yeah.

CAROL: The A.A. are the ones who put us in touch with you.

Gerry went.

He said they seemed like very nice people.

BERNIE: Very contrite.

You still go to church?

CAROL: No. Nobody goes to church anymore. (*Pause*) You still go to church?

BERNIE: I never went to church. Since I was a kid. Easter

CAROL: We should both go.

Renew our faith.

Gerry goes to church.

BERNIE: Yeah? Does he mean it?

CAROL: Who knows.

BERNIE: He might mean it. You never know . . . Some of 'em mean it.

Scene Two:

BERNIE: Goddamn, it's good to see you.
It's good to see you.
 CAROL: This apartment is very nice.
 BERNIE: I did it myself. Leslie, my friend, she helped.
Quite a lot, actually . . . to put the place in the state it's in now.
But the basic place . . . I furnished it.
Fixed it up.
Been here two years plus . . .
I'm glad you like it.
 CAROL: Our place is quite nice. You'll like it a lot. When you come see it. You have to come out. Very soon.
I did it myself.
It's so comfortable.
It's a real home, you know?
It's just five rooms.
It gets a little cramped when the kids are there.
Gerry's kids.
They sleep in the living room . . .
They're good kids.
Gerry has a study.
We're very comfortable there.
 BERNIE: You got a doorman?
 CAROL: Yes . . .
The building's very safe.
Lots of light and air.
We're thinking of building a house. (*Pause*)
This place really is lovely, Bernie.
 BERNIE: What can I tell you.

Scene Three:

CAROL: (*Sees bomber group picture*) Are you in there?
BERNIE: Yeah.
CAROL: I'm going to pick you out.
BERNIE: That's a long time ago.
CAROL: (*Indicates*) There!
BERNIE: That's me.

I haven't changed, huh?

CAROL: Bernie Cary. Army Air Corps.

BERNIE: Butch. They called me Butch then.

CAROL: Why?

BERNIE: . . . I couldn't tell you to save my life.

Those were strange times.

CAROL: What's this?

BERNIE: It's a medal.

Sit down. Sit down. It's nothing.

I fought. I did my bit.

If you want to know about your father

I was a tail gunner.

I shot a machine gun. Big deal.

They had a life expectancy of—you know what?—

Three missions. Three.

What the hell. You can get killed in a steel mill, right?

But I'm no hero.

They put you in a plane with a gun, it pays to shoot at the

guys who are trying to kill you.

Where's the courage in that . . .

But you didn't have to take anything.

From nobody.

That was all right.

Anybody get wise—some wiseass Lieutenant—I say:

"Shove it, Champ. I'm a fuckin' tail gunner on a B-17,

and I don't take no shit from some chicken Lieutenant."

And I didn't. From Anybody.

So what does that make me.

You would like England.

CAROL: I've been there.

BERNIE: You've been there? What? With your new husband?

CAROL: With him and by myself.

BERNIE: Where else you been?

CAROL: Jamaica. Around the States.

BERNIE: See America First, huh?

I worked a year in San Francisco. In a body shop.

CAROL: I've been in San Francisco.

BERNIE: Some fine people in San Francisco.

CAROL: Oh, yes.

BERNIE: And a lot of assholes.

CAROL: Lot of assholes all over.

BERNIE: Aah, people are people, you know?
Tell me about your new husband.
   CAROL: I want to know about you.
   BERNIE: And I want to know about you.
So. Does he love you?
I swear I'll kill the sonofabitch, so tell me the truth.
   CAROL: He loves me.
   BERNIE: And you love him?
   CAROL: Yes.
   BERNIE: So where's the story in that?
   CAROL: No story.
Just the usual.
   BERNIE: So it's not "the usual" for nothing.
These things work out. They work themselves out.
Is he a good guy?
   CAROL: He's . . .
He's a good guy. I think he's frightened of women.
   BERNIE: He's frightened of you? . . .
That's funny.
But you know, never having been a man, you don't know—
but a lot of men are frightened of women,
let me tell you.
Beautiful women especially can be frightening.
There's no shame in that.
He takes good care of you.
   CAROL: Yes.
   BERNIE: So what do you want?
   CAROL: I want to hear about you.
   BERNIE: What's to tell? You see it all here. Have a look
Fifty-three years old.
Ex-alcoholic.
Ex-this.
Ex-that.
Democrat.
You smoke pot?
   CAROL: No. You?
   BERNIE: Nope.
Tried it once. Don't like the taste.
When I was drunk I never drank anything but the best.
Saw no reason to change my style of life simply because I
happened to be an alcoholic.
Taste . . .

Never bummed for change. Waste of time.

Bill. Two bills, bounce a check.

Respectable.

If you're a drunk, you'd better be respectable . . .

1951 I lost my license. Fourteen citations for drunk driving in the month of December 1951.

You were what? Four.

I was living on the Cape.

You and your mother were in Newton.

CAROL: What were you doing?

BERNIE: In 1951 I was in the Vet's Hospital awhile with my back.

The rest of the time I was working for the Phone Company. Worked for the Phone Company ten years.

I was seeing this girl in Boston.

Your mother and I were split . . .

I got that court order in 1951.

You know . . .

Did you know I wanted to see you?

Did they tell you anything?

I wanted to come see you, you know.

I couldn't see you because of that court order.

CAROL: I don't know. They told me . . . something.

BERNIE: (*Pause*) I was a mover for a year.

Cross country.

I missed my brother's funeral. Your Uncle Alex.

You never met him. Did you ever meet Alex?

CAROL: Yes.

BERNIE: He's dead now. 1962.

And his wife, Lorraine, won't talk to me since I missed his funeral.

I'm sorry I missed it, too. But what the hell.

Life goes on. And when he died I was out west someplace with American Van Lines and I didn't even know about it 'til September . . .

You wanna hear a story?

CAROL: Sure do.

BERNIE: I'll tell you a story. So I'd been drunk at the time for several years and was walking down Tremont Street one evening around nine and here's this big van in front of a warehouse and the driver is ringing the bell in the shipping dock trying to get in (which he won't do, because they moved a couple of weeks ago and the warehouse is deserted. But he doesn't know that.)

So I say, "Hey, you looking for Hub City Transport?" and he says yeah, and I tell him they're over in Lechmere. So he says "Where?" So I tell him I don't know the address but I can take him there. Which was, of course, a bunch of shit, but I figured maybe I could make a couple of bucks on the deal.

And why not.

So I ride over to Lechmere.

I find the warehouse.

You ever been to Lechmere?

    CAROL: Just passing through.

    BERNIE: Very depressing.

So, anyway. He's in Lechmere to pick up a load.

And he offers me ten bucks to help him load the van.

So fine. Later we go across the street for a cup of coffee and he gives me this story. He just fired his partner, he likes the way I handle furniture, and do I want a job?

Hey, what the hell.

We finish the coffee and off we go.

And for one year I didn't get home, never shaved, wore the same goddamn clothes, slept in the cab, made some money, spent some money, saw the country. Alex died, and I missed his funeral.

Which, of course, is why Lorraine won't talk to me. Because I got back in September and I'm back a day or so and I go over to Alex's.

Lorraine answers the door and I tell her,

"Lorraine, tell your fat-ass husband to grab his coat because we are going to the track." He loved the track.

And she says: "If I ever catch you in my sight again, drunk or sober, I'm going to punch your fucking heart out."

Which were harsh words for her.

And to this day—she believed I was in town and drunk at the time of the funeral—not once have I seen or spoken to her in ten years . . .

And we were very close at one time.

She was a good woman.

Very loyal . . .

Alex fought in the war.

What the hell. How's your mother?

    CAROL: Good.

BERNIE: What about the guy she married?
CAROL: Good.
You know, he's a hell of a man.
BERNIE: No! Don't doubt it for a second.
I never met the sonofabitch, but I'd stake my life on it . . .
You got any kids?
CAROL: No.
BERNIE: Didn't think so. How long you been married?
CAROL: Two years. Gerry's got two kids.
BERNIE: You told me. How old?
CAROL: Twelve and eight. Boys.
BERNIE: How are they?
CAROL: They're good boys.
BERNIE: You like 'em?
CAROL: We get along.
BERNIE: They like you?
CAROL: You know how it is,
BERNIE: Their other mother died?
CAROL: Divorced.
BERNIE: . . . I like him, Gerry. He seems like an all right
guy.
A thoughtful guy . . .
Jesus, he gave me a moment, though,
I come into the restaurant and Frank—Frank's the owner
—he says, "Bernie, there's a guy outside askin' for Butch
Cary."
Now, I haven't called myself Butch since I'm on the wagon,
three years.
I was called Butch from the days in the Air Corps, and all my
old drunk partners know me as Butch. So. I figure it's some
old acquaintance looking for a handout, or a bill collector.
Because he called me Butch.
So I peek out the kitchen door and there's this real nice-
looking guy around forty—what am I telling you what he
looks like—
Anyway, it's obvious he's not a bill collector, and he's not
looking for a handout, and I don't know him from Adam.
So I get out of the kitchen—he probably told you this stuff—
I still got my coat on 'cause I just walked in the back door . . .
I guess I looked kind of suspicious—who wouldn't—and I go
over to him and he says,
"Are you Butch Cary?"

And I say, "Yeah, who are you?"
He says, "I'm Gerry Mindler. I'm Carol's husband.
Your daughter."
I told him I know who my daughter is.
I told him, "Mister, I am one tough sonofabitch, but I'll be
goddamned if I don't feel like I'm gonna bust out crying."
And I almost did.

Scene Four:

BERNIE: You got a brother you never met, you know, a
half-brother. Marty.
My and Ruth's kid. Ruth, my second wife. You could call her
your stepmother . . . if it made any sense.
I know your mother had another daughter.
CAROL: Barbara.
BERNIE: I know.
CAROL: We're very close.
BERNIE: I don't doubt it.
CAROL: We are.
BERNIE: Marty. You'd like him.
CAROL: How is he?
BERNIE: I haven't seen him now in several years. He's, say,
three years younger than you. He's a good kid.
CAROL: What does he do?
BERNIE: Do?
The last time I heard—and this might of changed—nothing.
CAROL: What was Ruth like?
BERNIE: Like your mother, I'm sorry to say.
Not that she wasn't a lovely woman.
And not that your . . .
CAROL: . . . It's okay.
BERNIE: Anyway, we didn't get along too long. And your
mother was not such a hotshot either, to get down to it.
Ruth never understood me. I take it back, she understood
me. When Marty was young. We got along.
CAROL: And then?
BERNIE: I left her. These things happen.
But, Jesus, he was a fine little kid.
Having kids, Carol, is something no one can describe.
Having your own kids is . . . indescribable.
I mean it.

You were quite a little kid.
We used to have a good time.
Going to the zoo . . .
Do you remember that? Do you remember what you used to
say when I came home?
Three years old?
I'd come in the door.
You'd say: "Hi there, Pop!"
I don't know where you picked that up. I guess your mother
used to coach you.
Do you remember that?
Do you remember going to the Science Museum?
We used to be over there every week. See the locomotive . . .
The steam engines, you remember that?
You were a beautiful kid.
You were everything to your mother and me.
I still got the pictures.
You want to see how cute you were? You wait here.
Just sit there.
You know who took those? Alex took those at his house . . .
Fourth of July 1950. It was the first year he had his new
house.
You probably don't remember.
Took them with his Brownie.
You were crying for some reason, and I said, "Look at the
camera, baby . . ." I'll be goddamned if I know where those
pictures are.

CAROL: It's okay.
BERNIE: They're around here somewhere.
CAROL: It's okay, Bernie.
BERNIE: But where can they be?
I look at 'em constantly . . .
You want some coffee?
CAROL: No, thanks.
BERNIE: You smoke too much.
CAROL: I know it.
BERNIE: Your husband smoke?
CAROL: Yes.
BERNIE: Does he tell you to cut down?
CAROL: Yes.
BERNIE: They're no good for you.
CAROL: I know.

BERNIE: He should set an example.

CAROL: He's my husband, Bernie, not my father.

BERNIE: I don't smoke.

I gave it up.

When I went on the wagon.

Did I tell you I'm thinking about getting married again?

CAROL: No.

BERNIE: It's not definite. Not yet.

I'm just thinking.

Leslie. She works at the restaurant. Gerry met her.

CAROL: Tell me about her.

BERNIE: . . . She knows me. I know her.

I respect her.

She's a good worker, she knows my past.

I think she loves me. She's about forty . . .

Was married once.

It's like a habit.

How would you, you know . . . feel if I got married again?

Would that . . . do anything to you?

I realize you don't have a long basis for comparison.

CAROL: I think it would be good for you.

BERNIE: You think that, huh?

CAROL: Yes.

BERNIE: Of course it wouldn't get in the way of our getting to know each other.

CAROL: Why are you getting married again?

BERNIE: . . . Companionship.

Scene Five:

BERNIE: But I'm a happy man now. And I don't use the term loosely.

I got a good job at the restaurant.

I've stopped drinking. I'm putting a little money away.

CAROL: I'm glad to hear it.

BERNIE: Well, there's nothing wrong with it.

For the first time in a long time I get a kick out of what I'm doing.

I enjoy it at work. Everybody knows me. They respect me.

I spend a lot of time walking. Just walking in the Common.

After all this time. Not to cadge a drink. Or to get laid.
Excuse me . . .
People always talk about going out to the country or getting
back to nature and all the time I say, "Yeah, yeah," and what
does it mean?
I see the logic of it, but it means nothing to me.
Because my entire life I'm looking for a way around.
Do you know what I mean?
Like drinking, certainly, or with your mother, or my second
wife . . . Being in debt—there was never a reason for all that
money trouble—and changing jobs all the time . . . so what
does it get me but dumber and dumber, and I'm a cynic.
But now . . .
On the other hand, it's about time—I mean, I'm fifty-three
years old. I've spent the majority of my life drinking and,
when you come right down to it, being a hateful
sonofabitch . . .
But you, married. Living well. You live well.
A nice guy. A fine guy for a husband.
Going to have . . . maybe . . . kids.
You shouldn't let it bother you, but you have a lot of
possibilities. Don't you feel that?

    CAROL: I do.

    BERNIE: Well, then. The rest is not very important.
It's for the weaklings,
No, really, And I like people as much as the next guy.
It's for the sissies and the drinkers—which I was—who need
it.
Otherwise   . What have you got to lose?
Take a chance.
You got to take your chance for happiness.
You got to grab it.
You got to know it and you got to want it.
And you got to *take* it.
Because all the possessions in the world can't take it for you.
Do you know what I'm talking about? . . .
It's a fucking jungle out there. And you got to learn the rules
because *nobody's* going to learn them for you.
You wanna drink? Go drink.
You wanna do *this*? Pay the price.
Always the price. Whatever it is.

And you gotta know it and be prepared to pay it if you don't
want it to pass you by.
And if you don't know that, you gotta find it out, and that's all
I know.

Scene Six:

BERNIE: I don't care.
1950, 1970. (*Pause*)
You know what I mean.
What's on my mind now is getting to know you.
And maybe getting married again.
You look good. Jesus, you are a good-looking young woman.
   CAROL: I get it all from you.
   BERNIE: Aaah . . .
   CAROL: I used to think you were the handsomest man I
ever saw.
You used to look just like Tonto.
   BERNIE: Tonto?
   CAROL: The Indian. The Lone Ranger's friend.
   BERNIE: I know who Tonto is.
   CAROL: It was my secret. I was sure you were Tonto.
I asked you once.
You remember?
   BERNIE: No.
   CAROL: You said, "No, of course not."
I was very upset. I didn't know why you were lying to me.
   BERNIE: I'm sorry.
   CAROL: I was about four.
I never told anyone.
I thought that it was our secret. (*Pause*)
You wanted me to keep our secret. (*Pause*)
   BERNIE: Thank you.
   CAROL: Bernie . . .
   BERNIE: What?
   CAROL: Bernie, you're wasted in the restaurant. Do you
know that?
   BERNIE: I like it at the restaurant.
I love it at the restaurant.
It's where I work. Leslie works there.
What do you mean?

CAROL: I mean . . .

BERNIE: I mean who do you think you're talking to?
This is not Tonto the Indian but Butch Cary, ex-drunk.
The only two worthwhile things I ever did in my life were
work for the Phone Company and fire a machine gun, and I
can't do either of them anymore, not that I feel sorry for
myself, but I'm just telling you.
I mean I am what I am and that's what happiness comes
from . . . being just that. Don't you agree? . . . I mean you
must remember that your mother was a very different sort of
person from me. As is, I'm sure, the guy she married. And
the way you're brought up, though all very well and good . . .
is not basically my life, as fine as it may be and I hope it brings
you a lot of happiness.
I mean, you haven't even *been* to the restaurant, for
chrissakes . . .
It's very clean and . . .

CAROL: No, I'm sure it's . . . I only meant . . .

BERNIE: I know what you meant.
I know what you're talking about.
But lookit, my life needn't be your life in any sense of the
word, you know?
I like it like I am, and if you find that the people you . . . go
with, your friends and so on . . .

CAROL: Don't be silly, Bernie.

BERNIE: I'm not being silly.

CAROL: Yes, you are, and that's the last I want to say about
it.

BERNIE: Okay, but . . .

CAROL: So for chrissakes, knock it off, okay?

Scene Seven:

BERNIE: I gotta admit it. I knew you were coming over. I
was scared.

CAROL: Yes, me too.

BERNIE: There's nothing wrong in that.

CAROL: No.

BERNIE: After all, what were we going to expect . . . Red
sails in the Sunset? . . .
What do you do now? I mean . . .

CAROL: I work for Gerry. At the Office.

BERNIE: You're a secretary?

CAROL: I'm just kind of . . . everything.

BERNIE: It sounds great.

CAROL: It actually has a lot of responsibility.

BERNIE: As long as you like it, right?

CAROL: (*Pause*) Right.

BERNIE: So quit . . .

Anyway, it's not the end of the world.

CAROL: No. (*Pause*) No. (*Pause*) We're not . . . sleeping together much anymore.

BERNIE: Oh.

CAROL: And that's only *part* of it.

BERNIE: What's the rest of it?

(*Pause*)

Come on, let me tell you something. You know what my advice to you is?

"Don't let it get you down."

CAROL: He's not such a great lover, anyway.

BERNIE: He seems like a nice enough guy.

CAROL: He's a lousy fuck.

BERNIE: That doesn't mean he isn't a nice guy, Carol.

CAROL: What do you know about it?

BERNIE: Speaking as your father and as a guy with quite an experience of the world . . .

CAROL: . . . whatever . . .

BERNIE: . . . not a hell of a lot. But I'll tell you, he's genuinely fond of you . . .

That's got to count for something . . .

Right?

Scene Eight:

CAROL: You know—when I was young they used to talk about Broken Homes.

Today, nothing. Everyone's divorced. Every kid on the block's got three sets of parents.

But . . .

It's got to have affected my marriage . . .

I came from a Broken Home.

The most important institution in America.

BERNIE: Life goes on. Your mother and me . . .

CAROL: . . . Oh, yeah, life goes on. And no matter how much of an asshole you may be, or may have been, life goes on.

Gerry's like that.

BERNIE: I'm not going to lie to you. I felt guilt and remorse and every other goddamn thing. I missed you.

What the hell.

I was mad. I was mad at your mother. I was mad at you.

I was mad at the fucking government that never treated me like anything but a little kid . . . saving their ass with daylight precision bombing . . .

Everybody hates the VA.

I mean, understand: I'm not asking you to understand me, Carol, because we've both been through enough.

Am I right?

(*Pause*)

CAROL: Gerry was in Korea.

BERNIE: Yes? And what does he have to say about it?

CAROL: Nothing.

Scene Nine:

BERNIE: Let me tell you a story.

One time—this was strange—when I'm working for the Phone Company. I'm out on the Cape. Lineman.

Repairs, on the street. I'm making out okay, what with that and my disability.

Bought myself a new Buick.

Beautiful sonofabitch. Used to drive into Boston and go out to Wonderland with Alex.

He loved that car. I think he was secretly envious.

And so I'm working out on the Cape. It's December thirtieth. I get invited to a New Year's party in Provincetown. I'm supposed to be working.

So I call in sick. What the hell, I had a good work record.

And it's New Year's Eve day and I'm getting ready to drive to Provincetown.

Put a hundred bucks in my wallet and I go to Mitchell's
—that's the tavern in Falmouth I used to hang out at—and
there's this Italian kid shooting pool. About twenty. I don't
know . . . Steve, something like that.

So I offer him twenty bucks to drive out to Provincetown with
me, stay in the car, and drive me home New Year's Day.

So fine. We get up to Provincetown, I go over to Kenny's
house . . . Kenny Hill. You would of liked him I think. He
would have liked you, I can tell you that. Had an eye for
younger women. Who could blame him.

And so we had a hell of a party.

That's one thing Kenny knew how to do is throw a party.

But the point is not the party but the next morning. So the
next morning I get up off the couch or wherever I was and
put on my coat and go out to the car to invite this kid Steve in
for a cup of coffee or something.

So there's the Buick but the kid is gone. Nowhere to be found.
Vanished. Along with my flashlight, which I don't find out, 'til
I rack the car up near Truro. (*Pause*) But hold on. (*He thinks
for a moment*)

I think he took my flashlight . . . (*Pause*)

So I go back in the house. Get myself together, and I figure
I'd better start back to Falmouth. I'm hung over as a sonofabitch. I say good-bye to my friends, grab a bottle, and into
the car.

It's snowing up a storm. I can hardly see anyway. I'm weaving
all over the road. Next thing I know I'm asleep. And the
following thing I'm wrapped around a telephone pole.

So I get out. Knocked the pole clean over; the hood of the
Buick is wrenched to shit. I go to get out the flashlight to try to
get a look at the engine, and the flashlight's gone.

There's no help for it, so I get back in and go to sleep.

Next thing I know here comes a Black and White. The cop
wakes me up, I happen to know him from around Falmouth,
and I convince him that it's all an accident, and I give him a
drink and he drives me home and promises to call the garage.

So you should be careful who you're calling a pig.

Any case, I no sooner get in bed than ten seconds later,
Wham! The telephone rings and it's Jim Daugherty, the
supervisor for the Cape.

"How are you feeling?" he asks.

"Like a big piece of cow shit," I tell him.

"You gotta come in today," he says.

"Jim," I tell him, "I'm sick, it's New Year's, get someone else."

"Everybody else is drunk," he says. "I'm the only one here, and some asshole knocked down a pole near Truro."

. . . So I tell him my car won't start. He says he's coming over in the truck to get me.

So I make some coffee and he comes and we go over to Truro to fix the pole.

He's cursing the whole way:

"Jagoff " this and "Asshole" that . . .

And what with the overtime and holiday pay and the twenty Jim slipped me for coming along I made about ninety bucks for one afternoon. And Jim was so mad, he did most of the work himself and I spent most of the time in the cab drinking.

Scene Ten:

BERNIE: But I can't work for the Phone Company anymore.

When they finally pulled my license, that was it.

I hit a cop car. Actually it sounds more exciting than it was. It was an unmarked car. He was parked anyway. Only time I ever got a ticket in Boston. A heartbreaker.

Anyway, I lost my license and that was it. I got fired and they meant it.

Jim Daugherty went down to Boston to talk to 'em.

No Dice.

He even wrote a letter to the Board of Trustees for me.

The Board of Trustees of the Phone Company.

No good.

He said if I got fired he was going to quit, too. . . . He didn't, though . . .

But he would've . . .

Broke him up, too. Best goddamn lineman on the Cape.

Eight years, best record.

We were very close . . .

Canned. Like that. Pension, benefits, seniority.

Shot . . .

It was probably for the best.

But I'll be goddamned if I can see how.

I used to drink a bit on the job. But who didn't?

Jim knew that. Nobody cared.

If it hadn't showed up in the accident report, I'd be working today.

What the hell.

CAROL: How long till you can get your license back?

BERNIE: Supposedly never, but, actually, in about a year. They review it.

They told me about it at the A.A. The guys there go up with you.

Their opinion is very respected.

CAROL: I was a teacher for a while.

BERNIE: You were? Where?

CAROL: In Newton. I taught sixth grade.

BERNIE: How about that! Where.

CAROL: At the Horace Mann School.

BERNIE: You were at the Horace Mann School?

CAROL: For a year and a half.

BERNIE: And I was right across the street?

CAROL: Where?

BERNIE: At the Garage.

The Company Garage is right across the street. I was out there all the time.

We used to eat at Mike's. Did you ever go in there?

CAROL: No. I went in for cigarettes once in a while.

BERNIE: I used to go in there all the time. I was there —easily—twice a week.

For years.

Goddamn.

When were you there?

CAROL: 1969.

BERNIE: . . . I haven't worked for the phone company since '55.

You want some tea?

CAROL: You have any coffee?

BERNIE: Yeah, sure. Instant.

CAROL: That's fine.

BERNIE: But I bet I saw you around. Boston, Boylston Street . . .

CAROL: We must've seen each other . . . in the Common . . .

A hundred times.

Scene Eleven:

BERNIE: I remember the day you turned twenty-one.
February fourth, 1968.
Your birthday.
I was going to call you up.
You probably don't believe it.
It's not important.
The actions are important.
The present is important.
I spent a couple of days in jail once.
What it taught me, you've gotta be where you are.
. . . While you're there.
Or you're nowhere.
Do you know what I mean?
As it pertains to you and me?
Because I think it's very important . . .
Does this make any sense to you?
CAROL: I want to get to know you.
BERNIE: And I want to get to know you. But that's not
going to magically wipe out twenty years . . .
In which you were growing up, which you had to do anyway,
and I was drunk . . .
I don't mean to get stupid about it.
But let's get up, go out, do this, go look at the locomotive if
they've still got it there, something . . . you know?
Because, all kidding aside, what's between us isn't going
nowhere, and the rest of it doesn't exist.

Scene Twelve:

BERNIE: So let me ask you something . . . you don t mind
if I get personal for a second, do you?
CAROL: What? (*Pause*)
BERNIE: What I want to know is why all of a sudden you
come looking for me. And it's not that I'm criticizing you.
CAROL: Why should I think you were criticizing me?
(*Pause*)
BERNIE: I mean, I could of come looking for *you* after you
were twenty-one. Not that I was sure how you'd feel about

seeing me . . . but you must of felt the same way? No.
I mean, it must of been . . . I'm guessing . . . some kind of
decision to get you to all of a sudden come looking for me.
How did you find me?

CAROL: Through the A.A.

BERNIE: And you just kind of decided and sent Gerry over
to meet me?

CAROL: Yes.

BERNIE: And why now?

CAROL: I felt lonely.

BERNIE: . . . Oh. (*Pause*)

CAROL: You're my father.

Scene Thirteen:

CAROL: I feel lonely.
(*Pause*)

BERNIE: Who doesn't?

CAROL: Do you?

BERNIE: Sometimes.

CAROL: I feel cheated.
And, do you know what? I never had a father.

BERNIE: Carol . . .

CAROL: And I don't want to be pals and buddies; I want
you to be my father.
(*Pause*)
And to hear your goddamn war stories and the whole thing.
And that's why now because that's how I feel.
(*Pause*)
I'm entitled to it.
Am I?
Am I?

BERNIE: Yes.

CAROL: I am. You're goddamn right.

BERNIE: You know what the important thing is?

CAROL: What?

BERNIE: To be together.
What's past is in the past . . . it's gone.
You're a grown woman . . . I'm on the wagon, your mother's
remarried, I got a good job, and there's no reason . . .
I can't make it up to you.

CAROL: Do you have to go to work tonight?

BERNIE: I don't work on Sundays. But Sandy got sick so I was supposed to come in but I called Frank and he told me he'd get someone else to cover so I don't have to go in tonight. You want to do something?

CAROL: Gerry was . . . he said he'd like it if we went out to dinner.
Would you like that?

BERNIE: Yeah. I'd like that.

CAROL: We could go out by ourselves if you want.

BERNIE: No. It's a good idea I think.
And it's no big thing in any case, right?

CAROL: . . . We could go out, just the two of us.

BERNIE: Whatever you want. What you want, Carol. That's what we'll do.

Scene Fourteen:

BERNIE: I got you something. Sit down. I'll give it to you.

CAROL: What is it?

BERNIE: I don't know. I found it on the bus.

CAROL: . . . It's beautiful.

BERNIE: Yeah.

CAROL: (*Reading inscription*) "To Carol from her Father. March eighth, 1973."

BERNIE: It's my fault. It's not their fault. My threes look like eights.
It's only five days off.
It's the thought that counts . . .
Ruth told me that you should never give anyone jewelry because then they'll always think they have to wear it when you're around . . .
So I never gave her any.

CAROL: It's real gold . . .
Thank you, Bernie.

BERNIE: I'm not going to tell you you don't have to wear it if you don't like it.
I hope you do like it.

CAROL: I do like it . . .

BERNIE: So what's the weather like out there?

CAROL: It's fine. Just a little chilly.

BERNIE: We should be getting ready, no? Shouldn't you call Gerry?

CAROL: Yes.

BERNIE: So you do that and I'll put away the things and then we'll go.

CAROL: The bracelet's lovely, Bernie.

BERNIE: Thank you.

Jeffrey Sweet

STOPS ALONG
THE WAY

Jeffrey Sweet

Born in Boston, raised in Evanston, Illinois, and educated at New York University with a major in film, Jeffrey Sweet is a very active playwright in the New York and Chicago theatre scenes.

A member of Lehman Engel's B.M.I. Musical Theatre Workshop since 1968, Mr. Sweet has a special interest in this field. Three of his musicals, for which he wrote both script and score, have been produced: *Winging It!* at the Milwaukee Repertory Theatre (1970); *Hitch,* directed by Beau Bridges (Los Angeles, 1972); and *Wicked John and the Devil,* commissioned and produced by the Corporation for Public Broadcasting (1973). The latter musical was also presented twice Off-Off-Broadway at the Cubiculo Theatre and the Manhattan Theatre Club. Mr. Sweet has also been director of special projects for the Encompass Theatre, which specializes in the presentation and development of American musicals. Two of his lyrics are published in the Lehman Engel's collection *Their Words Are Music.* At the time of this writing his new musical revue, *Holding Patterns,* is in rehearsals at Pittsburgh's Theatre Express.

His other writings include fiction and non-fiction for such diverse publications as *Newsday, Gallery, Ellery Queen, Alfred Hitchcock's Mystery Magazine, The Writer,* and *Chicago.* His book *Something Wonderful Right Away,* published in 1978, is an oral history of Chicago's famous improvisational group, The Second City, featuring interviews with Mike Nichols, Alan Alda, Gilda Radner, and other illustrious alumni. Sweet is also an Associate Editor of the *Dramatists Guild Quarterly* and a reporter for the *Dramatists Guild Newsletter,* and has served as editorial assistant for Scholastic Magazines and W.W. Norton & Co.

An actor as well as a writer, Mr. Sweet conducts workshops in improvisational theatre and playwriting, and recently conducted classes at the Goodman Theatre in Chicago, the O'Neill Center, and the Dramatists Guild.

His play *Porch,* which appeared in this series in 1976, was premiered at the Arena Stage in Washington, D.C., in 1977 with numerous subsequent productions at regional theatres, and was named "best drama of 1978" by the Society of Midland Authors. A full-length play, *Hard Feelings,* was produced in 1978 at Actors Studio in New York and at Victory Gardens in Chicago in 1979. Much of Mr. Sweet's writing was supported by grant assistance from The National Endowment for the Arts Literature Program.

Stops Along the Way, which appears in print for the first time in this collection, was chosen by Edward Albee for a bill of one-act plays scheduled for a six-week run at the Mitzi E. Newhouse Theatre at Lincoln Center in New York City in March, 1981. The play was given its first staged reading in 1980 at the North Light Repertory Theatre in Evanston, Illinois. With a sharp eye for detail and a keen ear for the sounds of intimacy, Mr. Sweet explores the necessary termination of a love affair between a teacher and a former student.

The play is dedicated to Mark and Bobbi Gordon and to Gary Bayer, with special thanks to the members of the New York Writers Bloc and Edward Clinton.

Characters:

DONNA, *early forties*
LARRY, *thirtyish*
RAY, *thirties or older*
WAITER
SERVICE STATION ATTENDANT
CLERK
BARTENDER
NOTE: *The latter four parts are to be played by one actor.*

Prologue:

Lights come up on Larry.

LARRY: (*To audience*) I had a lock on my gym locker in high school. A combination lock. All I had to do was dial 47-3-18. I had it written down on a piece of paper I kept in my wallet in case I should forget. Dial 47-3-18, give a little yank, and it would open. Bim-bam-boom, yank. I always thought that was pretty neat. (*A beat*) Ending things has always been a problem for me. Saying to someone that, I'm sorry, but I don't think we should go any further. But saying it in a way that doesn't hurt too much. I would like to know how to do that. The appropriate words, if there are any. I mean, is there some exactly appropriate combination of words and actions? Because, if there is, I would like to write it down and keep it in my wallet.

Lights fade up on the next scene.

Scene One:

A diner near a highway. Morning. Larry and Donna enter through the front door.

DONNA: I'm sorry. I should have eaten before we left.
LARRY: That's O.K.
DONNA: Between all the packing and getting ready . .
LARRY: It slipped your mind.

DONNA: I'll make it fast, I promise. Where do they hide the menus around here?

LARRY: On the wall.

DONNA: That means hunting up my glasses.

LARRY: I can read it for you.

DONNA: (*Fishing them out*) No, no, here they are. God, I hate being blind. Let me see . . .

LARRY: No hurry.

DONNA: I don't mean to delay.

LARRY: So we get there fifteen minutes later. Baltimore will still be there.

DONNA: Sure, Baltimore is eternal. The eternal city.

LARRY: I thought that was Paris.

DONNA: No, Paris is the city of light. Baltimore is the city of . . . blight.

LARRY: I thought you said eternal.

DONNA: Eternal blight. I don't know. It's too early. Give me a break. (*Indicating the placemats*) Oh, isn't this nice?

LARRY: What?

DONNA: The placemats, what they've got printed on them. "Games to play in the car." Hey, this could come in handy, don't you think?

LARRY: So what do you want?

DONNA: Oh, I can have what I want?

LARRY: Why not?

DONNA: O.K. How about we turn around and go back? (*A beat*) Just kidding.

LARRY: O.K.

(*A beat. Waiter enters*)

WAITER: Help you?

DONNA: I'll have the farm boy special.

WAITER: You want that tomato juice or orange?

DONNA: Orange.

WAITER: And is that coffee or tea?

DONNA: Coffee.

WAITER: How you want your eggs?

DONNA: Scrambled.

WAITER: And your toast?

DONNA: What?

WAITER: White, rye, whole wheat?

DONNA: Whole wheat.

WAITER: And you, sir?

LARRY: The same, but I'd like a double order of orange juice.

WAITER: I can give you a size large.

LARRY: Sure, that'll do.

WAITER: Thank you.

(*He exits*)

DONNA: You're gonna eat after all.

LARRY: As long as we've stopped . . .

DONNA: You're a nice guy, you know that?

LARRY: Sure.

DONNA: You could have just put me on a plane. A short hop to the airport, wave bye-bye, and it would have been over and done with. Or put me on Amtrak or a Greyhound.

LARRY: You think I'd put you on a bus?

DONNA: No, I'm saying it's something you could have done but didn't because you're nice. A nice person. It's a compliment.

LARRY: Thank you.

(*A beat. She laughs. A beat. She takes off her glasses, rubs her nose*)

DONNA: Jesus, I hate these frames! Make me look like I'm someone's Aunt Clara down in the basement, putting up preserves, for God's sake.

LARRY: You look fine in them.

DONNA: What do you know?

LARRY: Nothing.

DONNA: You have as much sense of fashion, of *style* as . . .

(*A beat*)

LARRY: Go on. I want to hear this.

DONNA: I'm trying to find a good metaphor.

LARRY: Simile.

DONNA: Hunh?

LARRY: Simile, not metaphor.

DONNA: Really?

LARRY: A simile is an explicit comparison. A metaphor is implicit.

DONNA: Hey, Teach, relax. You're not in your classroom. Any of your students ever call you that?

LARRY: Call me what?

DONNA: Teach.

LARRY: I think that went out with *Blackboard Jungle*.

DONNA: How would you know? You're not old enough to remember *Blackboard Jungle*.

LARRY: I saw it on TV.

DONNA: Well, *I* saw it in the movie theater when it first came out.

LARRY: Gee, you must be really *old*, hunh?

DONNA: So, what do they call you? Your students?

LARRY: Mr. Keller.

DONNA: I mean behind your back.

LARRY: I don't know. I've never been behind my back.

DONNA: Your nickname.

LARRY: I don't have a nickname.

DONNA: You had one in Baltimore.

LARRY: I did?

DONNA: You did.

LARRY: I don't think I want to hear this.

DONNA: I'm not going to tell you.

LARRY: Good.

DONNA: It was flattering, though.

LARRY: I'll bet.

DONNA: It was bestowed affectionately. We were very fond of you as a class. You were held in very high esteem. I ever tell you what Karen Persinger said?

LARRY: What did she say?

DONNA: This was—I don't know—maybe the second or third week. A few of us would go out for drinks afterward, and we'd get a little silly. You know, a couple drinks, that can happen. So we were talking about you and sort of having fun with the idea that you were our teacher and you were so young. And she sort of laughed and said, "You know, I can't decide whether I want to seduce him or adopt him."

LARRY: She didn't do either.

DONNA: Oh, did you want her to?

LARRY: Of course.

DONNA: Bullshit!

LARRY: You think so?

DONNA: She wasn't your type.

LARRY: For seducing or adopting?

DONNA: Either.

LARRY: You seem very sure of that.

DONNA: *Very* sure. *I* was your type, and whatever you

might choose to say about Karen Persinger, you can't say that she and I were in any way, shape or form the same type.

LARRY: Maybe I have more than one type.

DONNA: No, you've got one type. You and every man in the world've got one type.

LARRY: Yeah, what's that?

DONNA: Alive and breathing.

LARRY: You're right, that does leave out Karen Persinger. (*Donna laughs*)

DONNA: You're awful.

LARRY: Yeah, I know.

DONNA: She's a friend of mine.

LARRY: So why are you laughing?

DONNA: Because it's true.

(*They laugh*)

DONNA: Lady-Keller.

LARRY: What?

DONNA: That was your nickname. Lady-Keller. As in "lady-killer."

LARRY: You said you weren't going to tell me.

DONNA: I had my fingers crossed.

(*She gets up, goes over to the cigarette machine*)

LARRY: What are you doing?

DONNA: Getting . . . Oh, that's right.

LARRY: That's right.

DONNA: Old habits die hard.

LARRY: Will power.

DONNA: I know, I know. Nothing like the unaddicted telling the addicted how easy . . .

LARRY: I gave them up, too.

DONNA: Yeah, well, you have a talent for giving things up. Case in point.

(*A beat*)

LARRY: More kidding?

DONNA: What, am I allowed only one kid per half-hour? You going to ration my kidding?

LARRY: It's a long drive to Baltimore.

DONNA: I know.

LARRY: That's all.

DONNA: (*Picking up a placemat*) We can always play one of the games. "License plate." No, that's a boring one. Oh, here:

"Ghost." You've played "Ghost," haven't you?

LARRY: When I was a kid.

DONNA: That must have been all of two years ago, hunh?

LARRY: More like four.

DONNA: You said it. God, I feel so ancient.

LARRY: Practically a ruin.

DONNA: Go ahead and joke. When *you* hit your forties, we'll see who's taking Geritol.

LARRY: Iron-poor blood, hunh?

DONNA: Got to blame it on *some*thing.

LARRY: True, true.

DONNA: I want you to write to me.

LARRY: What—a letter?

DONNA: Letters. More than one. I mean, why would I want you to write me *a* letter? One letter?

LARRY: I don't know. Why would you?

DONNA: I wouldn't.

LARRY: O.K.

DONNA: What I'm talking about is correspondence.

LARRY: A stream of letters.

DONNA: Yes, going back and forth.

LARRY: Streams don't go back and forth.

DONNA: You know what I mean.

LARRY: Yes, I do. You want me to write more than one letter.

DONNA: I mean, do you think I would ask you to write just one letter?

LARRY: You might.

DONNA: Why?

LARRY: People do sometimes.

DONNA: Ask somebody to write just one letter?

LARRY: There are occasions. Say, if I were applying for a job or something, I might ask someone to write a letter for me.

DONNA: Of recommendation?

LARRY: Yes. Saying that I was bright and would do the work well and stuff like that.

DONNA: (*A joke*) Would you do that for me?

LARRY: What?

DONNA: Write a letter of recommendation?

LARRY: You want me to?

DONNA: Why not?

LARRY: O.K., what do you want me to write? For what position?

DONNA: I could make a joke.

LARRY: Hunh?

DONNA: You said, "For what position?" I've got a dirty mind.

LARRY: Oh.

DONNA: I'm just being silly.

LARRY: Yes.

DONNA: Which position would you recommend me for? No, never mind. I'm just being . . . I'm joking. But I want us to keep in touch.

LARRY: O.K.

DONNA: I mean, just because something's over on one level, doesn't mean that it has to be over on all, if you see what I mean.

LARRY: No, I agree with you.

DONNA: I'm a very good correspondent. I write very good letters. People don't very much, you know.

LARRY: Write letters?

DONNA: I was reading an article someplace. I don't remember exactly where. But it said how a major loss to historians and biographers is that people don't write letters any more.

LARRY: They phone.

DONNA: They call each other up, yeah. Well, I mean, it's terrific that there is such a thing as the phone, of course. But it means that these historians have less to work with. Primary sources, you know. I mean, if the phone had been invented back in the early days, say, there wouldn't have been any of that stuff between Jefferson and Adams. That would all have been lost. All that terrific correspondence. Instead, all you'd find in the archives would be bills for long-distance phone calls. You'd see that John Adams had made lots of calls to this number in Mount Vernon.

LARRY: Mount Vernon?

DONNA: Isn't that where Jefferson . . . ?

LARRY: I think that was Monticello.

DONNA: Maybe it was Monteverdi.

LARRY: Maybe.

DONNA: You have no sense of humor.

LARRY: Monteverdi. Ha-ha! That's a good one.

DONNA: Anyway, you'd see all these calls on John Adams's bill to Jefferson, and you know how long they talked, because there'd be these hour-long calls listed—time and charges —but what they said would be lost to history.

LARRY: Yes. You are right. That would be a shame, too.

DONNA: It *would*.

LARRY: Yes, it would.

DONNA: Anyway, what it said in this article was that they've got this program at Columbia University. An oral history program. The idea is to come up with a new primary source for historians to offset the loss of correspondence. What they do is they get these people who have, uh, *potential* for being historical people . . .

LARRY: Un-hunh.

DONNA: And they get them in this studio and they sit down and they interview them. Tape them and ask them questions about their important decisions. Really *in-depth, probing* questions.

LARRY: Mmmm.

DONNA: I think it's a good idea.

LARRY: You know what might be a better idea.

DONNA: What?

LARRY: If they got them drunk first.

DONNA: Drunk.

LARRY: Sure. Loosen 'em up a little. Break down those inhibitions. More likely they'd say what they really think. Say you get Dean Rusk. Or, no, you get Kissinger. You sit him down with a bottle of Cutty Sark or something and you get him just disgustingly drunk—I mean shit-faced—and you ask him about Cambodia. About why he bombed the shit out of Cambodia. Who knows what you'd get? Probably say he never liked the way they looked. "Too small. Too yellow."

DONNA: This is your idea of constructive?

LARRY: I think it's worth a shot. Or several. Get it? Worth a shot?

DONNA: Sometimes you *are* very young.

LARRY: Whereas Monteverdi was an example of mature wit.

DONNA: Anyway, all this is beside the point.

LARRY: What point is it beside?

DONNA: What I asked you.

LARRY: Yes, I'll write to you.

DONNA: You promise?

LARRY: Sure. Don't want to deprive the historians of primary sources.

DONNA: Good.

LARRY: I mean, if it's a choice between that and getting drunk with Kissinger . . .

DONNA: If you don't want to . . .

LARRY: I want to. Fine, sure, yes.

DONNA: We'll tell each other how we are, what's happening in our lives.

LARRY: I think it's an excellent idea.

DONNA: Because we've been close, and just because a relationship reaches an end to one stage, doesn't mean that must negate the possibility of other facets, other sides.

LARRY: Doesn't negate it at all.

DONNA: I mean, the sexual, romantic side is just one side. It's wonderful, but it's not all there is.

LARRY: No.

DONNA: And just because that side is over with.

LARRY: I agree with you.

DONNA: I want you to write.

LARRY: I will.

DONNA: I want real letters.

LARRY: O.K.

DONNA: Not notes.

LARRY: I understand.

DONNA: But real, meaty letters.

LARRY: O.K.

DONNA: And I'll do the same. I'll write. As soon as yours reaches me, I'll sit down and answer.

LARRY: Terrific. That's what we'll do then.

(A beat)

DONNA: Because it would be sad if we were to allow it to just . . . dwindle. It would be a waste.

(Waiter enters with their orders)

WAITER: Orange size large?

LARRY: Here.

WAITER: Enjoy your meal.

(He exits)

LARRY: Oh, Jesus, I can feel a cold coming on. I just know it.

DONNA: You want my juice?

LARRY: No, I ordered large.

DONNA: I don't need mine.

LARRY: A little Vitamin C won't hurt you.

DONNA: I'm not the one with a cold.

LARRY: Prevention. I mean, you don't want to give Elliot a cold first thing.

DONNA: That's awful considerate of you, thinking about my husband.

LARRY: I'm thinking about you.

DONNA: Elliot doesn't get colds.

LARRY: Probably drinks his orange juice.

(A beat)

DONNA: Actually, I think we both deserve to be congratulated—you and me. Really, hooray for us. In my considered and impartial opinion, we're being very adult. Handling it very well. You remember in physics, when they told about the atom, about splitting the atom?

LARRY: What about it?

DONNA: When they split an atom, all this energy gets released. When they separate the electrons from the protons —or maybe it's the won-tons. Anyway, there's this explosion of energy, and that's the basic principle behind the atom bomb, right? Well, I think it's the same with people. I mean, you take two people who've had a very tight, close thing, and you split them—for whatever reason, whether it's their idea or not—but you do with them like they're an atom, and there's all this energy that's released. And if it's the wrong kind of energy, you can have a Hiroshima on your hands. Hey, *that's* a metaphor, isn't it?

LARRY: That qualifies.

DONNA: But what I'm saying is it can be good energy, too, sometimes. In certain cases. Like in our case. Which surprises hell out of me, to tell you the truth. I'm in a good mood. I really am. Of course, I would have been even happier if it had worked out. Jeez, has it only been five weeks? Wow. Spooky. *(A beat)* Wouldn't it be terrific if you could insure emotions? Say you'd go to Prudential, and they'd sell you insurance against getting hurt or feeling guilty or something. Probably the premiums would be incredibly high, though. And can you imagine the claims adjusters, what they'd have to go through? Though right now I do wish I were covered. *(Larry looks uneasy)* No, I'm O.K. Actually, to tell you the truth, I think that this is going to turn out to be a very positive thing. Not that I'm glad it didn't work out. But even taking that into consideration, I can truthfully say I think it was a good thing. The whole experience. Taken as a whole. (*A beat*) It's sure as hell going to mean a change in things between Elliot and me. For the better, I think. O.K., the first few days I'm back, it's going to be a little awkward. But I predict, with a little time, he'll accept what happened. I mean, I don't expect him to come right out and admit it, but I bet you he'll come to see it was a good thing in the long run. He'll forgive. (*A beat*) No, fuck forgive! I don't want him to forgive. Or if he insists on forgiving me, well, two can play that game. I'll just forgive him right back. Believe me, there's a lot I could forgive. I don't have to tell you.

LARRY: No.

DONNA: Well, now he knows if he pushes me to it, I'm perfectly capable of leaving him. He's had the past five weeks to absorb that. But I think it will work out O.K. (*A beat*) You know, when it comes right down to it, you've probably helped my marriage. Isn't that funny? You're what they call a marital aid. (*He doesn't reply*) What's the matter?

LARRY: Nothing.

DONNA: You're so quiet.

LARRY: I'm just eating. That's all.

DONNA: (*Meaning it*) You're so damn cute. God damn, you've got to be the cutest guy I've ever met. Hey, is that a blush? Are you blushing? (*He makes a wry face to deflect her laugh. She smiles, looks into her purse*) Oh, damn!

LARRY: What?

DONNA: I can't believe I did that.

LARRY: Did what?

DONNA: I know I had it when I was in the john.

LARRY: Had what?

DONNA: My silver compact.

LARRY: Oh?

DONNA: The phone rang, and I must have just put it down and forgot about it.

LARRY: You think you left it in the apartment?

DONNA: Isn't that dumb? Damn, I wish I'd realized sooner! Could have gone back for it.

LARRY: Yes, that might have been possible sooner.

DONNA: Though we're only forty-five minutes away.
(A beat)
LARRY: Tell you what: I'll mail it to you first thing.
DONNA: That'd be really nice of you.
LARRY: As soon as I get back.
DONNA: You think it'll be safe? In the mail, I mean?
LARRY: I'll insure it.
DONNA: Because it's sort of an antique heirloom.
LARRY: I know.
DONNA: I mean, I know you're not a sentimental person, but you can understand.
LARRY: Do you want to go back and get it? Is that what you're saying?
DONNA: *(Retreating)* No. No, of course not. Wouldn't that put us off our schedule?
LARRY: Yes.
DONNA: It's nice of you to offer, but I don't think it's a very practical idea. Thank you anyway.
LARRY: I'll mail it to you.
DONNA: Yes. *(A beat)* I can live without it for a few days. Too small a thing to make a fuss over.
(A beat)
LARRY: *(Noticing she hasn't been eating)* I thought you were hungry.
(A beat. She smiles, picks up her fork as the lights fade)

Scene Two:

Inside a gas station. Various car products on shelves behind counter. Coke machine with rack attached to the side. Attendant and Larry are looking at a map. Larry is drinking a Coke.
ATTENDANT: You wanted Exit 31.
LARRY: Yeah, I can see that now.
ATTENDANT: You overshot.
LARRY: I guess she was confused by the map.
ATTENDANT: She was navigating?
LARRY: She had the map.
ATTENDANT: It's a skill.
LARRY: Yeah.

ATTENDANT: O.K., this is where we are. You see? Now, what you want to do is get over here.

LARRY: So how do we do that?

ATTENDANT: My best advice is to take this here through to Bradley.

LARRY: That's a town?

ATTENDANT: Just about ten minutes up the road, yeah. So you go through Bradley and, oh, about three-quarters of a mile past the far edge is Old Creek Road. Runs parallel to some railroad tracks they don't use any more.

LARRY: And I take a right there?

ATTENDANT: Right, yeah. Keep going on that, you'll hit the highway right about here. Got that?

LARRY: I think so.

ATTENDANT: How long's it been since you had that car of yours looked at?

LARRY: Oh, it's doing O.K.

ATTENDANT: Seems to me I heard the motor knocking some as you drove in. If I were you, I'd have someone look into it.

LARRY: Maybe when I get back home.

ATTENDANT: Suit yourself.

(Bell indicating another customer has arrived rings during the above. The Attendant begins to head out)

LARRY: Thanks for the directions.

ATTENDANT: My pleasure. Put the bottle in the rack when you're done, O.K.?

(Attendant exits. Larry sits alone for a second, drinking the Coke. Donna enters)

LARRY: You feeling better?

DONNA: Nothing happened.

LARRY: What do you mean nothing happened?

DONNA: I don't know. In the car I felt so queasy, I was so sure that any second . . . You know, sort of a hot burning feeling in my windpipe?

LARRY: Yes.

DONNA: But in the john, nothing. I just sort of stood there. Waiting. I felt kind of dopey, just standing there over the bowl with my mouth open. I even sort of tried to make it happen.

LARRY: You stick your finger down your throat?

DONNA: Why would I want to do that?

LARRY: Usually does the trick.

DONNA: Your finger?

LARRY: You said you were trying to make it happen. That's the way people usually try.

DONNA: That's not how I try.

LARRY: How do you try?

DONNA: I think of disgusting things. Things that, when you think of them, they make you sick to your stomach. Like dead animals on the road. Or sulphur in chemistry class. You remember that?

LARRY: But they didn't do the trick.

DONNA: Not this time, no.

LARRY: You should have tried your finger.

DONNA: I didn't know to do that.

LARRY: Well, you know now. You want to try that now?

DONNA: No. I think I'll try not to at all. Maybe I'll drink a Seven-Up.

LARRY: Seven-Up?

DONNA: That usually settles my stomach. You never do that?

LARRY: No.

DONNA: It really works. For me, I mean.

LARRY: (*Looking at the machine*) They don't have it here.

DONNA: How can they not have Seven-Up?

LARRY: They have Sprite.

DONNA: It's not the same.

LARRY: You take what you can get.

DONNA: Don't I know it.

LARRY: (*Giving her the bottle*) Here.

DONNA: Thanks.

LARRY: I was talking to the guy here—the attendant. He showed me how to get to the highway. It doesn't look too difficult.

DONNA: I screwed up.

LARRY: That's O.K.

DONNA: I never was much good at reading maps.

LARRY: You seemed pretty sure when we were back there.

DONNA: I was faking it.

LARRY: You had me fooled.

DONNA: I wasn't trying to fool you.

LARRY: I know.

DONNA: Is that what you think? That I was trying to fool you?

LARRY: No.

DONNA: What would be the point from my point of view? Getting lost just means driving more. More time for me to be carsick in. I don't exactly enjoy that.

LARRY: No, I don't guess you do.

DONNA: I don't.

LARRY: It was just a turn of phrase. An expression. I didn't mean anything by it. (*A beat*) I wasn't accusing you of anything.

DONNA: But you know how to get us back on course?

LARRY: Yeah, he showed me.

DONNA: What, we have to turn around?

LARRY: No, there's a road up ahead that connects.

DONNA: Will we be able to make up the time?

LARRY: Maybe some of it.

DONNA: How much you figure?

LARRY: We've lost an hour or so. No way around that.

DONNA: You figure I should call Elliot?

LARRY: What for?

DONNA: Tell him we're going to be late.

LARRY: What for?

DONNA: So he doesn't worry.

LARRY: Call him later.

DONNA: Why not now?

LARRY: O.K., call him now.

DONNA: He has a tendency to worry. Imagines the worst. That you've been hit by a car that's gone out of control or assaulted. Cheery stuff.

LARRY: Maybe you're right. Maybe you should call.

DONNA: Oh, well, no, I guess it can wait till later. Till we have an E.T.A.

LARRY: E.T.A.?

DONNA: Estimated time of arrival.

LARRY: Right.

DONNA: Not to be confused with E.R.A. Which is a detergent.

LARRY: Are you ready?

DONNA: Let me finish the Sprite, O.K.?

LARRY: Why don't you finish it in the car?

DONNA: Because I won't know till I'm finished how my stomach feels.

LARRY: (*A flash of irritation*) You'd finish it a hell of a lot quicker if you didn't talk so much.

(*A beat*)

DONNA: O.K.

(*She deliberately starts chugging the Sprite. She starts to choke on it. She puts the bottle down, coughing. Larry stands to the side, doesn't make a move. She gets control*)

LARRY: What was the point of that?

DONNA: You wanted me to finish.

LARRY: That's the kind of stunt I'd expect out of a kid.

DONNA: Look who's calling who a kid!

LARRY: You're a model of mature behavior?

DONNA: Don't you start lecturing me . . .

LARRY: What's next on the agenda? The death scene from *Camille*, for God's sake?

DONNA: What do you mean by that?

LARRY: I mean stalling.

DONNA: Stalling?

LARRY: Delaying tactics. This performance.

DONNA: That's what you call it.

LARRY: "I feel sick to my stomach. I'm going to throw up."

DONNA: I apologize for feeling sick. It is, of course, all my fault for feeling sick.

LARRY: Ever hear of psychosomatic?

DONNA: Would it have made you happier if I'd barfed all over the car?

LARRY: You want to know what would make me happier? Do you really want to know?

DONNA: Delaying tactics. To think I'd purposely prolong the pleasure of your company.

LARRY: All right, fine. Then don't. Let's get out of here and I'll get you back to Baltimore. Back to your . . . back to Elliot.

DONNA: It's better than staying here with you.

LARRY: Who's asking you to stay with me? Do you hear me asking you?

DONNA: You couldn't pay me enough. There isn't that much money in the world to compensate me for the . . .

LARRY: Yeah, sure, right.

DONNA: Five weeks with you, I'd be happy to return to

Elliot even if he were a fucking Nazi, which he's not. Not by a long shot.

LARRY: Then you should be very happy.

DONNA: I am. I'm delighted.

LARRY: I can tell.

DONNA: Believe me, I appreciate him a lot better now.

LARRY: The sooner you get in the car, the sooner you'll be with him to appreciate.

DONNA: That's fine by me. That's just fine by . . . (*She gags*) Oh, God . . .

(She runs off doubled over. Larry looks off after her, concerned. He starts to move to follow, but stops himself. He puts the empty bottles into the rack, then suddenly grabs the rack, holding onto it and shaking it as if they were bars of a cage. The lights fade)

Scene Three:

Counter of a small-town drug store. Clerk sits behind the counter listening to the radio. A beat. Larry enters.

CLERK: (*Turning down the radio*) Afternoon.

LARRY: I want something for carsickness.

CLERK: Dramamine.

LARRY: I guess.

(Clerk gets it)

CLERK: This should do it.

LARRY: (*Taking a ten from his wallet*) Take it out of this.

CLERK: Let me write it up.

(As the Clerk writes, Donna enters)

LARRY: (*To Donna*) What are you doing?

(She doesn't answer. She goes to the counter)

DONNA: You have Certs?

(Clerk points to where they are. She selects one)

LARRY: (*To Clerk*) Take that out of my ten, while you're at it.

DONNA: (*Rebelliously*) I can pay for it.

(She leaves some money on the counter)

LARRY: Hey, look, Donna, I'm sorry. I apologize.

(But she has exited in the middle of his apology. He sighs. Looks at the clerk)

LARRY: You know how it is.

CLERK: Sure.

(Clerk gives Larry change and the bag with his purchase. Larry exits. The lights fade)

Scene Four:

A motel room. Two beds. Doors to bathroom and outside. At rise, Donna is alone, attending to something in her suitcase. Larry enters from outside after a beat.

DONNA: You have any luck?

LARRY: The guy that drove the tow-truck put me onto someone.

DONNA: And?

LARRY: It'll be ready in the morning. That's what he says, anyway.

DONNA: Did he say what was wrong?

LARRY: Near as I can make out, something isn't feeding right. I don't know. All I know is it's costing me extra to get it done overnight.

DONNA: How much extra?

LARRY: Fifty.

DONNA: Talk about your highway robbery!

LARRY: It was either that or not have the car ready tomorrow.

DONNA: You want me to chip in?

LARRY: I can handle it.

DONNA: I can chip in a little if you want.

LARRY: Don't worry about it, O.K.? Anyway, it was about due to happen. It's an old car. I've had it since before grad school.

DONNA: If you're sure.

LARRY: It's only money. Easy come, easy blow. *(He flops onto one of the beds)* Jesus!

DONNA: Jesus what?

LARRY: Jesus H. Christ!

DONNA: Yes?

LARRY: An expression of temporary resignation.

DONNA: As in "My Lord, why hast Thou forsaken me?"

LARRY: That's catchy. I like that.

DONNA: So long as it's nothing serious.

LARRY: No.

DONNA: There's a pool out back. You want to frolic?

LARRY: Not really.

DONNA: What's the matter? Afraid you might enjoy it?

LARRY: I don't have a suit.

DONNA: We could probably come up with something for you. Maybe the guy at the front desk's got one you could borrow. Come on, probably do you good.

LARRY: If you want to swim, why don't you just go ahead and do it? You don't need me.

DONNA: It's no fun alone. What would it take to change your mind?

LARRY: A brain transplant.

DONNA: Ho-ho!

LARRY: Anyway, I thought you weren't feeling so hot. What do you want to go swimming for?

DONNA: I'm feeling better now. It was just a little carsickness. (*A beat*) Funny, hunh?

LARRY: What's that?

DONNA: I was just thinking. We had our first . . . thing in a motel. And here we are in another one. One at the beginning, one at the end. Sort of a classical symmetry, hunh?

LARRY: I guess.

DONNA: You're a real live wire tonight, aren't you?

LARRY: I told Elliot we were going to be delayed till tomorrow.

DONNA: You called?

LARRY: Somebody had to.

DONNA: I'm sorry. I just wasn't up to it.

LARRY: He asked to speak to you.

DONNA: What did you say?

LARRY: That you weren't up to it.

DONNA: You didn't.

LARRY: No. I said that you weren't around at the moment. And I said we'd probably hit Baltimore a little after noon.

DONNA: I'd like to hit Baltimore but good. (*A beat*) So what did he say to that?

LARRY: Just yes, that he'd see us.

DONNA: Did he sound disappointed?

LARRY: He didn't say.

DONNA: But did he *sound*?

LARRY: I don't know what he sounded.

(*A beat*)

DONNA: Did he ask if we were going to sleep in the same bed?

LARRY: No.

DONNA: Did you tell him we weren't?

LARRY: Now what do you think?

DONNA: You might have, just to put his mind at ease.

LARRY: I didn't say anything about who was sleeping where. I didn't exactly think it would be a smart thing to bring up.

DONNA: Right. Besides, there's no way to predict the future.

LARRY: Want to run that by me once more?

DONNA: Can't be certain about tonight until after it's over. Maybe not even then.

LARRY: You're going to sleep in that bed. I'm going to sleep in this one.

DONNA: What if I want it the other way round?

LARRY: Why?

DONNA: Maybe I want to be closer to the john.

LARRY: Sleep in whichever one you want. Whichever I'm not.

DONNA: If that's the way you want it, why'd you get just one room? Why didn't you get two?

LARRY: That was strictly an economic decision.

DONNA: If you say so.

LARRY: Look, I just don't think it would be a smart idea for us to sleep together.

DONNA: Is that how you decide whether you'll do something, if it's smart?

LARRY: I try. I don't pretend I'm always successful.

DONNA: I'll say.

LARRY: The subject is closed.

(A beat)

DONNA: What if I have a bad dream in the middle of the night and want you to keep the bogeyman away?

LARRY: Don't.

DONNA: I can't control what I dream. A bad dream doesn't ask permission.

LARRY: What do you say we get some dinner?

DONNA: What would it matter, one last time for old times' sake?

LARRY: *(Overlapping)* Maybe we can find one of those famous truck stops they always talk about.

DONNA: I think it would be nice, one last time.

LARRY: How do pork chops sound to you?

DONNA: I'm not that kind of hungry.

(A beat)

LARRY: Look, you're going back to your husband. I am taking you back to your husband.

DONNA: So?

LARRY: There's a responsibility there.

DONNA: Not to touch, hunh?

LARRY: I don't expect you to understand.

DONNA: I understand perfectly.

LARRY: Good, that means I don't have to explain any more. So let's get some dinner, O.K.?

DONNA: But what difference would it make?

LARRY: *(Choosing to make a joke)* Well, for one thing, we wouldn't be hungry any more.

DONNA: You know I wasn't talking about dinner.

LARRY: Donna . . .

DONNA: Would you really kick me out? If you woke up in the middle of the night and there I was next to you, would you really just shove me out?

LARRY: Yes.

DONNA: I don't believe you.

(A beat)

LARRY: Listen, are you going to join me for dinner or not? Because I'm hungry.

DONNA: You've got kind of a deal, don't you? You and Elliot.

LARRY: Deal?

DONNA: You keep hands off, and he relieves you of me.

LARRY: It's a little late for me to keep hands off.

DONNA: That's what I think.

LARRY: What would it accomplish?

DONNA: It wouldn't accomplish anything. The idea isn't to accomplish anything. Jesus, you talk like the introduction to a thesis or something! "What I hope to accomplish in this paper . . ."

LARRY: There's really no talking to you . . .

DONNA: You have *no right* to make a *deal* about me with *my husband*. I am not bound by your *deals*!

LARRY: There is no deal.

DONNA: O.K., then understanding. Spoken, unspoken, whatever. Your fucking code! Your fucking male, masculine code! I am not bound by it. I don't have to satisfy it just to make it easy for the two of you.

LARRY: I really don't know what you're talking about, you know that? What's more, I don't think you do either.

DONNA: I am not irrational. Don't you start with that bullshit!

LARRY: I'm not going to listen to any more of this.

(He turns to go)

DONNA: Well, what if I don't want to play along with you and Elliot? What if I don't want to go back to him?

(A beat)

LARRY: Don't be silly.

DONNA: Why is that silly?

LARRY: It was settled.

DONNA: Maybe I want it unsettled.

LARRY: You're just trying to start something.

DONNA: Maybe it never occurred to you that I might want to do something else?

LARRY: Like what?

DONNA: There are lots of possibilities. It's not as if I just have a choice between you and Elliot.

LARRY: All right. I can see that.

DONNA: There's a whole world of other people out there. Other things.

LARRY: You're absolutely right.

DONNA: Other options.

LARRY: Millions of them.

DONNA: There *are*.

LARRY: I know. A wealth of opportunity.

DONNA: You laugh. You think it's funny.

LARRY: Is there something you want to do? Something specific you have in mind?

DONNA: What difference would it make to you?

LARRY: I want to see you happy.

DONNA: Tell me another one.

LARRY: I'm not lying to you. If there's something you'd rather do, if you don't want to go back to Baltimore, just say the word.

DONNA: Yeah, and what would you do?

LARRY: I'll do what I can to help.

DONNA: A letter of recommendation, hunh?

LARRY: Whatever I can.

DONNA: I can just imagine how you'd help.

LARRY: I mean it.

DONNA: I know what you think. You think there's nothing I could do that anybody'd want to pay me for. You think I'd starve or shoplift or go on welfare.

LARRY: I think you're so good at figuring out what I think, you should become a professional mind reader! Travel the carnival circuit, tell fortunes. I'll be glad to find you a crystal ball.

DONNA: You're so damn clever!

LARRY: Then tell me. You've got something in mind, just tell me. You want to be a coal miner, I'll buy you a pick. You want to be a brain surgeon, I'll get you a scalpel. Only don't you put that on me. Don't you tell me that I'm forcing you to go back to Elliot, because it doesn't matter one damn to me if you go back to him or not.

DONNA: Just so long as I'm off your hands!

LARRY: (*Without thinking*) That's right! (*A beat*) I didn't mean that.

DONNA: You should have just put me on the bus. It would have been kinder.

LARRY: For you to ride all that distance alone?

DONNA: I would have managed. I'm stronger than you think.

LARRY: It wouldn't have been right.

DONNA: And this is?

LARRY: No.

(*A beat*)

DONNA: How long did you wait?

LARRY: For what? What do you mean?

DONNA: Before telling me it was over? You only said it the other night. But you must have *known* you were going to say it—what?—days ago. Maybe a week, maybe more. It must have been awful for you. All that time, knowing what you were going to have to say, what you were waiting for the right moment to say. And meanwhile, there I was, bouncing along. Piling on all this unwanted affection. I didn't have any idea. Tell you what kind of fool I am, I thought it was going pretty well. I thought we were hitting it off pretty good. And all that time, what was really going on was you were waiting, planning. (*A beat*) Just how well did you have it planned, Larry? How detailed? Did you outline it like you do with your lectures? Five-by-seven notecards held together with a rubber band?

LARRY: It wasn't like that.

DONNA: You mean that little speech of yours was extemporaneous? Then you have my admiration, boy. You really do. Because it came out a model of . . . I mean, tight and logical and well-proportioned.

LARRY: Just what is this supposed to . . .

DONNA: (*Interrupting*) Accomplish? Again "accomplish"? I want to *understand*. I want to know why we didn't work out. Because we should have. Or at least we should have lasted longer. I mean, five weeks—Christ! Even a banana republic lasts longer than five weeks.

LARRY: Why can't we just say that we turned out not to be right for each other and let it go at that?

DONNA: I left my husband for you.

LARRY: Did I ask you to? You just showed up.

DONNA: You let me in.

LARRY: And what was I supposed to do? Throw you out?

(*A beat*)

DONNA: Do you have any idea how I felt that night? I've never done anything like that before. Just left. I told Elliot to go to hell and I slammed out the door. With nothing. I didn't have anything. And I thought, "Jesus, I wish Larry hadn't moved to Boston, I want to be with him." And then I thought, why not? So you were in Boston. It's not like that was the end of the world. Boston. Why not? It was so clear and so right. I hailed a cab to the airport, leapt on the first plane I could, then another cab straight to your door. It wasn't until then, when I was ringing your bell, not till then that it occurred to me I hadn't called you first. I didn't even know if you were in. But then, when you did open the door . . . You didn't ask me anything. You just immediately held me and made me welcome. God, I loved you so much for that! (*A beat*) Is there any feeling left, or is it just a matter of responsibility?

(*A beat*)

LARRY: I don't know how to answer that.

DONNA: You just did. I mean, it doesn't touch you at all, does it?

LARRY: You know that's not true.

DONNA: And how would I know that?

LARRY: What would it take to convince you? Some demonstration? You want me to bleed?

DONNA: (*Ironically*) I don't think you have any blood *to* bleed.

LARRY: Thank you very much.

DONNA: Just motor oil or something.

LARRY: Thank you very much.

DONNA: No, I'm seriously concerned for you. Seriously. This remoteness of yours.

LARRY: I'm sorry if that's the way it comes across.

DONNA: Oh, I can handle your being remote from me. Not that it makes me happy, but I can deal with it. What really makes me sad is you seem to be remote even from you.

LARRY: Now you're playing with words.

DONNA: You know the real reason behind you breaking us up? You were beginning to *feel* something. For the first time in your life you were beginning to feel something, and it scared the shit out of you.

LARRY: Well, this is a relief. Here I thought you were going to say I'm a repressed homosexual.

DONNA: No such luck. They at least feel *something*.

LARRY: But I'm just a zombie, hunh? I'm a—what did you call me—cute? A cute zombie.

DONNA: O.K., laugh. Make a joke out of it.

LARRY: What do you *expect* me to do?

DONNA: No, I *expect* you to laugh. It's like I said—nothing touches you. Why should the truth be any different?

LARRY: O.K.

DONNA: I'm just sorry, that's all. I thought I saw real potential for a human being. I was wrong. You're just a clever facsimile.

LARRY: All this because I won't fuck you?

(*A beat*)

DONNA: You're a bastard!

LARRY: I know.

(*A beat*)

DONNA: No, you aren't.

LARRY: Yes, I am.

DONNA: Yes, you are.

LARRY: Thank you very much.
(A beat. She exits. The lights fade)

Scene Five:

A quiet corner in a bar. At rise, Larry is sitting at a table. He has obviously had a few, and is likely to have a few more. A beat. Then Donna enters. She looks around and sees him. She hesitates, then goes over to him.

DONNA: So here you are.

LARRY: Let me see. Yes, this is my hand, so I guess I must be.

DONNA: When I got back to the room, you were gone.

LARRY: What time did you get back to the room?

DONNA: A little after eight.

LARRY: Your story checks out so far.

DONNA: I waited for you.

LARRY: Did I show up?

DONNA: No.

LARRY: I didn't think so.

DONNA: Have you been drinking?

LARRY: Yes.

DONNA: I don't think I've ever seen you drunk before.

LARRY: I said I've been drinking. I did not say I was drunk.

DONNA: Then what are you?

LARRY: Fluid.

DONNA: Fluid?

LARRY: Yes, that is what I am. Fluid.

DONNA: What's the difference?

LARRY: If I were drunk, I couldn't say "fluid." My tongue would not be able to negotiate the letter "L." As long as I can say "L," I am in good shape.

DONNA: So you've been sitting alone, drinking all night?

LARRY: No. Before that I ate alone. Did you eat alone?

DONNA: I ate at Howard Johnson's.

LARRY: So you had all those flavors for company.

DONNA: Are you coming back to the room?

LARRY: I guess I will, sooner or later. Probably later.

DONNA: If you're so worried about getting a cold, you

should be taking care of yourself. Not sitting up all night, drinking.

LARRY: I'll be all right.

DONNA: Don't forget, we have to be getting up early tomorrow.

LARRY: I'll make it O.K., don't worry.

DONNA: I just want you to take care of yourself. You don't want to get a strep throat or something.

LARRY: I will be on my guard, I promise.

DONNA: Actually, you know what I think might be a good idea?

LARRY: What's that?

DONNA: If *I* drove.

LARRY: Drove the car?

DONNA: Yes.

LARRY: Tomorrow?

DONNA: Un-hunh.

LARRY: What makes that such a good idea?

DONNA: That way you could get some sleep. You could lie down in the back seat, get a little extra. Because you're going to need it. I know you're going to have to drive all the way back to Boston tomorrow. You've got to teach Monday morning, right?

LARRY: Thank you for reminding me.

DONNA: So you see, it makes sense. You'll get some sleep in the back, and I'll get us to Baltimore.

LARRY: And how can I be sure you won't get us lost again?

DONNA: I won't.

LARRY: You say that so earnestly, I almost believe you.

DONNA: I won't get us lost. You can plan it out if you want. You can mark the map.

LARRY: And you'll follow it, hunh?

DONNA: Yes.

LARRY: Just mark it and you'll . . .

DONNA: I'll follow it exactly.

LARRY: Shall I also mark the "X" where you'll ram us into something?

(A beat)

DONNA: I wouldn't do that.

LARRY: You won't ram us into, say, a big Wonder Bread truck?

DONNA: Why would I do something like that?

LARRY: I don't know. Why would you?

DONNA: I wouldn't.

LARRY: No?

DONNA: (*Half trying to play it as a joke*) I mean, that would be a very dangerous thing to do. We could get killed.

LARRY: Yes, my concern exactly.

DONNA: You think I'd do that? You really think I'd purposely do something like that?

LARRY: Maybe it wouldn't be purposely.

DONNA: You're talking crazy.

LARRY: Maybe not *on purpose*. But accidents happen.

DONNA: You have a very strange picture of me, you think I would be capable of that?

LARRY: Maybe.

DONNA: I don't find this funny.

LARRY: The thing is, with my luck you'd escape with only a scratch, but I'd end up sailing through the windshield head-first.

DONNA: I want to point out the fact that this is not me thinking these things, it's you.

LARRY: What are you saying?

(*A beat*)

DONNA: Why don't we go back to the room?

LARRY: I'm going to have another drink. Would you care for something?

DONNA: No.

LARRY: They might have Seven-Up here.

DONNA: No, thanks.

LARRY: Suit yourself. Mr. Bartender, sir, I would very much like another.

BARTENDER: Scotch and water?

LARRY: Yes, sir.

DONNA: I wish you wouldn't.

LARRY: You don't have to watch, if you don't want to. You can go back to the room. Turn on the TV or something. Why don't you do that?

DONNA: I don't want to.

LARRY: Suit yourself.

BARTENDER: Your drink.

(*Larry collects and pays for it*)

LARRY: Thank you.

(*A beat*)

DONNA: (*An attempt to be chatty*) Did you know they make surgical gloves here—in this town?

LARRY: For real and for true?

DONNA: I got into a conversation with this woman at Howard Johnson's. She works for this company that makes surgical gloves. It's not far from here.

LARRY: You're not proposing we visit?

DONNA: No, I just thought it was interesting. When you think of all the things we have and use, all the everyday things, we just sort of take them for granted. It doesn't occur to us that it all has to be made someplace. Even the most trivial things have to be made someplace. There's probably a great swizzle stick factory someplace.

LARRY: Sure, Swizzle, Montana.

DONNA: Right. Anyway, they also make rubbers, she said. This woman at Howard Johnson's. Rubbers as in prophylactics.

LARRY: The same people that make the surgical gloves?

DONNA: Yes.

LARRY: Do they make them out of the same material?

DONNA: I didn't ask.

LARRY: Because what I'm wondering is, if you are a doctor—that is to say, a man of medicine—and some nurse shows an inclination to get it on with you, and you don't happen to be prepared—you don't carry them in your wallet, say—and she, for one of many valid reasons, is not on the pill . . . Would it work, I wonder, if you were to snip off one of the fingers of a surgical glove?

DONNA: Don't you think it might be a little too small?

LARRY: That would depend.

DONNA: Yes, I guess it would.

LARRY: And who knows how elastic the material is. What is it—latex?

DONNA: I have no idea. I didn't ask.

LARRY: Food for thought.

(*A beat*)

DONNA: I wouldn't get us lost, and I wouldn't drive into a truck. Not even by accident. I just suggested my driving to help.

LARRY: I know. (*A beat*) This is not going at all the way I expected it to. We were going to be there by now. It would be over.

DONNA: You're looking forward to that, aren't you? It being over.

LARRY: Aren't you? Honestly now, aren't you just sick to death of me? I haven't given you what you wanted. Or what you, or what *anybody*, has a right to expect out of a person who . . . I mean, what do you hold on for? You called me a zombie.

DONNA: I was angry.

LARRY: You had a right to be.

DONNA: I'm sorry.

LARRY: Don't be. You had a right to be mad as hell. You were right. I am a card-carrying member of the zombie brigade. I *am*. You've seen *Night of the Living Dead*, right? Those are my buddies. We hang out together. If you prick us, not only do we not bleed, we . . . I don't know *what* we, actually, but you should definitely keep away. I'm saying this for your own good. Please believe me.

DONNA: You're no zombie. You're an asshole sometimes

LARRY: That's quite a range I've got. A to Z.

DONNA: Hunh?

LARRY: Asshole to zombie.

DONNA: You're not a zombie. I take it back.

LARRY: You giveth and you taketh away.

DONNA: I was mad.

LARRY: Yeah. (*A beat*) Hey, how many Californians does it take to change a light bulb?

DONNA: Four. One to change the bulb and three to share the experience.

LARRY: You've heard it before.

DONNA: It's an old joke.

LARRY: I just heard it the other day.

DONNA: Next you're going to tell me the news about the Titanic.

LARRY: Oh, did something happen to the Titanic?

DONNA: Smart-ass.

LARRY: You seem to be hung up on anal imagery tonight. "Asshole." "Smart-ass."

DONNA: Do you suppose that "anal" is the root of "analysis?"

LARRY: Probably. (*A beat*) How many feminists does it take to change a lightbulb?

DONNA: Five. One to change it and four to write about it.

LARRY: Damn, you know them all, don't you?

DONNA: That one I told you.

LARRY: You did?

DONNA: Yes. You thought it was very funny. You said it was a good one.

LARRY: Well, we've had *some* laughs, haven't we?

DONNA: I guess so.

LARRY: (*Getting up*) Stay here for a second.

DONNA: Where are you . . .

LARRY: There's somebody I met in here earlier. I think he's in the front room now.

DONNA: You're going off to talk to him?

LARRY: No, I want to bring him back here.

DONNA: What for?

LARRY: I'll be right back, O.K.?

(*He exits. She sits for a few seconds, then gets up, goes to the bar*)

BARTENDER: Help you?

DONNA: I think I will have a Seven-Up after all.

(*Bartender pours it, she takes it back to the table. Larry returns with Ray*)

LARRY: Ray, this is Donna. Donna, this is Ray.

RAY: (*Shaking hands*) Pleased to meet you.

(*Donna smiles a little in response*)

LARRY: You want something, Ray?

RAY: Oh, I'll go for another beer.

LARRY: Heineken?

(*Bartender nods and, during the following, brings it over to the table*)

LARRY: I was just telling Donna that I met you a little earlier, and then it occurred to me that, if you were still around, you might care to join us. Ray has a very interesting job.

DONNA: (*Not understanding what is going on*) Oh?

RAY: I don't know if it's all that . . .

LARRY: No, it's very interesting. I mean, *I* was interested.

RAY: Well, I enjoy it.

LARRY: Tell her.

RAY: Well, you know the Edwards motel chain?

DONNA: You aren't Mr. Edwards?

RAY: No such luck. What I do is visit all the Edwards motels and check their books, and also, you know, how they're keeping the places up.

DONNA: Kind of an auditor?

RAY: Yes, that's part of it.

DONNA: Yes, well, that is interesting.

LARRY: Well, what I liked—what particularly interested me—was that he doesn't have a set schedule.

DONNA: I don't follow.

LARRY: (*To Ray*) I'm sure you can explain it better.

RAY: Well, I'm supposed to visit each of them at least once every six months, but I can do it however I want. Map it out any way I want. You know, sort of zap in when they least expect me.

LARRY: Like Zorro.

RAY: I mean, if they know when to expect you . . .

DONNA: Then they can be prepared.

RAY: Cover their tracks, yeah. Some of the managers will try to pocket some of what should be going to the home office. I'm supposed to stop them.

DONNA: And do you? Do you catch people?

RAY: I've caught my share. Not to brag, but I'm pretty good at it.

LARRY: I'll bet you are.

RAY: Some of them, you know, they try to make a deal.

LARRY: What do you mean?

RAY: You catch them red-handed, and there's no question about it, and they're scared because, you know, it could be jail.

LARRY: Un-hunh, I can see that.

RAY: So they're scared.

LARRY: And they try to what? Bribe you?

RAY: I've been offered money, yes. I've been offered other things, too.

LARRY: Yeah?

RAY: You'd be surprised.

LARRY: Oh, yeah?

RAY: Because when someone is desperate . . .

LARRY: What kinds of things?

RAY: You mean, that they've offered?

LARRY: Women?

RAY: This one guy—I couldn't believe this. His daughter.

LARRY: You're kidding me!

RAY: Do you believe that? She was a teenager.

LARRY: His own daughter?

RAY: I mean, it takes a lot to make me angry, but that really pushed a button.

LARRY: What did you do?

RAY: Frankly, I wanted to belt him one.

LARRY: Did you?

RAY: I wanted to, but I didn't do it. But, can you imagine, he thought I was the kind of guy who would do that?

LARRY: Pretty sleazy.

RAY: He's not working for us anymore.

LARRY: I would guess not.

RAY: If he hadn't made that offer, I might have given him a second chance, but he put the nails in his own coffin. I have no regrets. His own daughter. Christ!

LARRY: You've got principles.

RAY: I don't know.

LARRY: No, don't be embarrassed. You are a principled man. That is a rare and wonderful thing to be.

RAY: I don't know. It just comes down to a matter of self-opinion. Being able to respect yourself.

LARRY: To look at the mirror in the morning when you're shaving.

RAY: You could put it that way.

LARRY: Sure, I know what you're talking about.

RAY: No big deal really.

LARRY: Still, there are a lot of people who would have taken him up on it.

RAY: Well, there are a lot of people who would do a lot of things. Doesn't mean you have to be one of them.

LARRY: That's exactly true. Don't you think so, Donna?

DONNA: (*Still confused*) Yes, you're right.

LARRY: No, you have my admiration.

RAY: (*Embarrassed*) Well, uh, thank you.

LARRY: I'm sorry, I can see I'm embarrassing you. We won't talk about it any more. So where are you off to now? The next place?

RAY: You mean, that I'm going to audit?

LARRY: We won't call ahead and warn them, I promise.

RAY: No, I thought I told you—Baltimore. We've got a few of them down that way.

DONNA: (*Seeing the light*) In Baltimore?

RAY: Four of them, actually. Four motels.

DONNA: In Baltimore?

RAY: Yes.

DONNA: O.K., *now* I understand. It took me a little while, but now dawn begins to break.

RAY: Excuse me?

DONNA: Let me just see if I've got this right. You are going to Baltimore, true?

RAY: Uh, yes.

DONNA: Well, it just so happens, *I* am going to Baltimore, too.

RAY: Oh. Are you going to visit relatives?

DONNA: In a manner of speaking. Yes, Larry, do you have something you want to say?

LARRY: It was an idea, that's all. I thought you might prefer . . .

DONNA: To ride with this kind gentleman to Baltimore instead of with you? No, it was very considerate. A very considerate idea. And logical. And economical, too, actually. Think of the gas you'll save. And this way, tomorrow you can just go straight back to Boston and not worry about being too tired for your Monday morning class. And, while you are driving back to Boston, Ray and I will be driving to Baltimore. And I think we're going to have a whale of a good time. Because I really do get a kick out of getting to know interesting new people, and I find you a very interesting person, Ray. What you've told us about your job—the work you do—I think is really fascinating. And I know from what you've said that I can trust you. I mean, a man who would turn down a free lay with somebody's pubescent daughter is obviously not going to take advantage. I know I won't suddenly find you patting my ass or squeezing my tits, which would be a drag. If I didn't want you to. But then, who can say about what I will or will not want? I mean, just sitting here, looking at you, I can tell you've got a pretty good body there, and you would probably satisfy me if I should be so inclined. Which, as I say, who knows, I might. No point in ruling anything out so soon, is there? Because the possibilities of what can happen between two people are limitless and thrilling. Don't you agree, Ray?

(*A beat. Ray stands up*)

RAY: (*Quietly*) I'm sorry if I've said something to offend you.

(*Ray exits. A beat*)

LARRY: I just thought it would be easier for you, that's all.
(*A beat. He reaches for her arm and she starts to leave*)
LARRY: Please . . .
(*A beat. She wrests her arm free. In a fury, she begins to sock him. He grabs her hands and they struggle with each other. She stops. She seems to be on the verge of tears*)
DONNA: I didn't realize you hated me that much!
LARRY: I don't hate you.
(*A beat. He kisses her. She begins to cry. They hold each other as the lights fade*)

Scene Six:

The motel room again. Donna is in bed. The other bed has not been slept in. It is morning. Larry is sitting, dressed, looking at the sleeping Donna. A few seconds. A horn honks outside. Donna stirs. She reaches out expecting to find him.

DONNA: Larry?
(*Not finding him, she sits up, suddenly wide awake*)
LARRY: It's all right. I'm over here.
(*A beat*)
DONNA: For a moment, I thought . . .
LARRY: No, I'm right here.
DONNA: You're dressed.
LARRY: Yes.
DONNA: How long have you been up?
LARRY: About a half hour.
DONNA: Couldn't you sleep?
LARRY: I just woke up, that's all.
DONNA: Not a nightmare?
LARRY: No, nothing like that.
DONNA: I personally slept terrific. Very deeply. Like a diving bell fathoms down.
LARRY: Sounds restful.
DONNA: Yes. I thank you.
LARRY: Well, you, too.
DONNA: It was very nice. (*He doesn't answer*) You're so funny.
LARRY: How?
DONNA: Oh, you're so serious. I remember, I think it was the fourth class. You'd assigned us to read *Pride and Prejudice*,

and we were all supposed to discuss it. Though I think most of us faked it with the movie. But you—you were so earnest. The way you leaned forward, jabbing the air with your pen, making all these wonderfully subtle points. It was something to see. I mean, here I was on the other side of forty, and it had been years since it occurred to me that *anybody* could be serious about Jane Austen, much less somebody . . . like you. I don't know. But there you were, talking like it really mattered, all those manners and mores. I really think that was the beginning for me. You and Jane Austen. (*A beat*) What time is it?

LARRY: It's still early. If you want to get some more sleep.

DONNA: I'll tell you what I want to get some more of. What do you say?

LARRY: I've already showered and shaved.

DONNA: Well, you wouldn't have to shave again.

LARRY: No, I don't think so. (*A beat*) Donna, last night . . .

DONNA: Yes?

LARRY: It shouldn't have happened.

DONNA: (*Sort of a joke*) It's my fault. You were drunk and I took advantage.

LARRY: No, I knew what I was doing.

DONNA: (*Still trying to joke*) Yes, you did, but you know it's not nice to brag about it.

LARRY: I'm trying to say something.

(*A beat*)

DONNA: (*A realization; a quiet statement*) Nothing's changed. Last night didn't change anything.

(*A beat*)

LARRY: No.

(*A beat*)

DONNA: Well, it was nice anyway.

LARRY: I did love you.

DONNA: Did?

(*A beat*)

LARRY: Do.

DONNA: But?

LARRY: I can't hack it. I just can't . . . (*He puts hands over his eyes as if to prevent tears*) Oh, shit!

(*A beat*)

DONNA: How long will it take you to get the car?

LARRY: Twenty minutes.

DONNA: Why don't you do that now? I'm going to shower and clean up a little. By the time you get back, I'll be ready to go. How does that sound?

LARRY: O.K.

DONNA: Then let's do it.

LARRY: All right.

(*A beat*)

DONNA: Hey!

LARRY: What?

DONNA: Come here for a second. (*He goes to her. They kiss*) I could have been very good for you. (*A beat*) Well, what are you waiting for?

LARRY: (*Phrasing it carefully*) You aren't going to do anything, are you?

DONNA: Now what do you think I would do?

LARRY: I don't know.

(*A beat. She smiles and shakes her head*)

DONNA: I'm going to take a shower. I think I owe Elliot *that* much, don't you? (*A beat. Then, as if to a child:*) Go on, scoot!

(*Larry, satisfied, smiles wanly and exits. She sits quietly for a second, then gets out of bed and dresses. She pulls out a pack of cigarettes, takes one out, is about to light it, then, impulsively, breaks it, tosses it and the pack into the trash. She goes to the window, draws the curtains aside a bit and cautiously looks out, as if she doesn't want to be seen. Then the moment has come. She picks up her purse and suitcase, opens the door and exits hastily, closing the door behind her as the lights slowly fade on the motel*)

Epilogue:

Lights come up on Larry.

LARRY: I called Baltimore several times over the next week or so, but Elliot didn't know where she was either. I think he was telling the truth. The thing is, when I got back home, I found this silver compact on the sink in the john, and I don't know what to do with it.

Fade to black

Jennifer Johnston

THE NIGHTINGALE
AND NOT THE LARK

Jennifer Johnston

The highly acclaimed Irish novelist Jennifer Johnston, hailed by reviewer R. M. Seaton as "a new star in the Irish literary sky," makes her playwriting debut in this series with the poignant character study *The Nightingale and Not the Lark*. Ms. Johnston brings to her theatre work the same sensitivity found in her novels, *The Captain and the Kings* (1972), *The Gates* (1973), *How Many Miles to Babylon?* (1974), *Shadows on Our Skin* (1977), and *The Old Jest* (1980). Of her novel *How Many Miles to Babylon?*, the story of three soldiers in World War I, the *Times Literary Supplement* said, ". . . her special talent is to distil and refine the whole tragicomic experience of Ireland and offer us, in remarkably spare, accurate little novels, a handful of people and scenes and smells that convey more about her country than volumes of analysis and documentation."

This tragicomic vision and telescopic detail pervades *The Nightingale and Not the Lark*. Here Ms. Johnston offers a moving portrait of Mamie, an elderly actress who has been reduced to eking out a living as the caretaker of an ancient hall rented by touring companies for play productions. Abandoned by her husband for another actress many years earlier, Mamie conjures up the rascal to vent her frustrations and unfulfilled aspirations. Mamie's past is skillfully counterpointed by the somewhat similar experiences of a young actress now performing in *Romeo and Juliet* in the hall where Mamie works, lives, and entertains her memories.

Ms. Johnston was born in Dublin and was educated there at Trinity College. She is married, has four children, and now lives in Derry, Northern Ireland.

Characters:

Scene:

A room at the top of an old hall in a provincial town, used by touring companies to perform plays, for concerts, lectures and occasional public meetings, etc. The room is fairly large, dusty, cold and generally unacceptable. At the back, a door leads into a small bedroom. To the right, another door leads out onto the landing at the top of a flight of stairs. A skylight gives what light there is to the stairs, and a naked, dusty bulb on each landing.

Mamie is the so-called caretaker of the building, though she hasn't taken much care of anything for years. Sometimes she sweeps down the stairs and empties the waste bins. She is supposed to check each night that the lights and electric fires are out and she keeps the keys of the building in her room. In age she would be in her late sixties, almost out of them, in fact. She is uncaring to the point of grotesqueness about her appearance. Her paltry wages are spent on whiskey and cigarettes. She is really pretty tired of being alive, but, like most of us, apprehensive about the alternative. Nothing good has happened to her for a very long time, but this is, of course, her own fault.

As the curtain rises, Mamie is sitting in the only armchair, half asleep, an empty teacup beside her on the floor, a glass, and an overflowing ashtray. Around the room her belongings are scattered rather than neatly stored, a poor accumulation of a lifetime's bits and pieces.

The stairs are unlit, but from below can be heard the rise and fall of voices on the stage. The play they are acting is Romeo and Juliet; *their style would appear to be somewhat flamboyant. There is a high-backed chair, almost a throne, downstage left, in which a man is sitting. We cannot see him clearly ever; he is, in fact, almost a shadow. He moves as little as possible, just the glimpse occasionally of white hands gesturing.*

There is applause from the distant audience which jolts Mamie from her sleep. She gropes on the floor for her glass and finds it empty. She thinks about this for a moment, then gets to her feet with difficulty and starts to wander round the room, looking for the bottle.

MAMIE: ". . . it was the nightingale and not the lark That pierced the fearful hollow of thine ear; Nightly . . . Nightly she sings . . ."
(She finds the bottle on the crowded draining board and brings it back to the glass)
"Nightly she sings . . ."
OWEN: "On yon pomegranate tree . . ." Pom . . . e . . . gran . . . ate.
MAMIE: Pomegranate.
(She pours whiskey into the glass and sits down again)
OWEN: A disagreeable fruit full of pips, I seem to recollect. Perhaps, of course, I was just unlucky. One had to keep spitting.
MAMIE: Pomegranate. Yes. I didn't remember.
OWEN: You never remembered. I can tell you if you'd eaten one, you'd have remembered, all right.
MAMIE: No one sent for you. I didn't ask for you to come. No . . . I don't remember. Go away! I don't want you here tonight. I . . . don't . . . feel well.
OWEN: When did you last feel well? Ha-ha-ha!
MAMIE: Just go away.
OWEN: I'll go in my own good time.
MAMIE: You always did that. I remember that. I remember . . . What *do* I remember?
OWEN: Like everyone else, you remember what you *want*.
MAMIE: Do I? Not even that.
(Her head droops. Her glass tilts dangerously)
OWEN: You're going to spill your drink.
MAMIE: Wha . . . ? Oh . . . yes . . . thanks.
(She takes a long drink)
OWEN: You always used to tell me . . .
MAMIE: You remember . . . you actually remember?
OWEN: . . . you promised your father . . .
MAMIE: Be careful what you say about poor Daddy!
OWEN: . . . that you wouldn't drink.

MAMIE: I took the pledge. He held my hand and made me promise. . . . I'd have done anything for Daddy. A great, great man. Why did you bring up the subject of Daddy? You know it always upsets me.

OWEN: Yes.

MAMIE: You always said such terrible things about Daddy. You never understood. A man you'd never even met and you used to say such . . .

OWEN: I didn't like what I'd heard about him. The gun was never my weapon.

MAMIE: Shoneen!

OWEN: The word is mightier than the sword.

MAMIE: Renegade!

OWEN: Oh, God, how you used to throw those words at me.

MAMIE: He used to plait my hair for me in the mornings and tie great big silk bows on the ends of the plaits.

OWEN: Green, no doubt.

MAMIE: I had beautiful hair. Right down to my waist. Wavy and soft. He used to sing to me. "Let Erin remember the days of old." His fingers were gentle, not like my mother's; she used to pull the head off me . . . "Ere her faithless sons betrayed her."

OWEN: You were his beautiful Cathleen ni Houlihan.

MAMIE: Yes. How did you know? Yes, I was.

OWEN: You told me twice a week for three years.

MAMIE: "When Malachi wore the collar of gold . . .

(She takes another drink)

Which he won from the proud . . ."

(She nods off as she sings)

OWEN: So . . . useless . . .

(A light goes on on the stairs. A door bangs below. There is the sound of footsteps. Janet appears. She calls up the stairs)

JANET: Mrs. Hall? Mrs. Hall? *(She runs up the stairs and bangs on the door)* Mrs. Hall?

(Mamie stirs and looks around. Carefully, she puts the glass down on the floor and rubs at her face to wake herself up)

JANET: Mrs. Hall?

MAMIE: Coming. Patience. Coming. Old bones move slowly.

(She gets up slowly and goes to the door. It is chained and locked.

She fumbles with the lock and then cautiously opens the door on the chain)

MAMIE: Who is it? What do you want?

JANET: It's only me, Mrs. Hall. Janet. You know . . . Janet. I'm afraid I've lost the key again, the one for the big storeroom . . . I mean mislaid, really, I always find things in the end. I just seem to have no system. I'm sorry. I just wondered if I could borrow yours. Only for half an hour or so.

MAMIE: Oh, yes, Janet.

(She closes the door, unchains it, then opens it)

MAMIE: Come on in, dear. The keys . . . close the door behind you, it's perishing up here. Under the roof. It's always . . . The keys? Now, where . . . ? You never can tell these days. It's always better to keep the door locked.

JANET: I'm sorry to bother you. You must be sick of the sight of me, the way I keep running up and getting things from you. I just have this weakness for mislaying things. Tom says I'm totally disorganized.

MAMIE: Keys.

(She is searching ineffectually around)

JANET: If it wasn't for the fact that no one wants to be an A.S.M. *(Assistant Stage Manager)*, I'm sure they wouldn't keep me a second. We have to clear out tonight. Get everything packed up and all that. It's so stupid of me!

MAMIE: Keys, Keys. Keys. Would you have a cup of tea?

JANET: Well . . . no, really. Not now, anyway. Perhaps later, when I bring the keys back.

MAMIE: A drink?

JANET: No, thanks.

MAMIE: A cigarette? At least have a cigarette.

JANET: I . . .

MAMIE: Maybe you don't smoke? I didn't smoke when I was your age. It's only . . .

JANET: I smoke, all right. I keep meaning to give it up . . . apart from anything else, it's so expensive. But I haven't the will power.

MAMIE: There by the chair. Help yourself. Light one for me.

(Janet picks up the box and opens it. It is empty)

JANET: I'm afraid . . . all gone.

MAMIE: No cigarettes? What'll I do without a cigarette? The nights are so long. I'll never get through the night without . . . You wouldn't understand how bad the nights are.

JANET: I could run out to the pub and get some for you.

MAMIE: Would you do that? That would be a real kindness. But perhaps you wouldn't have the time.

JANET: That's all right. I'll run out now while you're looking for the key. I'll be back in five minutes.

MAMIE: Yes. I'll find the keys.

JANET: So, if you could give me the, well, the money . . .

MAMIE: Yes. Of course. *(Her bag is on the table. She fumbles in it for her purse. She takes out a pound and hands it to the girl)* Gold Leaf. They have Gold Leaf. I know that. Twenty. I'll get out tomorrow. I didn't have time today. There seemed to be so many things to do. You'd be surprised how many things there are to do. Odds and ends. Keeping the place together. It's really a job for a . . . but then . . . I suppose it's good to have a roof over my head.

JANET: And you'll look for the keys? You won't forget?

MAMIE: I'll find them. Don't you worry. I'll lay my hands on them in a moment. They've just walked a little. You know how things walk sometimes.

JANET: I'll be straight back.

(She goes out and closes the door, then runs down the stairs. Mamie pours herself another drink and sits down again in her chair)

MAMIE: Damn keys! Damn walking keys! I tell you one thing, I don't feel a bit well today. Not a bit well.

OWEN: Nor yesterday, nor last year, nor last century.

MAMIE: You never liked me, did you?

OWEN: Not much. You were pretty enough.

MAMIE: Yes, I was, wasn't I? It wasn't just my hair. I was a very beautiful girl.

OWEN: For a while. An instant joy . . . but then . . . oh, then you long for something else. I knew that when you stopped being pretty there would be nothing left. Only a resentment.

MAMIE: That was your fault. *(She shouts suddenly)* You destroyed me! *(He laughs)* Laugh! That's all you ever did. You'd laugh and then you'd walk out and leave me.

OWEN: Nothing ever changed. I came back so many times and nothing had ever changed. It seemed impossible for you to learn.

MAMIE: *You* changed!

OWEN: No. Moved logically on where I had always meant to go. I was lucky. Think of all those poor sods still playing bit parts in dirty halls in Dungarven, Sneem, Ballyshannon. Clothes never out of a suitcase. Chilblains in the winter. Only now they're old. Rheumatism. Telling their grandchildren about their great days in the sticks.

MAMIE: Good days!

OWEN: You don't remember.

MAMIE: "There's rosemary, that's for remembrance; pray love, remember; and there's pansies, that's for thoughts."

OWEN: You were terrible!

MAMIE: "There's fennel for you, and columbines; there's rue for you; and here's some for me; we may call it herb of grace o' Sundays; I would give you some violets, but . . ."

OWEN: No! No! You never could remember your lines. "O, you must wear your rue with a difference."

MAMIE: ". . . they withered all when my father . . . died." When my father died.

OWEN: That was fifty years ago.

MAMIE: I see him there in my mind's eye coming in the gate, smiling, always smiling. Feel his hands plaiting my hair. Why did they have to murder him?

OWEN: Presumably to stop him murdering them.

MAMIE: Everyone was king to me, except you.

OWEN: I married you, didn't I? Wouldn't you call that kindness? What more did you want? You wanted to be my Cathleen ni Houlihan, too. I understood too late.

MAMIE: A home, children, love . . .

OWEN: And what about me?

MAMIE: Most men are happy with that.

OWEN: You're drinking yourself to death.

MAMIE: That's my business.

OWEN: Of course . . . I just thought I'd mention it.

MAMIE: We could have been happy.

OWEN: I only wanted to be an actor. Happiness never came into it. A giant. You wanted to keep me small, tame, someone of insignificance.

MAMIE: No. You could have been the best actor in Ireland.

OWEN: I had the world in mind. I wanted a good fight. I had to get out of this bloody pond.

MAMIE: You never gave it a chance.

OWEN: No. I admit that. My instinct for self-preservation was too strong. I saw myself, the father of seven, each one more like your father than the last, playing Hamlet at the age of fifty, because nobody dared suggest it was time for me to play Claudius instead. You, an eternal, terrible Ophelia. I remember everything.

MAMIE: I wish that girl would hurry up with the cigarettes.

OWEN: You also smoke too much.

MAMIE: It's something to do.

OWEN: I remember . . .

MAMIE: It was all so long ago.

OWEN: Nonetheless . . .

MAMIE: There were good times. No matter what you say.

OWEN: The odd bit of fun . . .

MAMIE: More than that. Do you remember the year we played *Othello*?

OWEN: '38. Cork, Limerick, Galway, Sligo.

MAMIE: Belfast. We even played Belfast. I hated the grey, dirty streets. We couldn't understand what the stagehands said, remember that? They might have been foreign. We laughed.

OWEN: You cried because they didn't give you Desdemona.

MAMIE: No.

OWEN: In those rooms we had in Baggot Street, with the tiny windows looking west over the mountains. The evening sun used to make the walls all golden. You cried. You tried to make me force them.

(Mamie pours out another drink)

MAMIE: That's not true!

OWEN: Yes. Please, you said to me, *please*. Make them! Push them! Please!

MAMIE: I would have been good.

(Owen laughs)

MAMIE: Better than that bitch!

OWEN: Your Emilia was adequate. No more than that.

MAMIE: Denise. Wasn't that her name?

OWEN: Who?

MAMIE: You know quite well who!

(There is a long silence. A light comes on at the bend in the stairs. A door opens and shuts. There is the sound of laughter for a moment)

MAMIE: Where is the girl?

OWEN: You smoke too much.

MAMIE: It's my life . . . my . . . Denise was her name all right! Maybe it wasn't such a good tour after all.

OWEN: It was much the same as any other.

MAMIE: The last one. Was it the last?

OWEN: *Night Must Fall.* Then . . .

MAMIE: You went.

OWEN: I went.

MAMIE: She . . .

OWEN: You had no one to blame but yourself. I asked you to come. Asked and asked. God knows why, but I did. You were my . . .

MAMIE: Yes. Wife.

OWEN: Wife.

MAMIE: We were all right here. What sort of a life would that have been for me? Trailing round after you. Bit parts here and there. No ground under my feet. And she . . . That's no life.

OWEN: What life have you had? Sour with hating. Success, success all the way?

MAMIE: *(Yells at him)* Go back to hell!

(The landing light goes on and Janet runs up the stairs with the cigarettes in her hand. She hears Mamie's voice and pauses for a moment outside the door before knocking)

If it hadn't been for you . . .

(Janet knocks)

MAMIE: Yes? Who's that?

JANET: Mrs. Hall? It's me, Janet. I have your cigarettes for you.

MAMIE: Come in, dear, it's open. Just turn the handle.

(Janet comes in, with her a dreary band of light)

JANET: Gosh, it's dark. Will I . . . ? Maybe you prefer the dark?

MAMIE: I hadn't noticed. It never makes much difference one way or another. Turn on the light, there's a girl. The switch is by the door.

(Janet turns on the light and looks around with surprise. Mamie blinks)

JANET: I hope I'm not bursting in on you. I thought I heard . . .

MAMIE: I'm on my own. Always glad . . . Come in, dear. Shut that door behind you. Drafts, as you get on . . . drafts . . . It's a cold and drafty place, even in summer. No warmth seems to creep in at all. Maybe it's just because I'm getting . . .

JANET: I thought I . . .

MAMIE: Maybe I coughed. I cough a lot. Everyone says I smoke too much.

JANET: There are your cigarettes, and the change.

MAMIE: Thank you, dear. *(She spills the change onto her knee and into the chair and greedily opens the packet. She searches for matches)* I thought I had some here. Things walk, walk. *(She gets up and goes over to the gas ring. She picks up the matches)* Ah! You see. I knew there'd be some around somewhere. Now . . . Have a cup of tea, dear? You must do that after running an errand for me. It won't take a second.

(She turns on the gas jet and fumbles with the matches. The first one she strikes goes out before she can light either the gas or her cigarette. She breaks the next one as she strikes it)

JANET: Here, let me do it. I won't have a cup of tea, thanks. I really haven't time. It's the keys . . . did you find them? *(She lights Mamie's cigarette for her)* Will you have a cup yourself or will I turn off the gas?

MAMIE: Gas?

JANET: Will I light it?

MAMIE: Keys . . .

JANET: Or will I turn it off?

MAMIE: We'll have a cup of tea. I'll just look for those keys. Light it, light it, dear. Gas is so dangerous. Just put a few drops of water in the kettle. It won't take a moment to boil. You may as well have a cup while you're here. I remember when I was your age, I always liked a cup of tea to keep me going during the show. I never drank, you know. I took the pledge just before my father . . . he didn't drink himself.

(Janet pours some water in the kettle and puts it on the gas)

JANET: Did you work in the theatre? There. How amazing! Where do you usually put the keys?

MAMIE: Long ago. You wouldn't even have been born, I don't suppose. Before the war. A little bit during the war, too, but then things started to . . . well . . . tail off a bit . .

nothing was ever the same . . . before the war . . .

JANET: Wow!

MAMIE: I suppose you might say I was stage-struck. It wasn't in my background at all. No. But I just couldn't keep away from the theatre.

JANET: I do understand that, so well. I've never wanted to do anything else.

MAMIE: I had talent.

JANET: Would they be in any of these drawers?

MAMIE: I knew my limitations. That's half the battle. A charming talent. No! Don't touch those drawers.

JANET: Sorry. I just thought . . .

MAMIE: Personal. Those are my private and personal . . . Long ago, folded neatly, not like now . . . folded neatly. Two drawers of my neatly folded past.

JANET: I have a book I stick reviews into. Anything I've been involved in, you know. I, actually, I, well, no one's actually mentioned me yet. Not my name. But all the same . . . they'll be fascinating to look back on some day . . . when I'm . . . well, you know, in the years . . .

MAMIE: Pass me the teapot. Thanks. And the tea. There in that tin. I played Juliet, you know. Just run a little water into the pot to warm it. Some people say it isn't necessary, but it is. The aroma, the true aroma, only bursts out of the leaves when you put them into a warm pot. Juliet and Ophelia and . . . em . . . Desdemona. *(She glances nervously towards Owen)* Desdemona. You have to make absolutely sure that the water is furiously boiling. Yes. I never liked Desdemona. Rinse out a cup for yourself. I have one over by the chair.

JANET: We're doing *Othello* next season.

MAMIE: Will you be playing Desdemona?

JANET: Oh, no . . . I'm not . . . I've really only been working in the theatre a very short time. I only left drama school last year. I went to drama school in England. London. This is my . . .

MAMIE: The keys . . .

JANET: Tom . . . my . . . well, the man I'm going to marry . . . he will be playing Othello. He's fantastic. Really fantastic! One day he'll be . . . really something. Better than Burton. He has that sort of power. It really gets you when you're watching him. He's playing Mercutio at the moment. He thinks it's a far more interesting part than Romeo. He's fantastic! He has the audience absolutely glued . . . glued . . .

MAMIE: Do you think that milk has turned? Smell it. I think it's all right. What key did you say you wanted?

JANET: The big storeroom. No, it's O.K., thanks. I like mine black.

MAMIE: I wouldn't get married if I were you. Not to an actor, anyway.

JANET: Why ever not?

MAMIE: I was married.

JANET: Was your husband an actor?

MAMIE: That's it. That's the one you want. I knew it couldn't be too far away. The storeroom. Yes. An actor.

JANET: Where is he now? I mean . . . why . . . ?

MAMIE: Dead. A long, long time dead.

JANET: I'm sorry.

MAMIE: Long, long. I like a drop of whiskey in my tea. Jizzes it up a bit. Makes you feel less . . . less.

JANET: Less what?

MAMIE: Just less. Feel less. No need to be sorry. He left me and went to London. He didn't want to stay here. He wanted fame and fortune. Fame, anyway. Couldn't see a future for himself here. *(She laughs)* Didn't have any future there either. Hitler killed him. If he hadn't left me he'd still be alive. Playing old men in plays by Chekhov, Leonid Andreyevitch Gaev—Polonius, Uncle Peter. If he hadn't left me . . .

JANET: Was he in the army?

MAMIE: Oh, God, no! Name in lights . . . what am I saying? There were no lights in war time. Name metaphorically in lights. West End. Moving up the ladder, just as he would have wanted and then one night Hitler put a stop to it all. I cried when I heard.

JANET: I'm sure you were very upset.

MAMIE: Tears of joy! When I stopped crying I laughed.

JANET: Honestly, I . . .

MAMIE: It's true. I'm not embarrassed by the thought. She was killed, too. Hand in hand maybe, they left this world.

JANET: She?

MAMIE: She. Bitch! Don't marry.

JANET: All marriages aren't like that. We . . .

MAMIE: Everyone starts out saying we. You end up alone.

JANET: We'll be all right. You can take that from me. Better than all right. We have so much in common. That's very important, don't you think?

MAMIE: The key.

JANET: Oh, yes, thanks.

MAMIE: Have another cup of tea?

JANET: No. I'd better fly. I'll be murdered as it is. I really shouldn't have stayed so long.

MAMIE: You'll bring them back, won't you? I have to have the keys here in case of emergencies.

JANET: Of course. I'll bring back all the keys. Maybe we could have a drink. I'd like you to meet Tom. I might bring him up for a few minutes.

MAMIE: Tom?

JANET: My . . . who I'm going to marry.

MAMIE: Ah, yes. Tom. Bring Tom. I like to have a chat from time to time. Not many people come to see me.

JANET: I'll do that, then. I promise. We'll be up later. Au revoir, then. I'll only say that. *(She opens the door)* You're right about the draft. It's horrible out here. I must rush. See you later, then.

MAMIE: Yes.

(She moves over to the door and after Janet has closed it and run down the stairs, she carefully locks it again)

OWEN: Afraid of burglars?

MAMIE: You never know these days. You hear such terrible things. Read in the papers such . . . old people . . .

OWEN: Or a rapist maybe? Crazy with lust?

MAMIE: You always were crude! *(She goes over to the drawers and brings them one by one over to her chair. She sits down and begins to fumble through the bits and pieces in them. She pours out some whiskey and takes a good drink)* Crude! I always hated crudeness. Vulgarity. Did you and she leave the world hand in hand?

OWEN: Don't be so damn stupid! We weren't even in the same room. I was taking off my make-up. The theatre got a direct hit. One of Hitler's major gestures to the world, a theatre full of actors rubbing furiously at their faces with cotton wool, glistening with cold cream. Here one minute, gone the next! I was changing slowly from Mark Antony back to the anonymous Mr. X. I always enjoyed that process. I don't remember why. My own face always looked so pale and anxious as it appeared from under the make-up. Pale anxiety.

MAMIE: Anxiety! What a vision you had of yourself. You didn't know the meaning of the word!

OWEN: You didn't know me. Only the roles I played.

MAMIE: And she?

OWEN: Oh . . . I don't know. We had certain thoughts that were alike. Our dream was the same.

MAMIE: And look where it got you.

OWEN: What a bitter old hag you are!

MAMIE: I had reason to become bitter.

OWEN: No. Hate and bitterness are destroyers and you were too stupid to see that. You still are. You know quite well I didn't leave you out of passion for some other lady. Self-preservation. You and this country, you would have drowned me in your mediocre charm.

MAMIE: I would have done anything for you.

OWEN: You wouldn't come away with me.

MAMIE: That was too much to ask. Anyway, it was too late then . . . she . . .

OWEN: She was irrelevant.

MAMIE: She was terrible as Desdemona. I remember that. Terrible!

(She imitates a voice from the past)
"I never did
Offend you in my life; never lov'd Cassio
But with such general warranty of heaven
As I might love. I never gave him token."

OWEN: It's a pity you couldn't remember your own lines like you seem to be able to remember hers.

MAMIE: Hand in hand . . .

OWEN: You know nothing about it.

MAMIE: I saw you walk hand in hand to the boat.

OWEN: Did you? I never knew that.

MAMIE: How could you know? You never looked round to see if I were there.

OWEN: That's true. Oh, God, the joy of leaving it all behind. I couldn't have believed I would have felt such joy. Such lightness of spirit.

MAMIE: Here it is. *(She pulls out a newspaper cutting, holds it out in front of her and reads from it in a singsong voice)* "Brilliant young Irish actor killed by direct hit on West End theatre." Dee da dee da Owen Hall dadada great loss dadada and a picture. Makes you look like the young Cary Grant. Maybe it *is* the young Cary Grant. No. It's you all right. Too good to be true. *(She tears up the paper and throws the pieces on the floor)*

OWEN: So much for the young Cary Grant!

MAMIE: They never mentioned her. Not one mention anywhere. She can't have been hitting the high spots. Of course, she wasn't Irish, was she? Trust you to run away with an English woman! Here, listen to this. The . . . um . . . *Irish Times,* September, 1937. "Owen Hall has more than a touch of genius." Remember that?

OWEN: I . . .

MAMIE: *Independent,* May, something. "This sensitive actor can do little wrong." Here *The Times* again, "witty interpretation." The bloody works! *(She tears the papers up and has a drink)* Brilliant. Witty. Sensitive. Dead!

OWEN: I don't know why I stay and listen to all this nonsense.

MAMIE: You have to stay this time. You have to stay until I want you to go. You are merely a figment of my imagination.

OWEN: How lucky for me I didn't have to stay *before*. I might have ended up like you. Better dead, Mamie, dear. Much, much better.

MAMIE: Oh, how my father would have despised you!

OWEN: Daddy always has to have his say.

MAMIE: He died for Ireland. You just died. Died for nothing. Died because you left me. Good old Hitler.

OWEN: Why do you call me back?

MAMIE: Good old Hitler.

OWEN: Always the same recriminations. The same boring words. Over and over again. The only words we have ever been capable of saying to each other.

MAMIE: Good old Hitler. *(Furiously she tears up the papers, scatters the contents of the drawers onto the floor)* One word of kindness, that's all. You loved me once, didn't you?

OWEN: I don't remember. What does loving mean? The spring? Flowers? A pretty girl? Being young? Oh, God, the old myths! No one tells you the truth. You have to find it all out for yourself and then it's too late. Then the energy has faded.

(Mamie stands up with great difficulty)

MAMIE: I was a pretty girl. Like a bird, some people used

to say. It wasn't just my father thought I was beautiful. What
sort of a bird was I like, Owen? Why don't you answer? One of
those long-legged ones that dance on the edge of the sea?
And cry? Mew really, like a cat. They peck as they dance.
Foraging in the damp sand. Or a wren? They are charming
little birds. I think I would have liked that. Why won't you
speak? You could be kind, gallant when you felt like it.

(She moves towards the cooker. She picks up the kettle and fills it)
If my father had been alive . . . if they hadn't . . . I should
never have cut my hair. You never saw it when I wore it long.
Like silk. In the winter sparks would fly out of it when I
brushed it. A hundred strokes a day I always gave it. He
would have seen through you. He always used to say that
there would be no man in the world good enough for me. As
his fingers plaited my hair he used to tell me great stories.
Great . . . I needed someone to look after me.

*(She puts the kettle on the gas and turns on the jet. She strikes a
match, which falls from her trembling fingers to the floor. The box
is now empty. She begins to search vaguely for another box)*
Someone on whom I could lean. He was so strong. You *seemed*
to have strength. I was wrong about that. You only cared
about yourself. Why did you destroy my life? What right had
you to do that? When my mother told me what they'd done to
Daddy, I thought I wouldn't live another day. Men cried at his
funeral. Then I had my hair cut off. I'd never have . . .

*(She wanders over to the chair and looks around. She knows she
is supposed to be looking for something, but can't remember what
it is. She drains the remainder of the bottle into her glass. Takes
a drink)*
Crowds and flowers and men crying. I often wondered what
they did with the little bits of *your* body. And hers. I suppose
her family . . . you had no one. Why do I call you back? Is
that what you asked me? To tell you how much I hate you.
You see, if I didn't have you here beside me I might forget
that. And it's only that hate that keeps me alive. Keeps me
warm. Are you listening? I hate you! You never loved me
enough to hate me. Just despised me, didn't you? Didn't you?
Why don't you answer me? Owen! Owen! Where are you?
Don't go. Please don't leave me alone. I'm . . . afraid on my
own. Owen!

(She searches in her bag and then throws it on the floor)

Keys . . . no, I am afraid! So now you see . . . you have to look after me . . . like Daddy . . . you mustn't leave me alone. Not keys. Matches, matches. Owen!

(There is a burst of clapping from below. She stands quite still and listens, then slowly makes her way to the front of the stage. She bows to the audience, smiles, almost young. She holds her arms out towards them)

Thank you, oh, thank you!

(She holds up a hand. The clapping dies away)

On behalf of . . . on behalf of us all here . . . I would like to thank you for being such a wonderful audience. Wonderful. Goodnight and God bless you all!

(She bows again. Steps back and takes the hands of the imaginary actors on each side of her. She bows again. Head up smiling to the gallery. Below a door opens and Janet and Tom, a young man, appear. Mamie turns and slips on the papers on the floor. She makes a grab for the arm of her chair and doesn't quite make it. She falls on to her knees)

MAMIE: "And will he not come again?
And will he not come again?
No, no, he is dead;
Go to . . ."

JANET: Only for a tick, darling . . . Just to say hello to the old girl. I promise we won't stay. Please!

MAMIE: ". . . thy death bed;
He never will come again."

TOM: No! I said no. We'll be there for hours. You know perfectly well. We'd never get away. It's our last night here and I'm damned if I spend it with that drunken old cow! Come on, there's a girl. They're waiting for us in the pub.

JANET: One minute.

MAMIE: "He never will . . . come . . ."

TOM: I'm not coming a step further and that's that. I'm parched. You go up and hold her hand, if that's what you want. I'll be in the pub when you've finished.

MAMIE: ". . . again."

(Her head falls on to the chair)

JANET: Don't go without me. Wait. I'll just hand her in the keys and . . .

TOM: No messing about.

(She runs up the stairs. She stands at the door for a moment, not quite knowing what to do)

TOM: For God's sake, Janet, get on with it. There's no point in wasting good drinking time.

(He goes)

JANET: Tom! Wait!

(She hangs the keys over the door knob and turns and runs down the stairs after him)

JANET: Tom! Wait! You greedy pig, wait for me!

(Soon there is only silence and the curtain falls)

Brian Friel

AMERICAN WELCOME

Brian Friel

In 1966 Brian Friel, then recognized on both sides of the Atlantic as one of Ireland's most talented and successful young short story writers, exploded onto the Broadway scene with his portrait of a young Irishman's farewell to his native country and family in *Philadelphia, Here I Come*. Overnight, the Irishman was heralded as an international playwright of the first order. Upon achieving this success Friel gave up his teaching career, which he had pursued while gaining his reputation as a master of the short story.

Other theatrical triumphs soon followed. His next play was *The Loves of Cass McGuire*, which gave actress Ruth Gordon one of her most noteworthy roles. Friel then wrote two one-act plays, *Winners* and *Losers*, presented in New York under the title *Lovers*, which Walter Kerr praised in *The New York Times* as ". . . effortlessly hilarious, thoroughly in charge of its own raffish and rambunctious tone from first gasp to last."

His next play, *Crystal and Fox*, moved from Dublin to Los Angeles. This was followed by *The Mundy Scheme*, a satirical look at Ireland's socio-political scene. Friel again delighted Dublin theatregoers with a different aspect of Irish life with the offshore inhabitants of *The Gentle Island*. Following shortly was *The Freedom of the City* with virtually simultaneous premiers at The Abbey Theatre and at the Royal Court Theatre in London.

His most recent productions include *Volunteers*, produced at Northampton, Massachusetts in 1977; *Faith Healer*, produced on Broadway in 1979; *Aristocrats*, presented at The Abbey Theatre in 1979; *Translations*, which opened in Northern Ireland in 1980; and a new adaptation of Chekhov's *Three Sisters*, commissioned by The Abbey Theatre.

American Welcome was first presented at Jon Jory's Actors Theatre of Louisville during the marathon fourth Festival of New American Plays in March, 1980. During this event which took place in a forty-eight hour period, audiences could view five full-length plays, a cabaret musical, an hour-long monodrama, two one-act plays, and an anthology of ten sketches. Friel's play was one of the ten-sketch set of satirical jibes at American mores, written by non-American, English-speaking playwrights. Among the other playwrights sharing the bill were Brian Clark, Wole Soyinka, and Athol Fugard.

American Welcome is an impish satire on an American stage

director trying to distort the new script of a dumbfounded European playwright. No doubt most playwrights, domestic as well as foreign, have had similar experiences, but the parable extends to any situation in which ego attempts to prevail over ability.

Characters:

THE EUROPEAN
THE AMERICAN

A hotel lobby. Piped music in background. Two chairs, one on each side of a small table. On one chair sits The European, a large brown envelope on his lap. He casually surveys his surroundings. After a few seconds, The American enters, carrying a briefcase. He looks around, spots The European, bears down on him. The American is young. He speaks very rapidly and gives excessive emphasis to several words in each sentence.

AMERICAN: It *is* Mr. Smith, isn't it? Mr. John Smith? I'd recognize that distinguished head anywhere! I'm Bert —remember? We've corresponded. I'm directing your play. Welcome, Sir! Welcome to America!
(They shake hands)
No, no. Don't get up—please. *(He sits)* May I? Well! You've made it! You're here! Gosh! And may I tell you, Sir, how honored and how privileged we are to have you here with us. I'm sure you're still groggy with jet-lag, are you? Can I get you something to eat, something to drink? How's your hotel? Had you a good flight? Can I get you a coffee? Tea? Beer? May I call you Joe? Thank you. And may I make a personal comment? You look so European—it's uncanny!
(Without breaking his speech he opens his briefcase and takes out a script and a large notepad)
Wonderful. Okay. Let's get down to business. But before we do, Jim, may I tell you just once more how magnificent, how truly magnificent your play is—I mean that—and how honored and privileged I am to be associated with it. I really mean that. You see, Bill, what you have given us is a perfectly conceived and perfectly executed analysis of the human condition the world over. It's so perfect it—it—it's frightening. Beautiful form. Electrifying language. Subtle wit. Penetrating insights. I mean to say that's art—that's real art —that's European art, if you know what I mean. What I'm trying to say, Tom, is this: you have entrusted me with this

delicate perfection—and I'm scared. I say to myself: "Bert, can you handle it? Are you worthy of it?"
You're tired. Can I get you something? Coffee? Tea? Beer? Okay. Fine. What have I got here? A few questions. Do you mind if I ask you a few silly questions? Just for my own enlightenment, I knew you wouldn't mind. And may I tell you, Chuck, how honored and how privileged we are to have you here with us? First problem: language. Frankly, we're uneasy with the language. I mean to say we're not uneasy with the language—it's just that there's a lot of it we don't understand. Simply a question of usage; or to be more accurate, simply a question of our ignorance of your usage. I've made a list here—words like "boot," "bumper," "chemist" —there are maybe a dozen of them. Frankly, we don't know what you mean. And since you want to communicate with American audiences and since we want them to understand you, I mean to say what we did was this. We went to our most distinguished American playwright—and you've got to meet him while you're here; he just adores your work—and what he did for us was this. He took all those little confusing words—five or six thousand approximately—and with wonderful delicacy and skill and with the utmost respect for the rhythms and tones of your speech, he did this most beautiful job of translating the play into the language we speak and understand. I hope you'll approve. I know you'll approve.
Can I get you something? Coffee? Tea? Beer? Gosh! I really can't believe it, Mike! You're actually here! I'm just knocked-out!
Okay. Second problem: the form of your play. We're uneasy with the form. I mean to say we're not uneasy with the form—it's just that you've written this wonderful naturalistic play but you've written it in monologue form! A naturalistic play in monologue form, for God's sake! I mean to say a monologue is just not naturalistic if you don't mind my saying so. Let me qualify that instantly. The monologue may be naturalistic in Europe but it is not "natural" to us. We talk, we exchange, we communicate. And since you want to communicate with American audiences and since we want them to understand you, I mean to say what we did was this. We went to our most distinguished American playwright—and you've got to meet him while you're here; he just reveres your

work—and what he did for us was this. He took your little monologue and with wonderful delicacy and skill and with the utmost respect for the rhythms and tones of your speech, he did this most beautiful job of transforming your script into a four-character, two-act, single-set comedy that is just—how can I tell you?—just breathtaking. I hope you'll approve. I *know* you'll approve.

You're suffering from jet-lag—I can see it. Can I get you something? Gin? Whisky? Brandy? Gosh! I really can't believe it, Dan! You're actually here! I'm just knocked-out!

(He sits back, relaxes, smiles, contentedly)

Well, that wasn't too bad now, was it? And here we are, all set to go. And let me tell you this. We think—*hell, we know!*—that we've got the most distinguished, the funniest, the most sensitive, the most disturbing, the most enlightening and the most moving play of the season—a big, big, big hit that is going to make us all rich and famous.

And may I tell you once more how honored and how privileged we are to have you here with us. May I shake that distinguished hand again?

Welcome, Tony Brown, welcome to America!

(He takes the European's hand and pumps it with enthusiasm)

Blackout

Christopher Durang

SISTER MARY IGNATIUS EXPLAINS IT ALL FOR YOU

Christopher Durang

Christopher Durang, like his contemporaries David Mamet, Michael Christofer and Albert Innaurato, received his first professional productions in a regional theatre—the Yale Repertory Theatre under the management of Robert Brustein, at that time Dean of Yale School of Drama. Mr. Durang's first offering there in the 1974–75 season was *The Idiot's Karamazov*, an iconoclastic travesty of Western literature written in collaboration with Albert Innaurato (whose play *The Transfiguration of Benno Blimpie* appeared in *The Best Short Plays 1978*).

Other productions followed in rapid succession: *Das Lusitania Songspiel* and *Titanic* appeared in 1976, the first a satire on Bertolt Brecht, for which Durang and his co-author Sigourney Weaver received Drama Desk acting award nominations, the latter a satire on sexuality, which *New Yorker* critic Edith Oliver called ". . . a merry and (innocently) obscene farce." In 1977 Yale Repertory premiered *The Vietnamization of New Jersey (A American Tragedy)*, a burlesque of David Rabe's *Sticks and Bones*. Also in 1977, *A History of the American Film*, a play with music by Mel Marvin (developed at Lloyd Richard's O'Neill National Playwrights Conference), was staged in separate productions within a two month period at the Hartford Stage Company in Connecticut, the Mark Taper Forum in Los Angeles, and the Arena Stage in Washington, D.C. In the 1978–79 season, Durang's translation of *Tales from the Vienna Woods* by Odon von Horvath was presented by the Yale Repertory Theatre.

Mr. Durang made his Broadway debut with another production of *A History of the American Film*, presented at the ANTA Theatre in March of 1978. The play and its music parody and satirize dozens of American films from *The Grapes of Wrath* through *Earthquake*, and film stars from Bette Davis through Anthony Perkins. Richard Eder, writing in the *New York Times*, described it as ". . . a very funny carnival . . . authentic, inspired and possessed." The production gleaned a Tony nomination for Best Book of a Musical, and many regional and college productions followed.

Raised in a Catholic family in Berkeley, New Jersey, Mr. Durang started writing musicals while still in high school. During his senior year he considered entering the priesthood, but decided instead to go to Harvard, where he majored in English. While there he took a playwriting course with

William Alfred, author of *Hogan's Goat.* Durang continued his studies at Yale School of Drama, where he held a playwriting fellowship.

Mr. Durang's most recent play, *Beyond Therapy,* a full-length comedy about two confused lovers and their therapists, was commissioned by the Phoenix Theatre and produced in January, 1981, at Marymount Manhattan.

The influence of Mr. Durang's Catholic training and his criticism of certain elements of it are unmistakable in *Sister Mary Ignatius Explains It All For You.* In this outrageous satire on the rigidity of dogma, a traditional nun is confronted by former students whose lives she has failed to control. Terry Curtis Fox in the *Village Voice* raves: ". . . [it] is a hysterically funny, bitter, anguished, out-of-control moral comedy that stands as a rebuke to all 'bad taste humor' which refuses to acknowledge the implications of its attacks. Durang reveals himself to be as angry as Lenny Bruce . . . he has . . . dared to let the laughs drop for part of his play in order to make his audience squirm. It is one of those grand moments where an unbridled talent finally shows what he is capable of doing."

Presented at Curt Dempster's Ensemble Studio Theatre in New York in December of 1979, the play received an Obie award for the author and the leading lady. It was presented with the following cast:

SISTER MARY IGNATIUS   Elizabeth Franz
THOMAS   Mark Stefan
GARY SULLAVAN   Gregory Grove
DIANE SYMONDS   Ann McDonough
PHILOMENA ROSTOVITCH   Prudence Wright Holmes
ALOYSIUS BUSICCIO (BENHEIM)   Don Marino

Director: Jerry Zaks

Characters:

SISTER MARY IGNATIUS
THOMAS
GARY SULLAVAN
DIANE SYMONDS
PHILOMENA ROSTOVITCH
ALOYSIUS BENHEIM

Enter Sister Mary Ignatius, dressed in an old-fashioned nun's habit. The stage is fairly simple. There should be a lectern, a potted palm, a few chairs. There is also an easel, or some sort of stand, on which are several drawings made on cardboard, the only one we can see at the top of the play is either blank or is a simple cross. Sister looks at the audience until she has their attention, then smiles, albeit somewhat wearily. She then begins her lecture, addressing the audience directly.

SISTER: *(Crossing herself)* In the name of the Father, and of the Son, and of the Holy Ghost, Amen. *(Shows the next drawing on the easel, which is a neat if childlike picture of the planet earth, the sun, and moon)* First there is the earth. Near the earth is the sun, and also nearby is the moon. *(Goes to next picture which, split in three, shows the gates of heaven amid clouds, some sort of murky area of paths, or some other image that might suggest waiting, wandering, and a third area of people burning up in flames, with little devils with little pitchforks, poking them)* Outside the universe, where we go after death, is heaven, hell, and purgatory. Heaven is where we live in eternal bliss with our Lord Jesus Christ. *(Bows her head)* Hell is where we are eternally deprived of the presence of our Lord Jesus Christ *(Bows her head)*, and are thus miserable. This is the greatest agony of hell, but there are also unspeakable physical torments, which we shall nonetheless speak of later. Purgatory is the middle area where we go after death to suffer if we have not been perfect in our lives and are thus not ready for heaven, or if we have not received the sacraments and made a good confession to a priest right before our death. Purgatory, depending on our sins, can go on for a very, *very* long time and is fairly unpleasant. Though we do not yet know whether there is any physical torment in purgatory, we do know that there is much psychological torment because we are being delayed from being in the presence of our Lord Jesus Christ. *(Bows her head)* For those non-Catholics present, I bow my head to show respect for our Saviour when I say His Name. Our Lord Jesus Christ. *(Bows head)* Our Lord Jesus Christ. *(Bows head)* Our Lord Jesus Christ. *(Bows head)* You can expect to be in purgatory for anywhere from three hundred years to seven hundred billion years. This may sound like forever, but don't forget in terms of eternity seven hundred billion years *does* come to an end. All things come to an end except our Lord Jesus Christ. *(Bows head. Points to the drawing again, reviewing her point)* Heaven, hell, purgatory. *(Smiles. Goes to the next drawing which, like that of purgatory, is of a murky area, perhaps with a prison-like fence, and which has unhappy baby-like creatures floating about in it)* There is also limbo, which is where unbaptized babies were sent for eternity before the Ecumenical Council and Pope John XXIII. The unbaptized babies sent to limbo never leave limbo and so never get to heaven. *Now* unbaptized babies are sent straight to purgatory where, presumably, someone baptizes them and then they are sent on to heaven. The unbaptized babies who died before the Ecumenical Council, however, remain in limbo and will never be admitted to heaven. Limbo is not all that unpleasant, it's just that it isn't heaven and you never leave there. I want to be very clear about the Immaculate Conception. It does not mean that the Blessed Mother gave birth to Christ without the prior unpleasantness of physical intimacy. That is true but is not called the Immaculate Conception; that is called the Virgin Birth. The Immaculate Conception means that the Blessed Mother was herself born without original sin. Everyone makes this error, it makes me lose my patience. That Mary's conception was immaculate is an infallible statement. A lot of fault-finding non-Catholics run around saying that Catholics believe that the Pope is infallible whenever he speaks. This is untrue. The Pope is infallible only on certain occasions, when he speaks "ex cathedra," which is Latin for "out of the cathedral." When he speaks ex cathedra, we must accept what he says at that moment as dogma, or risk hell fire; or, now that things are becoming more liberal, many, many years in purgatory. I would now like a glass of water. Thomas. *(Enter Thomas dressed as parochial school boy with tie and blazer. It would be nice if he could look age seven)* This is Thomas, he is seven years old and in the second grade of Our Lady of

Perpetual Sorrow School. Seven is the age of reason, so now that Thomas has turned seven he is capable of choosing to commit sin or not to commit sin, and God will hold him accountable for whatever he does. Isn't that so, Thomas?

THOMAS: Yes, Sister.

SISTER: Before we turn seven, God tends to pay no attention to the bad things we do because He knows we can know no better. Once we turn seven, He feels we are capable of knowing. Thomas, who made you?

THOMAS: God made me.

SISTER: Why did God make you?

THOMAS: God made me to show forth His goodness and share with us His happiness.

SISTER: What is the sixth commandment?

THOMAS: The sixth commandment is thou shalt not commit adultery.

SISTER: What is forbidden by the sixth commandment?

THOMAS: The sixth commandment forbids all impurities in thought, word or deed, whether alone or with others.

SISTER: That's correct, Thomas. *(Gives him a cookie)* Thomas has a lovely soprano voice which the Church used to preserve by creating castrati. Thomas unfortunately will lose his soprano voice in a few years and will receive facial hair and psychological difficulties in its place. To me, it is not a worthwhile exchange. You may go now, Thomas. What is the fourth commandment?

THOMAS: The fourth commandment is honor thy mother and thy father.

SISTER: Very good. *(Gives him a cookie. He exits)* Sometimes in the mornings I look at all the children lining up in front of school, and I'm overwhelmed by a sense of sadness and exhaustion thinking of all the pain and suffering and personal unhappiness they're going to face in their lives. *(Looks sad, eats a cookie)* But can their suffering compare with Christ's on the cross? Let us think of Christ on the cross for a moment. Try to feel the nails ripping through His hands and feet. Some experts say that the nails actually went through His wrists, which was better for keeping Him up on the cross, though of course most of the statues have the nails going right through His palms. Imagine those nails being driven through: pound, pound, pound, rip, rip, rip. Think of the crown of thorns eating into His skull, and the sense of infection that He must have felt in His brain and near His eyes. Imagine blood from His brain spurting forth through His eyes, imagine His vision squinting through a veil of red liquid. Imagine these things, and then just *dare* to feel sorry for the children lining up outside of school. We dare not; His suffering was greater than ours. He died for our sins! Yours and mine. We put Him up there, you did, all you people sitting out there. He loved us so much that He came all the way down to earth just so He could be nailed painfully to a cross and hang there for three hours. Who else has loved us as much as that? I come from a large family. My father was big and ugly, my mother had a nasty disposition and didn't like me, and there were twenty-six of us. It took three hours just to wash the dishes, but Christ hung on that cross for three hours and *He* never complained. We lived in a small, ugly house, and I shared a room with all my sisters. My father would bring home drunken bums off the street, and let them stay in the same room as himself and my mother. "Whatever you do to the least of these, you do also to Me," Christ said. Sometimes these bums would make my mother hysterical, and we'd have to throw water on her. Thomas, could I have some more water please? And some chocolates?

(Enter Thomas)

Who made you?

THOMAS: God made me.

SISTER: What is the ninth commandment?

THOMAS: The ninth commandment is thou shalt not covet thy neighbor's wife.

SISTER: What is forbidden by the ninth commandment?

THOMAS: The ninth commandment forbids all indecency in thought, word and deed, whether alone or with thy neighbor's wife.

SISTER: Thank you. Go away again. *(He exits)* Bring the little children unto me, Our Lord said. I don't remember in reference to what. I have your questions here on little file cards. *(Reads)* If God is all powerful, why does He allow evil in the world? *(Goes to next card with no reaction. Reads)* Tell us some more about your family. *(Smiles)* We said grace before every meal. My mother was a terrible cook. She used to boil chopped meat. She hated little children, but they couldn't use birth control. Let me explain this one more time. Birth control is wrong because God, whatever you may think about the wisdom involved, created sex for the purpose of procreation, *not* recreation. Everything in this world has a purpose. We eat food to feed our bodies. We don't eat and then make ourselves throw up immediately afterward, do we? So it should be with sex. Either it is done for its proper purpose, or it is just so much throwing up, morally speaking. Next question. *(Reads)* Do nuns go to the bathroom? Yes. *(Reads)* Was Jesus effeminate? Yes. *(Reads)* I have a brain tumor and am afraid of dying. What should I do? Now I thought I had explained what happens after death to you already. There is heaven, hell and purgatory. What is the problem? "Oh ye of little faith," Christ said to someone. All right. As any seven year old knows, there are two kinds of sin: mortal sin and venial sin. Venial sin is the less serious kind, like if you tell a small lie to your parents, or when you kick a barking dog. If you die with any venial sins on your conscience, no matter how many of them there are, you can eventually work it all out in purgatory. However—mortal sin, on the other hand, is the most serious kind of sin you can do—murder, sex outside of marriage, hijacking a plane, masturbation—and if you die with any of these sins on your soul, even just one, you will go straight to hell and burn for all of eternity. Now to rid yourself of mortal sin, you must go make a good confession and vow never to do it again. If, as many of you know, you are on your way to confession to confess a mortal sin and you are struck by a car or bus before you get there, God may forgive you without confession if before you die you manage to say a good act of contrition. If you die instantaneously and are unable to say a good act of contrition, you will go straight to hell. Thomas, come read this partial list of those who are going to burn in hell.

(Enter Thomas)

THOMAS: *(Reads)* Christine Keeler, Roman Polanski, Zsa Zsa Gabor, the editors of *After Dark* magazine, Linda Lovelace, Georgina Spelvin, Big John Holmes, Brooke Shields, David Bowie, Mick Jagger, Patty Hearst, Betty Comden, Adolph Green.

SISTER: This is just a partial list. It is added to constantly. Thomas, how can we best keep from going to hell?

THOMAS: By not committing a mortal sin, by keeping close to the sacraments, especially going to confession and receiving communion, and by obeying our parents.

(She gives him a cookie)

SISTER: Good boy. Do you love our Lord, Thomas?

THOMAS: Yes, Sister.

SISTER: How much?

THOMAS: This much. *(Holds arms out wide)*

SISTER: Well, that's very nice, but Christ loves us an infinite amount. How do we know that, Thomas?

THOMAS: Because you tell us.

SISTER: That's right. And by His actions. He died on the cross for us to make up for our sins. Wasn't that nice of Him?

THOMAS: Very nice.

SISTER: And shouldn't we be grateful?

THOMAS: Yes, we should.

SISTER: That's right, we should. *(Gives him a cookie)* How do you spell cookie?

THOMAS: C-o-o-k-i-e.

SISTER: Very good. *(Gives him a cookie)* Mary has had an argument with her parents and has shot and killed them. Is that a venial sin or a mortal sin?

THOMAS: That's a mortal sin.

SISTER: If she dies with this mortal sin on her soul, will she go to heaven or to hell?

THOMAS: She will go to hell.

SISTER: Very good. How do you spell ecumenical?

THOMAS: *(Sounding it out)* Eck—e-c-k; you—u; men—m-e-n; ical—i-c-k-l-e.

SISTER: Very good. *(Gives him a cookie)* What's two plus two?

THOMAS: Four.

SISTER: What's one and one and one and one and one and one and one and one and one?

THOMAS: Nine.

SISTER: Very good. *(Gives him a cookie)* Because she is afraid to show her parents her bad report card, Susan goes to the top of a tall building and jumps off. Is this a venial sin or a mortal sin?

THOMAS: Mortal sin.

SISTER: And where will she go?

THOMAS: Hell.

SISTER: Sit on my lap. *(He does)* Would you like to keep your pretty soprano voice forever?

THOMAS: Yes, Sister.

SISTER: Well, we'll see what we can do about it. *(Sings)*
Cookies in the morning, cookies in the evening,
Cookies in the summertime,
Be my little cookie,
And love me all the time.
God, I've done so much talking, I've got to rest. Here, you take care of some of these questions, Thomas, and I'll sleep a little. *(To audience)* I'll just be a minute.

(She closes her eyes, he looks at cards)

THOMAS: *(Reads)* How do we know there is a God? We know that there is a God because the Church tells us so. And also because everything has a primary cause. Dinner is put on the table because the primary cause, our mother, has put it in the oven and cooked it. *(Reads)* If God is all powerful, why does He allow evil? *(Skips that one; next one)* What does God look like? God the father looks like an old man with a long white beard.

SISTER: I'll take the next one. *(Reads)* Are you ever sorry you became a nun? I am never sorry I became a nun. *(Reads)* It used to be a mortal sin to eat meat on Fridays, and now it isn't. Does that mean that people who ate meat on Fridays back when it was a sin are in hell? Or what? People who ate meat on Fridays back when it was a mortal sin are indeed in hell if they did not confess the sin before they died. If they confessed it, they are not in hell, unless they did not confess some other mortal sin they committed. People who would eat meat on Fridays back in the fifties tended to be the sort who would commit other mortal sins, so on a guess, I bet many of them *are* in hell for other sins, even if they did confess the eating of meat. *(Reads)* What exactly went on in Sodom? *(Irritated)* Who asked me this question? *(Reads)* Why is St. Christopher no longer a saint, and did anyone listen to the prayers I prayed to him before they decided he didn't exist? The name Christopher means Christ-bearer and we used to believe that he carried the Christ child across a river on his shoulders. Then sometime around Pope John XXIII, the Catholic Church decided that this was just a story and didn't really happen. I am not convinced that when we get to heaven we may not find that St. Christopher *does* indeed exist and that he dislikes Pope John XXIII; however, if he does not exist, then the prayers you prayed to him would have been picked up by St. Jude. St. Jude is the patron saint of hopeless causes. When you have a particularly terrible problem that has little hope of being solved, you pray to St. Jude. When you lose or misplace something, you pray to St. Anthony. *(Reads)* I am an Aries. Is it a sin to follow your horoscope? It is a sin to follow your horoscope because only God knows the future and He won't tell us. Also, we can tell that horoscopes are false because according to astrology Christ would be a Capricorn, and Capricorn people are cold, ambitious and attracted to Scorpio and Virgo, and we know that Christ was warm, loving, and not attracted to anybody. Give me a cookie, Thomas. *(He does)* I'm going to talk about Sodom a bit. Thomas, please leave the stage. *(He does. She talks softer)* To answer your question, Sodom is where they committed acts of homosexuality and bestiality in the Old Testament, and God, infuriated by this, destroyed them all in one fell swoop. Modern day Sodoms are New York City, San Francisco, Amsterdam, Los Angeles, . . . well, basically anywhere where the population is over 50,000. The only reason that God has not destroyed these modern day Sodoms is that Catholic nuns and priests live in these cities, and God does not wish to destroy them. He does, however, give these people body lice and hepatitis. It's so hard to know why God allows wickedness to flourish. I guess it's because God wants man to choose goodness freely of his own free will; sometimes one wonders if free will is worth all the trouble if there's going to be so much evil and unhappiness, but God knows best, presumably. If it were up to me, I might be tempted to wipe out cities and civilizations, but luckily for New York and Amsterdam, I'm not God. *(Reads)* Tell us some more about your family. *(Smiles, pleased)* I had twenty-six brothers and sisters. From my family five became priests, seven became nuns, three became brothers, and the rest of them were institutionalized. My mother was also institutionalized shortly after she started thinking my father was Satan. Some days when we were little, we'd come home and not be able to find our mother and we'd pray to St. Anthony to help us find her. Then when we'd find her with her head in the oven, we would pray to St. Jude to make her sane again. *(Reads)* Are all our prayers answered? Yes, they are; what people who ask that question often don't realize is that sometimes the answer to our prayer is "no." Dear God, please make my mother not be crazy. God's answer: no. Dear

God, please let me recover from cancer. God's answer: no. Dear God, please take away this toothache. God's answer: all right, but you're going to be run over by a car. But every bad thing that happens to us, God has a special reason for. God is the good shepherd, we are His flock. And if God is grouchy or busy with more important matters, His beloved mother Mary is always there to intercede for us. I shall now sing the Hail Mary in Latin. *(Sister motions to the lighting booth, and the lights change to an apparently pre-arranged special spotlight for her, atmospheric with blue spill and back lighting, the rest of the stage becomes fairly dim. Sings)*

Ave Maria,
Gratia plena,
Maria, gratia plena,
Maria, gratia plena,
Ave, Ave! . . . (etc.)

> *(As Sister sings, enter four people, ages 28–30, they are a woman dressed as the Blessed Mother, a man dressed as St. Joseph, and two people, a man and a woman, dressed as a camel. The Blessed Mother sits on the back of the camel, which is lead in by St. Joseph. Because of the dim lighting, we don't see them too clearly at first. Sister, either sensing something happening due to the audience or else just by turning her head, suddenly sees them and is terribly startled and confused)*

ST. JOSEPH: We're sorry we're late.

SISTER: Oh, dear God! *(Kneels)*

ST. JOSEPH: Sister, what are you doing?

SISTER: You look so real.

ST. JOSEPH: Sister, I'm Gary Sullavan, and *(Pointing to the Blessed Mother)* this is Diane Symonds. We were in your fifth grade class in 1959, and you asked us to come today. Don't you remember?

SISTER: 1959?

GARY: Don't you remember asking us?

SISTER: Not very distinctly. *(Louder, to lighting booth)* Could I have some lights please? *(Lights come back up to where they were before. To Gary)* What did I want you to do?

GARY: You wanted us to put on a pageant.

SISTER: That camel looks false to me.

PHILOMENA: Hello, Sister. *(She's the front of the camel)*

SISTER: I thought so.

PHILOMENA: It's Philomena, Sister. Philomena Rostovitch.

ALOYSIUS: And Aloysius Benheim. *(He's the back of the camel)*

SISTER: I don't really recognize any of you. Of course, you're not in your school uniforms.

DIANE: 1959.

SISTER: What?

DIANE: You taught us in 1959.

SISTER: I recognize you. Mary Jean Mahoney?

DIANE: I'm not Mary Jean Mahoney. I'm Diane Symonds.

SISTER: This is all so confusing.

GARY: Don't you want to see the pageant?

SISTER: What pageant is it?

GARY: We used to perform it at Christmas in your class; every class did. You said it was written in 1948 by Mary Jean Mahoney, who was your best student, you said.

DIANE: You said she was very elevated, and that when she was in the seventh grade she didn't have her first period, she had a stigmata.

SISTER: Oh yes. They discovered it in gym class. Mary Jean Mahoney. She entered a cloistered order of nuns upon her graduation from twelfth grade. Sometimes late at night I can hear her praying. Mary Jean Mahoney. Yes, let's see her pageant again. *(To audience)* She was such a bright student. *(Vague)* I remember asking them to come now, I think. I wanted to tell you about Mary Jean Mahoney, and the perfect faith of a child. Yes, the pageant, please. Thomas, come watch with me.

(Thomas enters and sits on Sister's lap)

GARY: *(Announcing)* The pageant of the birth and death of Our Beloved Saviour Jesus Christ, by Mary Jean Mahoney as told to Mrs. Robert J. Mahoney. The setting: a desert near Bethelem. St. Joseph and the Virgin Mary and their trusty camel must flee from the wicked King Herod.

DIANE: *(Sings, to tune of "We Gather Together to ask the Lord's Blessings")*

Hello, my name's Mary,
And his name is Joseph,
We're parents of Jesus,
Who's not been born yet,

We're fleeing from Herod,
And nobody knows if,

We'll make it to the town,
But we'll try, you can bet.

And I'm still a virgin,
And he's not the father,
The father descended
From heaven above,

And this is our camel,
He's really not much bother,
We're off to Bethlehem,
Because God is love.

GARY: Here's an Inn, Mary. But there doesn't look like there's any room.

DIANE: Well, ask them, Joseph.

GARY: *(Knocks on imaginary door)* Excuse me, you don't have room at this Inn, do you? *(Listens)* He said they don't, Mary.

DIANE: Oh, dear. Well, let's try another Inn.

GARY: *(Knocks)* Excuse me, you don't have room at this Inn, do you? *(Listens)* He says they don't allow camels.

DIANE: Let's try the third Inn.

GARY: *(Knocks)* Excuse me, you don't have room at your Inn, do you? *(Listens)* I thought not . . . what? You would? Oh, Mary, this kind Innkeeper says that even though he has no room at the Inn, we can sleep in his stable.

DIANE: Do I look like a barn animal?

GARY: Mary, we really haven't any choice.

DIANE: Yes, we do. Sister says we have choice over everything, because God gave us free will to decide between good and evil. And so I choose to stay in the stable.

GARY: Well, here it is.

DIANE: Pew! It smells just like the zoo Mommy took me and Cynthia to visit last summer. We liked to look at the animals, but we didn't like to smell them.

GARY: I don't think there are any sheets.

DIANE: I don't need sheets, I'm so tired, I could sleep anywhere.

GARY: Well, that's good. Goodnight, Mary.

DIANE: But I do need pillows.

GARY: Mary, what can I do? We don't have any pillows.

DIANE: I can't sleep without pillows.

GARY: Let's pray to God then. If you just pray, He answers your prayers.

DIANE: Sometimes he says no, Joseph.

GARY: I know, but let's try. Dear God, we beseech thee, hear our prayer.

DIANE: Pillows! Pillows! Pillows!

GARY: And behold God answered their prayers.

CAMEL: *(Philomena)* We have an idea, Mary and Joseph. We have two humps, and you can use them as pillows.

DIANE: Thank you, God! Come on, Joseph. Let's go to sleep.

CAMEL: *(As Mary and Joseph start to sleep, sings a lullaby:)*
Rockaby, and good night,
May God keep you and watch you,
Rockabye, and good night, (etc.)
(They sleep. Aloysius makes baby crying noises, tosses out a doll onto the floor)

DIANE: *(Seeing the doll)* Joseph, He's born. Jesus is born.

GARY, DIANE, and CAMEL: *(Sing)*
Joy to the world, the Saviour's come,
Let earth receive her king,
La la la la la la la la,
La la la la la la la la,
Let heaven and nature sing,
Let heaven and nature sing,
Let heaven, and heaven, and nature sing!

GARY: *(To doll)* Can you say Poppa, Jesus? Can you say Momma?

DIANE: He's not that kind of child, Joseph. He was born without original sin like me. This is called my Immaculate Conception, which is not to be confused with my Virgin Birth. Everyone makes this error, it makes me lose my patience. *We* must learn from *him,* Joseph.

GARY: *(To audience)* And so Jesus instructed His parents, and the priests in the Temple, and he said many unusual things, many of them irritating to parents. Things like "Before Abraham was, I am." And "Do you not know that I must go about my father's business?" after we'd been worried to death and unable to find Him for hours and hours. And He performed many miracles.

DIANE: He turned water into wine.

GARY: He made cripples walk.

DIANE: He walked on the water.

GARY: And then came the time for His crucifixion. And his mother said to him:

DIANE: *(To doll)* But why, Jesus, why? Why must you be crucified? And what do you mean by "I must die so that others may know eternal life"?

GARY: And Jesus explained that because Adam and Eve, especially Eve, had sinned that mankind was cursed until Jesus could redeem us by dying on the cross.

DIANE: But that sounds silly. Why can't God just forgive us? And it's Adam and Eve anyway, not us.

GARY: But Jesus laughed at her and He said, "Yours is not to reason why, yours is but to do and die." And then He said, "But seriously, mother, it is not up to God to justify His ways to man; rather man must have total and complete faith in God's wisdom, he must accept and not question, just like an innocent babe accepts and doesn't question his parents." And then Mary said:

DIANE: I understand. Or rather, I understand that I am not supposed to understand. Come, let us go to Golgotha and watch you be crucified.

GARY: And Mary and the apostles and the faithful camel, whose name was Misty, followed Jesus to the rock of Golgotha and watched Him be nailed to a cross. *(Gary has a hammer and nails, and nails the doll to a little cross, then stands it up that way)*

DIANE: And Jesus looked at the two thieves crucified on either side of him, and He said to one:

GARY: Thou art saved; and to the other, He said:

DIANE: Thou art condemned for all eternity.

GARY: And then He hung there for three hours in terrible agony.

DIANE: Imagine the agony. Try to feel the nails ripping through His hands and feet. Pound, pound, pound, rip, rip, rip. Washing the dishes for three hours is nothing compared to hanging on a cross.

GARY: And then He died. He's dead now, Mary.

DIANE: *(Sad, lost)* Oh!

GARY: Let's go for a long walk.

DIANE: Oh, Joseph, I feel so alone.

GARY: So do I, Mary.

DIANE: *(Truly wondering)* Do you think He was just a nut? Do you think maybe the Holy Ghost isn't His Father at all, that

I made it all up? Maybe I'm not a virgin . . . Maybe . . .

GARY: But then Misty said . . .

CAMEL: *(Philomena)* Do not despair, Mary and Joseph. Of course, He is God, He'll rise again in three days.

DIANE: If only I could believe you. But why should I listen to a dumb animal?

CAMEL: *(Philomena)* O, ye of little faith.

DIANE: *(Sad)* Oh, Joseph, I'm losing my mind.

GARY: And so Mary and Joseph and the camel hid for three days and three nights, and on Sunday morning they got up and went to the Tomb where Christ was buried. And when they got there, standing by the Tomb was an angel. And the angel spoke.

ALOYSIUS: *(Back of camel)* Mary and Joseph, your son has risen from the dead, just like your dumb animal Misty told you He would.

DIANE: I can't see the angel, can you, Joseph?

ALOYSIUS: O doubting Thomases of the world, must you see and touch everything in order to believe? Mary and Joseph! Your son Jesus wishes you to go out into the world and tell the people that unless they have the faith of the dumb animal Misty they shall not enter the Kingdom of Heaven. For, yea I say to you, at the end of the world the first in the class will be the last in the class, the boy with A in arithmetic will get F, the girl with F in geography will graduate with honors, and those with brains will be cast down in favor of those who are like dumb animals. For thus are the ways of the Lord.

GARY: And then Mary and Joseph, realizing their lack of faith, thanked Misty and made a good Act of Contrition. And then Jesus came out from behind the tree where He was hiding, they spent forty days on earth enjoying themselves and setting the groundwork for the Catholic Church, and then Jesus, Mary, Joseph and Misty ascended into heaven and lived happily ever after.

(Diane and Gary, holding the doll between them, stand in front of the camel. All sing the final jubilant phrase of "Angels We Have Heard on High" Christmas carol, as Diane and Gary mime ascension by waving their arms in a flying motion)

ALL: *(Singing)*

Glor-or-or-or-ia! In Excelsis Deo!

(All four bow. Sister applauds enthusiastically. After their bow, the

four quickly get out of their costumes, continuing to do so during some of Sister's next speech if necessary. Their "regular" clothes are indeed regular and not too noteworthy: Diane might wear slacks or jeans but with an attractive sweater or blouse and with a blazer, Gary might wear chinos, a nice shirt with even a tie, or a vest—casual but neat, pleasant, Philomena might wear a dress, Aloysius a shirt and slacks [or, if played as a bit formal, even a suit])

SISTER: Oh, thank you, children. That was lovely. Thank you. *(To audience)* The old stories really are the best, aren't they? Mary Jean Mahoney. What a good child. And what a nice reunion *we're* having. What year did you say you were in my class again?

GARY: 1959.

SISTER: 1959. Oh, those were happy years. Eisenhower, Pope Pius still alive, then the first Catholic president. And so now you've all grown up. Let's do some of the old questions, shall we? *(To Aloysius)* Who made you?

ALOYSIUS: God made me.

SISTER: Quite correct. What is the seventh commandment?

PHILOMENA: The seventh commandment is thou shalt not steal.

SISTER: Very good. *(To Diane)* What is contrition? You.

DIANE: Uh . . . being sorry for sin?

SISTER: *(Cheerfully chastising)* That's not how we answer questions here, young lady. Thomas?

THOMAS: Contrition is sincere sorrow for having offended God, and hatred for the sins we have committed, with a firm purpose of sinning no more.

DIANE: Oh, yes. Right.

SISTER: *(Still kindly)* For someone who's just played the Virgin, you don't know your catechism responses very well. What grade are you in?

DIANE: I'm not in a grade. I'm in life.

SISTER: Oh, yes, right. Well, cookies anyone? Thomas, go bring our nice guests some cookies. *(Thomas exits)* It's so nice to see you all again. You must all be married by now, I imagine. I hope you all have large families like we encouraged?

PHILOMENA: I have a little girl, age three.

SISTER: That's nice.

ALOYSIUS: I have two boys.

SISTER: I like boys. *(To Gary)* And you?

GARY: I'm not married.

SISTER: Well, a nice looking boy like you, it won't be long before some pretty girl snatches you up. *(To Diane)* And you?

DIANE: I don't have any children. But I've had two abortions.

(Sister is stunned. Enter Thomas with cookies)

SISTER: No cookies, Thomas. Take them away. *(Thomas exits immediately. To Diane)* You are in a state of mortal sin, young woman. What is the fifth commandment?

DIANE: Thou shalt not kill.

SISTER: You are a murderer.

DIANE: *(Unemotional)* The first one was when I was raped when I was eighteen.

SISTER: Well, I am sorry to hear that. But only God has power over life and death. God might have had very special plans for your baby. Are you sure I taught you?

DIANE: Yes, you taught me.

SISTER: Did I give you good grades?

DIANE: Yes. Very good.

SISTER: Have you told these sins in confession?

DIANE: What sins?

SISTER: You know very well what I mean.

DIANE: I don't go to confession.

SISTER: Well, it looks pretty clear to me, we'll just add you to the list of people going to hell. *(Calling)* Thomas, we'll put her name right after Comden and Green. Somebody, change the subject. I don't want to hear any more about this.

GARY: *(Trying to oblige)* Ummmm . . . it certainly is strange being able to chew the communion wafer now, isn't it?

SISTER: What?

GARY: Well, you used to tell us that because the communion wafer was really the body of Christ, if we chewed it, it might bleed.

SISTER: I was speaking metaphorically.

GARY: Oh.

SISTER: *(Pause)* Well, I still feel shaken by that girl over there. *(Points to Diane)* Let's talk about something positive. You, with the little girl. Tell me about yourself.

PHILOMENA: Well, my little girl is three, and her name is Wendy.

SISTER: There is no Saint Wendy.

PHILOMENA: Her middle name is Mary.

SISTER: Wendy Mary. Too many y's. I'd change it. What does your husband do?

PHILOMENA: I don't have a husband. *(Long pause)*

SISTER: Did he die?

PHILOMENA: I don't think so. I didn't know him for very long.

SISTER: Do you sign your letters Mrs. or Miss?

PHILOMENA: I don't write letters.

SISTER: Did this person you lost track of *marry* you before he left?

PHILOMENA: *(Sad)* No. *(Cries)*

SISTER: Children, you are making me very sad. *(To Philomena)* Did you get good grades in my class?

PHILOMENA: No, Sister. You said I was stupid.

SISTER: Are you a prostitute?

PHILOMENA: Sister! Certainly not. I just get lonely.

SISTER: The Mother Superior of my own convent may get lonely, but does she have illegitimate children?

ALOYSIUS: There was that nun who stuffed her baby behind her dresser last year. *(Sister stares at him)* It was in the news.

SISTER: No one was addressing you, Aloysius. Philomena, my point is that loneliness does not excuse sin.

PHILOMENA: But there are worse sins. And I believe Jesus forgives me. After all, he didn't want them to stone the woman taken in adultery.

SISTER: That was merely a *political* gesture. In private Christ stoned *many* women taken in adultery.

DIANE: That's not in the Bible.

SISTER: *(Suddenly very angry)* Not everything has to be in the Bible! *(To audience, trying to recoup)* There's oral tradition within the Church. One priest tells another priest something, it gets passed down through the years.

PHILOMENA: *(Unhappy)* But don't you believe Jesus forgives people who sin?

SISTER: Yes, of course, He forgives sin, but He's *tricky*. You have to be *truly* sorry, and you have to *truly* resolve not to sin again, or else He'll send you straight to hell just like the thief He was crucified next to.

PHILOMENA: I think Jesus forgives me.

SISTER: Well, I think you're going to hell. *(To Aloysius)* And what about you? Is there anything the matter with you?

ALOYSIUS: Nothing. I'm fine.

SISTER: But are you living properly?

ALOYSIUS: Yes.

SISTER: And you're married?

ALOYSIUS: Yes.

SISTER: And you don't use birth control?

ALOYSIUS: No.

SISTER: But you only have two children. Why is that? You're not spilling your seed like Onan, are you? That's a sin, you know.

ALOYSIUS: No. It's just chance that we haven't had more.

SISTER: And you go to Mass once a week, and communion at least once a year, and confession at least once a year? Right?

ALOYSIUS: Yes.

SISTER: Well, I'm very pleased then.

ALOYSIUS: I am an alcoholic, and I beat my wife, and I keep thinking about suicide.

SISTER: Within bounds, all those things are venial sins. At least one of my students turned out well. Of course, I don't know how hard you're hitting your wife; but with prayer and God's grace . . .

ALOYSIUS: My wife is very unhappy.

SISTER: Yes, but eventually there's death. And then everlasting happiness in heaven. Some days I long for heaven. *(To Gary)* And you? Have you turned out all right?

GARY: I'm okay.

SISTER: And you don't use birth control?

GARY: Definitely not.

SISTER: That's good. *(Looks at him)* What do you mean, "definitely not?"

GARY: I don't use it.

SISTER: And you're not married. Have you not found the right girl?

GARY: In a manner of speaking.

SISTER: *(Grim)* Okay. You do that thing that makes Jesus puke, don't you?

GARY: Pardon?

SISTER: Drop the polite boy manners, buster. When your mother looks at you, she turns into a pillar of salt, right?

GARY: What?

SISTER: Sodom and Gomorrha, stupid. You sleep with men, don't you?

GARY: Well . . . yes.

SISTER: Jesus, Mary, and Joseph! We have a regular cross section in here.

GARY: I got seduced when I was in the seminary. I mean, I'd been denying it up to then.

SISTER: We don't want to hear about it.

GARY: And then when I left the seminary I was very upset, and then I went to New York and I slept with five hundred different people.

SISTER: Jesus is going to throw up.

GARY: But then I decided I was trashing my life, and so I only had sex with guys I had an emotional relationship with.

SISTER: That must have cut it down to about three hundred.

GARY: And now I'm living with this one guy who I'd gone to grade school with and only ran into again two years ago, and we're faithful with one another and stuff. He was in your class too. Jeff Hannigan.

SISTER: He was a bad boy. Some of them should be left on the side of a hill to die, and he was one.

GARY: You remember him?

SISTER: Not really. His type.

GARY: Anyway, when I met him again, he was still a practicing Catholic, and so now I am again, too.

SISTER: I'd practice a little harder if I were you.

GARY: So I don't think I'm so bad.

SISTER: *(Vomit sound)* Blah. You make me want to blah. Didn't any of you listen to me when I was teaching you? What were you all doing? *(Mad, trying to set the record straight again)* There is the universe, created by God. Eve ate the apple, man got original sin, God sent down Jesus to redeem us. Jesus said to St. Peter, "Upon this rock," rock meaning Peter, "I build my Church," by which he meant that Peter was the first Pope and that he and the subsequent Popes would be infallible on matters of doctrine and morals. So your way is very clear: you have this infallible Church that tells you what is right and wrong, and you follow its teaching, and then you get to heaven. Didn't you all *hear* me say that? Did you all have wax in your ears? Did I speak in a foreign language? Or what? And you've all sinned against sex—*(To Aloysius)* not you,

you're just depressed, you probably need vitamins—but the rest of you. Why this obsession with sex? The Church has been very clear setting up the guidelines for you. *(To Philomena and Diane)* For you two girls, why can't you simply marry one Catholic man and have as many babies as chance and the good Lord allows you to? Simple, easy to follow directions. *(To Gary)* And for you, you can *force* yourself to marry and procreate with some nice Catholic girl—try it, it's not so hard—or you can be celibate for the rest of your life. Again, simple advice. *(Suddenly furious)* Those are your options! No others. They are your direct paths to heaven and salvation, to everlasting happiness! Why aren't you following these paths? Are you insane?

DIANE: You're insane.

SISTER: You know, you're my least favorite person here today. I mean, the little effeminate one over there *(Points to Gary)* makes me want to blah, but I can tell he once was nice, and he might get better with shock treatments and aversion therapy. But I can tell shock treatments wouldn't help you. You're fresh as paint, and you're nasty. I can see it in your face.

DIANE: You shouldn't be teaching children. You should be locked up in a convent where you can't hurt anybody.

SISTER: Me hurt someone. You're the one who runs around killing babies at the drop of a hat.

DIANE: It's a medical procedure. And even the Church admits it can't pinpoint *when* life begins in the womb. Why should you decide that the minute the sperm touches the ovum that . . .

SISTER: Don't talk filth to me, I don't want to hear it! *(Suddenly very suspicious)* Why did you all come here today? I don't remember asking you.

GARY: It was Diane's idea.

SISTER: What? What was?

PHILOMENA: We wanted to embarrass you.

ALOYSIUS: None of us ever liked you.

SISTER: What do you mean? My students always loved me. I was the favorite.

ALOYSIUS: No. We thought you were a bully.

SISTER: I was the *favorite.*

ALOYSIUS: You never let me go to the bathroom when I needed to.

SISTER: All you had to do was raise your hand.

ALOYSIUS: There were sixty children, and I sat in the back of the room; and I did raise my hand, but you never acknowledged me. Every afternoon my bladder became very full, and I always ended up wetting my pants.

SISTER: Big deal.

ALOYSIUS: I spoke to you about recognizing me sooner, and about my problem, but all you said then was "big deal."

SISTER: I remember you. You used to make a puddle in the last row every day.

ALOYSIUS: I have bladder problems to this day.

SISTER: What a baby. You flunked. I was giving you a lesson in life, and you flunked. It was up to you to solve the problem: don't drink your little carton of milk at lunch; bring a little container with you and urinate behind your desk; or simply hold it in and offer the discomfort up to Christ. He suffered three hours of agony on the cross, surely a full bladder pales by comparison. I talk about the universe and original sin and heaven and hell, and you complain to me about bathroom privileges. You're a ridiculous crybaby! *(Cuffs him on the head)*

PHILOMENA: You used to hit me, too.

SISTER: You probably said stupid things.

PHILOMENA: I did. I told you I was stupid. That was no reason to hit me.

SISTER: It seems a very good reason to hit you. Knock some sense into you.

PHILOMENA: You used to take the point of your pencil and poke it up and down on my head when I didn't do my homework.

SISTER: You should have done your homework.

PHILOMENA: And when I didn't know how to do long division, you slammed my head against the blackboard.

SISTER: Did I ever break a bone?

PHILOMENA: No.

SISTER: There, you see! *(To Gary)* And what about you?

GARY: You didn't do anything to me in particular. I just found you scary.

SISTER: Well, I am scary.

GARY: But my lover Jeff doesn't like you cause you made him wet his pants, too.

SISTER: All this obsession with the bladder. *(To Diane)* And you, the nasty one, why did you want to embarrass me?

DIANE: *(Said simply)* Because I believed you. I believed how you said the world worked, and that God loved us, and the story of the Good Shepherd and the lost sheep; and I don't think you should lie to people.

SISTER: But that's how things are. I didn't lie.

DIANE: When I was sixteen, my mother got breast cancer, which spread. I prayed to God to let her suffering be small, but her suffering seemed to me quite extreme. She was in bad pain for half a year, and then terrible pain for much of a full year. The ulcerations on her body were horrifying to her and to me. Her last few weeks she slipped into a semi-conscious state, which allowed her, unfortunately, to wake up for a few minutes at a time and to have a full awareness of her pain and her fear of death. She was able to recognize me, and she would try to cry, but she was unable to; and to speak, but she was unable to. I think she wanted me to get her new doctors; she never really accepted that her disease was going to kill her, and she thought in her panic that her doctors must be incompetent and that new ones could magically cure her. Then, thank goodness, she went into a full coma. A nurse who I knew to be Catholic assured me that everything would be done to keep her alive—a dubious comfort. Happily, the doctor was not Catholic, or if he was, not doctrinaire, and they didn't use extraordinary means to keep her alive; and she finally died after several more weeks in her coma. Now there are, I'm sure, far worse deaths—terrible burnings, tortures, plague, pestilence, famine; Christ on the cross even, as Sister likes to say. But I thought my mother's death was bad enough, and I got confused as to why I had been praying and to whom. I mean, if prayer was really this sort of button you pressed—admit you need the Lord, then He stops your suffering—then why didn't it always work? Or ever work? And when it worked, so-called, and our prayers were supposedly answered, wasn't it as likely to be chance as God? God always answers our prayers, you said, He just sometimes says no. But why would He say no to stopping my mother's suffering? I wasn't even asking that she live, just that He end her suffering. And it can't be that He was letting her suffer because she'd been bad, because she hadn't been bad and besides suffering doesn't seem to work that way, considering the suffering of children who've obviously done nothing wrong. So why was He letting her suffer? Spite? Was the Lord God actually malicious? That seemed possible, but far fetched. Maybe He had no control over it, maybe He wasn't omnipotent as you taught us He was. Maybe He created the world sort of by accident by belching one morning or getting the hiccups, and maybe He had no idea how the whole thing worked. In which case, He wouldn't be malicious, just useless. Or, of course, more likely than that, He didn't exist at all, the universe was hiccupped or belched into existence all on its own, and my mother's suffering just existed like rain or wind or humidity. I became angry at myself, and by extension at you, for ever having expected anything beyond randomness from the world. And while I was thinking these things, the day that my mother died, I was raped. Now I know that's really too much, one really loses all sympathy for me because I sound like I'm making it up or something. But bad things sometimes happen in clusters, and this particular day on my return from the hospital I was raped by some maniac who broke into the house. He had a knife and cut me up some. Anyway, I don't really want to go on about the experience, but I got very depressed for about five years. Somehow the utter randomness of things—my mother's suffering, my attack by a lunatic who was either born a lunatic or made one by cruel parents or perhaps by an imbalance of hormones or whatever, etc. etc.—*this randomness seemed intolerable.* I found I grew to hate you, Sister, for making me once expect everything to be ordered and to make sense. My psychiatrist said he thought my hatred of you was obsessive, that I just was looking for someone to blame. Then he seduced me, and he was the father of my second abortion.

SISTER: I think she's making all this up.

DIANE: He said I seduced him. And maybe that's so. But he could be lying just to make himself feel better. *(To Sister)* And of course your idea that I should have had this baby, either baby, is preposterous. Have you any idea what a terrible mother I'd be? I'm a nervous wreck.

SISTER: God would have given you the strength.

DIANE: I suppose it is childish to look for blame, part of the randomness of things is that there is no one to blame; but basically I think everything is your fault, Sister.

SISTER: You have obviously never read the Book of Job.

DIANE:　I have read it. And I think it's a nasty story.

SISTER:　God explains in that story why He lets us suffer, and a very lovely explanation it is, too. He likes to test us so that when we choose to love Him no matter what He does to us that proves how great and deep our love for Him is.

DIANE:　That sounds like "The Story of O."

SISTER:　Well there's obviously no talking to you. You don't want help or knowledge or enlightenment, so there's nothing left for you but an unhappy life, sickness, death, and hell.

DIANE:　Last evening I killed my psychiatrist and now I'm going to kill you. *(Takes out a gun)*

GARY:　Oh, dear. I thought we were just going to embarrass her.

SISTER:　*(Stalling for time)* And you have, very much so. So no need to kill me at all. Goodbye, Diane, Gary, Aloysius . . .

DIANE:　You're insane. You shouldn't be allowed to teach children. I see that there's that little boy here today. You're going to make him crazy.

SISTER:　Thomas, stay offstage with the cookies, dear.

DIANE:　I want you to admit that everything's your fault, and then I'm going to kill you.

PHILOMENA:　Maybe we should all wait outside.

SISTER:　Stay here. Diane, look at me. I was wrong. I admit it. I'm sorry. I thought everything made sense, but I didn't understand things properly. There's nothing I can say to make it up to you but . . . *(Seeing something awful behind Diane's head)* LOOK OUT! *(Diane looks behind her, Sister whips out her own gun and shoots Diane dead. Sister like a circus artist completing a stunt, hands up:)* Ta-da! For those non-Catholics present, murder *is* allowable in self-defense, one doesn't even have to tell it in confession. Thomas, bring me some water.

GARY:　We didn't know she was bringing a gun.

(Thomas brings water)

SISTER:　I remember her now from class. *(Looks at her dead body)* She had no sense of humor.

ALOYSIUS:　I have to go to the bathroom.

SISTER:　*(Aims gun at him)* Stay where you are. Raise your hand if you want to go to the bathroom, Aloysius, and wait until I have acknowledged you. *(She ignores him now, though keeps gun aimed at him most of the time)* Thomas, bring me a cookie. *(He does)* Most of my students turned out beautifully, these are the few exceptions. But we never give up on those who've turned out badly, do we, Thomas? What is the story of the Good Shepherd and the Lost Sheep?

THOMAS: The Good Shepherd was so concerned about his Lost Sheep that he left his flock to go find the Lost Sheep, and then He found it.

SISTER: That's right. And while he was gone, a great big wolf came and killed his entire flock. No, just kidding, I'm feeling lightheaded from all this excitement. No, by the story of the Lost Sheep, Christ tells us that when a sinner strays, we mustn't give up on the sinner. *(Sister indicates for Thomas to exit, he does)* So I don't totally despair for these people standing here. Gary, I hope that you will leave your friend Jeff, don't even tell him where you're going, just disappear, and then I hope you will live your life as a celibate. Like me. Celibate rhymes with celebrate. Our Lord loves celibate people. And you, Philomena, I hope you will get married to some nice Catholic man, or if you stay unmarried then you, too, will become a celibate. Rhymes with celebrate.

ALOYSIUS: Sister, I have my hand up.

SISTER: Keep it up. And you, Aloysius, I hope you'll remember not to kill yourself, which is a mortal sin. For if we live by God's laws even though we are having a miserable life, remember heaven and eternal happiness are our reward.

GARY: Should we help you with the body, Sister?

SISTER: The janitor will help me later, thank you. You two may go now, so I can finish my lecture.

GARY: Why don't you let him go to the bathroom?

SISTER: Gary?

GARY: Yes, Sister?

SISTER: You still believe what you do with Jeff is wrong, don't you? I mean, you still confess it in confession, don't you?

GARY: Well, I don't really think it's wrong, but I'm not sure, so I do still tell it in confession.

SISTER: When did you last go to confession?

GARY: This morning actually. I was going to be playing Saint Joseph and all.

SISTER: And you haven't sinned since then, have you?

GARY: No, Sister.

(Sister shoots him dead)

SISTER: *(Triumphantly)* I've sent him to heaven! *(To Philome-*

na) Okay, you with the little girl, go home before I decide your little girl would be better off in a Catholic orphanage. *(Philomena exits in terror. To audience)* I'm not really within the letter of the law shooting Gary like this, but really if he did make a good confession I have sent him straight to heaven and eternal, blissful happiness. And I'm afraid otherwise he would have ended up in hell. I think Christ will allow me this little dispensation from the letter of the law, but I'll go to confession later today, just to be sure.

ALOYSIUS: Sister, I have to go to the bathroom.

SISTER: Wait until I recognize you, Aloysius.

ALOYSIUS: I'm going to leave now.

SISTER: *(Angry, emphasizing the gun)* I've used this twice today, don't tempt me to use it again. Thomas! *(He enters)* Who made you?

THOMAS: God made me.

SISTER: Why did God make you?

THOMAS: God made me to show forth his goodness and to share with us his happiness.

ALOYSIUS: If you don't let me go to the bathroom, I'm going to beat my wife when I go home.

SISTER: We all have free will, Aloysius. Thomas, explain about the primary cause again.

THOMAS: Everything has a primary cause. Dinner is put on the table because the primary cause . . .

SISTER: Thomas, I'm going to nap some, I'm exhausted. *(Hands him gun)* You keep that dangerous man over there covered, and if he moves shoot him; and also recite some nice catechism questions for us all while I rest. All right, dear?

THOMAS: Yes, Sister. *(Sister sits on a chair and naps. Thomas sits on her lap, aiming the gun at Aloysius, and recites from memory)* "What must we do to gain the happiness of heaven?"

To gain the happiness of heaven, we must know, love, and serve God in this world.

(Lights start to dim)

"From whom do we learn to know, love and serve God?"

We learn to know, love, and serve God from Jesus Christ, the Son of God, who teaches us through the Catholic Church. "What are some of the perfections of God?"

Some of the perfections of God are: God is eternal, all-good, all-knowing, all-present, and almighty.

(Lights have dimmed to black)

Author's Notes For Production

Since scripts are so open to interpretations, I wanted to suggest some things to avoid, as well as to aim for, in presenting this play, and to make a few clarifications.

The casting of Sister Mary is obviously of the utmost importance. For starters, it's a mistake to have an actress play (or, worse, seem to be) mean. Though a strident bullying approach may work in an audition and even be funny, it can't really sustain for the whole play; we see Sister kill two people at the end of the play, but we shouldn't expect her to do so five minutes after we first see her. Also, perhaps more importantly, the strength and power of figures like Sister Mary (or, say, Jean Brodie) is in their charm; we believe them because they take us in. If Sister were obviously a horror, we'd know not to believe her.

In line with this, the relationship between Sister and Thomas should have warmth and even love. It's true that she presents him as one might present a dog doing tricks; and yet he does all the tricks well, and she rewards him not only with cookies but also with warmth, approval, bounces on the knee, etc.

The actress playing Sister should avoid commenting on her role. (All the actors should avoid commenting.) The humor works best when presented straight. That is, it's fine that we as an audience think it outrageous that Sister contemplates Thomas' castration to save his pretty voice; the actress should not indicate her own awareness of this outrageousness (that kind of comic-wink acting that is effective sometimes in a skit, rarely in a play). Sister thinks nothing is wrong with her contemplation, and it's only her feelings we should see.

Thomas should be seven or eight, and be smart and polite. There should be no attempt to play up his being child (like having him not be able to read the list of names going to hell; he should read them easily). An older child could play it, but seven or eight has a genuine innocence that can't be faked —an innocence which is central to the play's meaning.

The tone of the pageant is tricky. It should be childlike, as opposed to childish. It is thirty year olds performing it, so they shouldn't pretend to be children, but they can't act like adults precisely either. They should be simple and direct, presenting the story as if we didn't know it and as if it didn't have a child's imprint on the writing. Lots of busy stage business making fun of clunky amateur productions will get in the way.

There is an enormous trap to be avoided in the playing of the four ex-students, and that centers around their apparent plot to come to Sister's lecture to "embarrass" her. For starters, you mustn't play the plot as a subtext in the pageant or really anywhere before it's mentioned because the audience simply won't know what you're doing. Plus, there's a further trap: if you choose to play that the four have come to embarrass Sister by telling her how much they've strayed from her teaching (Philomena's illegitimate child, Gary's being gay), those revelation scenes won't work comically (as they're intended) because the comedy is based partially on Gary and Philomena not meaning to reveal what Sister drags out of them.

John Gruen
NEVER TELL ISOBEL

John Gruen

Widely recognized as a biographer and writer who covers the art world, John Gruen makes his debut in this series with *Never Tell Isobel,* an abstract, lyrical play which examines male and female roles in a questioning social milieu.

Mr. Gruen was born in Paris, France and received his early education in Berlin and Milan. The son of a journalist, Mr. Gruen continued his education in New York, where he attended the City College of New York, and in Iowa, where he received his B.A. and M.A. degrees from the University of Iowa. Upon graduating, he married the Iowa-born painter, Jane Wilson, a fellow student at the university. Armed with a Ph.D. fellowship to the Institute of Fine Arts of New York University, Gruen began studies in art history, but soon felt compelled to abandon further academic training in favor of pursuing a career as a journalist.

As early as 1960, Gruen began writing short plays, several including *Never Tell Isobel* produced by New York's La Mama Experimental Theatre Club. His one-act play *Smut and the Baritone* was performed at Lee Strasberg's Actors Studio in the early seventies.

In 1962 Mr. Gruen was employed by the *New York Herald Tribune* as critic of music and art, a post he held until the paper's demise in 1968. He established himself as major writer with a number of publications in the fields of music, art and dance. His first book *The New Bohemia,* a study of New York's creative avant-garde that included an in-depth look at the emerging playwrights of the sixties generation, appeared in 1968. *Close-up,* a collection of interviews with people in the arts, was published in 1969. That same year saw publication of the esteemed biography *The Private World of Leonard Bernstein.* In 1973 he wrote an assessment of the art scene during the 1950s, *The Party's Over Now.* This was followed in 1975 by a provocative study of the dance world, *The Private World of Ballet.* His biography of the composer Gian Carlo Menotti was published in 1978, and his acclaimed biography of the great Danish dancer *Erik Bruhn* appeared the next year.

John Gruen has written articles and reviews for countless periodicals and newspapers, has served as art critic for the *Soho Weekly News,* and has been a cultural contributor for the *New York Times* since 1968. He is an Associate Editor of *Dance Magazine* and a Contributing Editor for *Art News.* Since 1975 he has been the host of the popular radio program, *The Sound of Dance,* broadcast weekly over WNCN in New York, Long Island and Connecticut. His *Masterpieces of the Dance,* a study of sixty-two major ballets, is scheduled for publication in the fall of 1981.

Mr. Gruen and his wife make their home in New York City, where their daughter, Julia, is a student at Columbia University.

Characters:

FRANCESCA and DOUGLAS ⎫
ISOBEL and SAM   ⎪
MELINDA and BARNABY   ⎬ *Five Couples in their early*
LAURA and JACOB   ⎪ *thirties*
TINA and ROGER   ⎭
CLAUDE, *The Observer, and somewhat older*

NOTE: *This is not a play about marriage. It is a play about unalterable ties. It is more like a dance of unalterable sequence. The play may be highly choreographed. But the director must never lose the sense that each couple is unalterably tied.*

Scene:

A stark, bare setting. All the Couples and the Observer are on stage.

FRANCESCA: Incredible as it may seem, Douglas and I are going to be married. Or was that just another one of your idle proposals, darling?

DOUGLAS: No, love. For some odd reason, I do want to marry you.

ISOBEL: But how marvelous! How splendid!

SAM: Well, I think it's about time. Listen, everybody. Yoo-hoo, everybody. Listen to this. Francesca and Douglas will be wed! They will be wed. It's official! They've just announced it. All in favor say "Aye!"

EVERYBODY: Aye!!!

(Blackout. Lights up again. Same setting. Same people)

FRANCESCA: Incredible as it may seem, Douglas and I are going to be divorced. Or was that just another one of your idle proposals, darling?

DOUGLAS: No, love. For some odd reason, I do want to divorce you.

ISOBEL: But how marvelous! How splendid!

SAM: Well, it's about time. Listen, everybody. Yoo-hoo, everybody. Listen to this. Francesca and Douglas will be divorced! They will be divorced. It's official. They've just announced it. All in favor say "Aye!"

EVERYBODY: Aye!!!

(Lights dim. A soft, slow tango. Everyone begins to dance, with the exception of Claude, who moves forward, addressing the dancers. However, they are not listening, but are deeply engrossed in their dancing)

CLAUDE: When all else fails, a tango is the cure. Oh, you mad couples, with your feet moving, your hearts beating, your minds reeling. But that's difficult to tell, isn't it —whether your minds are reeling or not? What are you dreaming of, you mad couples? Are your minds following the rhythm of your dark and private thoughts? Or are you merely swaying in some vague discontent? You puzzle me. You are so peculiar. You are so strange. Holding on to one another like that. Tina, with your sad look. Roger—with your insistent, critical ways. Melinda, with your troubled and questioning eyes. Laura, with your empty, frightened smiles. All you couples being led by each other—moving in such a stately fashion toward some obscure and confused goal. Sam, my friend. You are really the only one, Sam. Jacob, my enemy. A man who fears men. A blind man. Douglas, a man with far too many faces. And silly Francesca. What drives you, Francesca? What propels you into constant shallowness? What acute discomfort and personal failures account for your mindlessness? And you, Barnaby? Have you found a way to escape? And Isobel, are you forever and always reaching out for something . . . anything?

(The music stops. Couples stand frozen, facing each other)

When the music stops, life goes on.

(Couples arrange themselves as at a cocktail party. Claude is among them)

MELINDA: Oh, Barnaby. Make things happen for me. I don't want to feel empty and useless. Can't you think of something? I am tired of myself. I am tired of my feelings and of my thoughts. Isn't there anything you can do?

FRANCESCA: Incredible as it may seem, Douglas and I are going to have a baby!

ISOBEL: But how marvelous! How splendid!

LAURA: Well, call it intuition, if you like, but I *knew* you'd use that against me. Really, Jacob, it was the most innocent kind of flirtation. I'll just stay home next time, that's all. You will be happier that way. I know you will be happier.

ISOBEL: Oh, Sam. These odd, peculiar things come over me. Everything is so thrilling to me. I'm so startled by everything. Everyone is such a constant surprise to me. Isn't it marvelous? Isn't it splendid? Oh, Sam. I truly *do* walk in wonderment. Oh, I think so *much* of everyone here. Everyone here is just *so* kind and good I am truly, truly, the luckiest of women! To have such wonderful, wonderful friends!

TINA: Well, Roger, I've done what you asked me to. I've worn what you wanted me to wear. I've combed my hair just the way you like it. I'm wearing the earrings you suggested I wear. The color of my eyeshadow is the color you insisted I wear this evening. And, of course, the perfume as well. Am I exactly the way you want me? Am I fulfilling all your visual needs? Well, Roger, now what am I to do for you?

BARNABY: What am I going to do with you, Melinda? How can I make things happen for you? How can I make you less tired of yourself? Look at Tina. Look how beautiful she is. Perhaps you should change your life, my darling. Why not start with your outside look? I'm sure the inside will follow suit.

JACOB: It's your smile, Laura. It's much too personal. I mean, you smile at a man—and it's a total, complete invitation. It's the way you smile, and the way you look at men, Laura. You have a way of doing that which suggests the suggestive. What's more, you're aware of it, and that hurts. I would much rather you didn't smile, Laura. Much rather you didn't smile.

DOUGLAS: For some odd reason, Francesca and I are going to have a baby.

ISOBEL: But how marvelous! How splendid!

SAM: Well, it's about time. Listen everybody. Yoo-hoo, everybody. Listen to this. Francesca and Douglas will have a baby. They will have a baby. It's official. They've just announced it. All in favor say "Aye!"

EVERYBODY: Aye!!!

(*Blackout. Everyone has exited except Sam and Isobel*)

SAM: Well, how about that? Francesca and Douglas will have a baby!

ISOBEL: Oh, Sam. Doesn't that make you feel just so wonderful?

SAM: Not really.

ISOBEL: Why, Sam? Why?

SAM: Babies don't interest me, Isobel. They have their faces and their eyes, and their tiny bodies, and their incredible vacuity. I don't respond to babies. I find no pleasure in their gurgling. Their wailing upsets me. The only interesting thing about babies is that they put us in contact with the process of growth. But basically . . . babies are a bore.

ISOBEL: Oh, Sam. How wonderfully you express yourself. I admire your brain so much. I guess you're right. Babies are boring. Sam, I really think you should be a writer. Then everybody would know what a beautiful brain you have. Don't you want to share your brain with everyone? Think of it, Sam! To share your thoughts with millions. I think that would be just so thrilling. And you're so right about babies. With their little faces, and little eyes, and tiny bodies, and their incredible vacuity. Oh, Sam. You expressed that so well!

SAM: You're a wonderful girl, Isobel. I like you. You're special. You're my kind of girl. I'm glad we're having these moments together—just you and I—without the others. I've been meaning to ask you a question, Isobel.

ISOBEL: Go ahead, Sam. Ask me anything.

SAM: Why do you agree with everything I say? Why do you agree with everything *everybody* says? Why are you such an agreeable person?

ISOBEL: Why, Sam! That's not for me to say. That's for others to decide. It would be immodest for me to answer such a question.

SAM: You're an astonishing girl, Isobel. Tell me, my dear, isn't there anything you *don't* agree with?

ISOBEL: Well, I suppose I may as well tell you. I don't agree with people who have bad manners.

SAM: No shit?

ISOBEL: That's right. Because—well . . . Sam, what did you just say?

SAM: Forget it, Isobel.

ISOBEL: Well, Sam, for example, I feel that there are so many beautiful words in the world, why use ugly ones? Would you like to hold me in your arms, so that we can be close?

SAM: Not particularly. Basically, holding people in my arms doesn't really interest me. You see, ultimately we will have to disengage ourselves—and then, we'll again be quite alone. Don't you find that to be true?

ISOBEL: Oh, I do, Sam. Obviously you have studied philosophy.

SAM: You might say I am a nihilist-pessimist. That means I'm a very depressed person.

ISOBEL: Yes, but your depressions are never destructive. You have the ability to love while being depressed. That's such an admirable and poetic character trait.

SAM: You're a sweet girl, Isobel. Shall we join the others?

ISOBEL: I'd love to.

(Blackout. Same couples dancing as before. Claude again addresses the dancers)

CLAUDE: Sweet loving couples! Opening their hearts to one another. Letting their thoughts commingle, like so many bittersweet perfumes in the air. What could be more charming or pleasing? As for me? My joys are the joys of observation. Of voyeurism, if you like. I am aroused by the passions of others. I seek out that which is private in others and am stimulated by what it is I uncover. It is a lonely occupation, true, but wonderfully instructive and satisfying. Often, these revelations yield me my life. I construct my emotions around the emotions of others—and particularly of strangers. All these people are strangers to me. Oh, yes—I know their names—and some of their qualities. But they are strangers, nonetheless. Look at Melinda and Barnaby. There is a certain magic in the way they dance—don't you agree? The length of any relationship may be measured by how smoothly the dancing goes. Melinda and Barnaby have executed their dance for lo, these many years. See how perfectly their motions match. But their dance is slow and measured and very careful indeed. A passive kind of dance. I find much resignation in their dancing.

(Blackout. All exit except Barnaby and Melinda)

MELINDA: I am almost always afraid. The fear begins at night, of course. I seem always to be on the brink of discovering that which frightens me, and my mind tries to fix itself on that revelation which moves closer and closer. But inevitably nothing is revealed. That which frightens me eludes me. Just as I have it—it becomes blurred and vague. Barnaby, why am I always so frightened?

BARNABY: Fear becomes you, my angel. It gives you depth and substance. And it makes you sensitive to others. I have never known you when you weren't afraid. So it must be a natural state. Fear is sensed, of course. That is why everyone treats you with such care. People are very careful never to let you know what your fears might be. They sense that it's your greatest area of attraction and strength. Should they expose or reveal your fears to you, their interest in you would diminish. You would rob them of all kinds of fantasies they may have about you. And that would be a pity, Melinda —because by being so fearful, my darling, you make others less afraid—and that's a rare quality to have. People need you, my sweet. And I need you. Somehow you seem to serve others as a receptacle for all their own fears. You have but to walk into a room when everything everyone has ever been afraid of seems already to be deposited and dwelling within you. This makes everyone instantly less afraid. Doesn't that knowledge make you a little happier?

MELINDA: I suppose so. Have you not grown tired of me, Barnaby?

BARNABY: Certainly not, dearest. I need you. I am comforted by your presence. It's just that I can't help you. The fact is, I don't want to help you. Let us go on this way, please. You with your fears, I with my need of your fears. You understand, don't you, my darling, that your constant state of anxiety gives me so much freedom, so much liberty. Your being who you are gives me tremendous latitude for the liberty I constantly seek.

MELINDA: Then I do make you happy, Barnaby.

BARNABY: Totally. Except for your appearance, of course. I wish you could change the way you look. Can't you emulate Tina? She knows exactly how to look. You seem incapable of knowing how to look.

MELINDA: Tell me how you want me to look.

BARNABY: Just like Tina. I adore the way she combs her hair. Her taste in clothes is impeccable. Her perfumes are always so understated. And the way she moves! There is nothing awkward about Tina.

MELINDA: I can only look like myself, Barnaby.

BARNABY: That is sad.

MELINDA: And frightening.

BARNABY: Yes. Well . . . would you like to join the others?

MELINDA: I'm afraid I would.

(Blackout. All the men are seated facing each other)

ROGER: Being a man is difficult. But I am a man.

SAM: So much responsibility is foisted upon us.

BARNABY: Men are not like women.

JACOB: I am a man. But I am not like other men.

DOUGLAS: Men are better than women.

CLAUDE: Men and women are sad.

ROGER: Women teach us to be men.

SAM: But it is difficult to be a man.

BARNABY: We learn very slowly what is expected of us.

JACOB: Finally, no one prepares us to be men.

DOUGLAS: Not even our mothers.

CLAUDE: Not even our fathers.

ROGER: Men decide amongst themselves how to be men.

SAM: It is a secret agreement.

BARNABY: And women secretly agree to be women.

JACOB: It is good to be a man.

DOUGLAS: Even today it is good to be a man.

CLAUDE: Today it is better to be a man than to be a woman.

ROGER: I am happy to be a man.

SAM: I am *extremely* happy to be a man.

BARNABY: I am *most* happy to be a man.

JACOB: I am *very* happy to be a man.

DOUGLAS: I am *so* happy to be a man.

CLAUDE: I am *always* happy to be a man.

ROGER: Let us promise always to be men together.

SAM: Because it is good to be a man.

BARNABY: Because it is noble to be a man.

JACOB: Because men understand one another.

DOUGLAS: Despite their weaknesses.

CLAUDE: Of which there are so many.

(Blackout. The men exit. Each woman comes out singly)

LAURA: I cannot help the way I smile. That is how I smile. I realize it has a certain effect on men. But that same smile also has an effect on women. It is a different effect. When a woman sees me smiling she says to herself, "That girl has a great capacity for friendship." But in truth, I have no women friends. Because I do not make enough of an effort. Friend ship is really very difficult. To sustain, that is. Why am I not able to make friendships with women? I do not know. Somehow, friendship to me implies a total giving of oneself. And I cannot give myself totally to a woman. Although I have secret longings to do so. You see, I do not understand friendship, at all. No man has ever taught me about friendship with women. And no woman has ever taught me about friendship with men. No one has ever prepared me for friendship. And yet I would like very much to be somebody's friend.

TINA: I have no wish to explain myself to anyone. In short, I wish to remain a mystery. It's better that way. It makes people like me. They can invent things about me. I offer no difficulties, no obstacles. I make no demands. I remain passive. It's really the best way. But I always look my best. I am told to do so, and I do so. Often I change my appearance. That is good for other people's imagination. There will be more invention about me. That is the way I like it. The effort is really all on their side. That is good enough for me.

FRANCESCA: Incredible as it may seem, I am really a very deep person. I feel things deeply. And I am a committed person. I have been married. I have been divorced. I have had a baby. And I am a very kind person. I am constantly in touch with life. This makes me a very compassionate person as well. People think I'm frivolous. Naturally they are wrong. I only wish to appear frivolous because that makes me seem very affable and easy to be close to. Actually, I am a serious woman. No one is as serious as I am. Consider my great love and respect for human frailty. The mistakes men and women make—I do not exclude myself—are spectacles which I understand perfectly. Without the benefit of analysis I have come to learn that *money* and not sex rules the world. Money is the motivating factor behind our deepest feelings. I feel very deeply about that. Money is the key. Yes, money is the key. I love money. Money is beautiful. Oh, I am *mad* about money. God, I love money! Yes, yes. Money is everything. And money is my passion. That is why I am kind, and good, and in constant touch with life. You do understand what I mean, don't you?

ISOBEL: There are so many beautiful words in the world. Why not use them to live by? Like: indubitably. Like: trenchant. Like: consequential. Like: Scandinavian! I spend a good deal of time on beautiful words. I think words are better than thoughts. When I sit listening to someone talk, I always agree with them because, inevitably, no matter what it is they may be talking about, some remarkable word pops up—and that's what I respond to. I mean if someone utters the word "clandestine," well . . . I just go to pieces. Not because of what the word means, but because of the way it sounds. Or take a word like "singular." Why . . . that word just sings! I also like to be held in a man's arms. That's the only other thing that I truly respond to. It's not just being held, you understand, it's that someone is actually using their hands and arms to enfold me. And so I think about that. Nestling in someone's arms, I think about their hands and their arms. That, too, is something to live by. Basically, I am in a constant state of euphoria. And I don't care what anybody says.

MELINDA: I am almost always afraid. That is to say, fear and its burden inhabit me. And yet it has brought me a certain wisdom—perhaps even a certain depth. One's thinking process becomes more alive to the alternatives of fear —such as happiness and the sense of joy. Can it be that I am frightened at the possibility of experiencing either? Somewhere, at the darkest point of my fear there appears a dim light. I can barely make it out—but I know it's there. This curious, pale glimmer gives me hope. I have tried but cannot successfully change my appearance. I am chained and tied to it. Frankly, I am not dissatisfied with my appearance, although it saddens me when others find it wanting. The fact is, my appearance is not my area of interest. I am far more interested in my fears. And I am particularly interested in the soft gray light which seems to announce, if not promise, some long-awaited respite.

(Blackout. The men and women face each other. Claude stands to the side)

CLAUDE: Have these people nothing meaningful to say to one another? They seem vaguely to sense each other. I should like to see them play a game—a knotty, difficult game.

DOUGLAS: Give me your hand, Francesca.

FRANCESCA: It is yours.

DOUGLAS: *Now* I've got you. What have you called our child?

FRANCESCA: Gilbert. And you're hurting me.

DOUGLAS: Why have you not called him Douglas, as I've asked you to?

FRANCESCA: Because my will is stronger than yours. And you're hurting me!

DOUGLAS: You fool! You empty foolish woman! Calling him Gilbert only proves how little you understand me or your son. Gilbert is wrong! You should have called him Douglas, as I've asked you to. Had you called him Douglas you would have loved me more—you would have loved *me* more.

FRANCESCA: Douglas, you are hurting me! Let me go! You left your son at the height of my pregnancy. You were not present at his birth. You were off—you were gone—vanished!

DOUGLAS: That was settled before his birth, Francesca.

FRANCESCA: It was your name I screamed, Douglas. *Your* name, Douglas! When our child was born, it was your name I screamed.

DOUGLAS: Had you called him Douglas, you would have loved me more.

FRANCESCA: Incredible as it may seem, I loved only your frailties. Weak men interest me. I am drawn to them—I seek them out. Weak men need women like me—it makes them strong. That is why men have always left me. That is why you left me. Give me a weak man, and after a year or two they emerge full of strength they never knew they had. My money has made men strong. It has made you strong. But once you felt your strength, you left me. I expected that, of course. You left me as all the others have left me. You see, I am not a frivolous, empty foolish woman. It is my mission in life to give men their strength. I married you because you were the weakest of all the men I'd ever met. It was perfectly thrilling to meet a man so terribly weak. I shuddered in ecstasy at the thought of all your weaknesses! Oh, Douglas, I did love you. I so admired your sense of failure. I cherished your insecurities. I truly responded to your vague, tormented, unresolved ways.

DOUGLAS: But you hadn't counted on our son?

FRANCESCA: Gilbert is an investment. He is still a weak baby. But Mummy will make him strong. His maleness will be intact, have no fear. He will be such a challenge to me! When I'm through with Gilbert he will be the strongest man of all. I will send him into the world a Colossus. Mark my words. Gilbert is an investment. I will pour millions into Gilbert.

Because money makes men strong. When it will be Gilbert's turn to leave me, you and the world will know what it means to be a man.

DOUGLAS: Come close, Francesca. Let me drive nails into your soul. Let me break your heart. Let me extinguish your breath. Let me stifle your spirit. I want to crush you against me, and want my bones to be the spikes that annihilate you.

FRANCESCA: I am constantly in touch with life.

DOUGLAS: So you are! So you are!

FRANCESCA: No one is as serious as I am. I am a woman unlike other women. And now, Douglas, please dance with me. You've promised me the next dance. We have only a few dances left, you and I. Why not dance the dances we have left?

(They dance off)

CLAUDE: As for me, I'll take Roger. He's such an ambiguous soul. A fellow of many parts, you might say. Such an imagination! Come here, Roger. Let's have a chat. How is your life?

ROGER: In turmoil, as usual.

CLAUDE: How so, dear Roger?

ROGER: Well, you know, when I was a child, I knelt before the Pope. Yes, the Pope. The incident had an extraordinary effect upon me. I must have been twelve. I knelt before him, and he extended his hand. And I kissed his ring. His hand was red. A red hand. And his ring was black. And, of course, I thought he was God. I thought I was in the presence of God. After I kissed his ring, he touched my head. I supposed it was a blessing. Then I rose. And he looked into my eyes. What a look that was. Full of compassion. Full of goodness. But there was something else in that look. Right in the center of that compassion and goodness there was also something mocking —something overly familiar—something fiercely insinuating. I wonder what it was he read in *my* eyes. Fear and awe, I suppose. At any rate, that same afternoon I was seduced by my friend Paul.

CLAUDE: Were his eyes as blue as yours?

ROGER: In a way, they were bluer. He was far more intense than I. We built a raft together. And we placed it in a stream, and became eternal navigators. I remember the sun, and I remember the heat, and I remember the love. Everything assailed me so in those days. Everything had such power! The days contained a million assaults—both pleasurable and painful. And everything had such fierceness! That is why I have become so critical of everything. The fierceness is gone. The taste of joy and the taste of anger have diminished. And I've become so terribly afraid of tenderness . . .

CLAUDE: How so, dear Roger?

ROGER: Tina is so beautiful! And yet, I have lost my tenderness toward her. Why is that? I am so critical of Tina! I thought I could rediscover myself through her. And in so many ways! Let me talk to her. Let me find out why all this has happened. Come here, my beautiful Tina.

TINA: I've worn my hair just the way you like it, Roger.

ROGER: I know. You're constantly changing yourself for me. You've always done everything I've asked you to. You've been so good to me.

TINA: I've tried to be what you wanted me to be.

ROGER: Have you a clue as to why?

TINA: It seems so important to you. I have no wish to fight it.

ROGER: Why do you give in to my dissatisfactions so easily?

TINA: It's easy to do. It was difficult at first. At first I thought it was really *me*. I thought I needed devastating repair. And this troubled me, of course. When the manner in which I talked displeased you, I altered my speaking habits. When you thought the manner in which I moved seemed too abrupt, I altered my movements. When you criticized my tastes, I managed to change them. When the clothes I wore displeased you, I quickly discarded them and found attire that met with your approval. When the shape of my eyes proved distracting, I resorted to new, more deceiving cosmetics. When the color of my nails became irritating, I found more pleasing alternate colors. When the intonation of my voice offended you, I succeeded in altering its timbre. I suited my desires to yours. In short, I completely gave way to your need for illusion.

ROGER: But has it brought *you* satisfaction?

TINA: Of course. I understand your needs. I know precisely why you ask these things of me.

ROGER: Why, Tina? Why?

TINA: Because you wish to be me. Because you need to be me. I can partially fulfill your need to be me, by doing all the things you ask of me. I understand you, Roger, and have no wish to lose you. I know that something in you needs me desperately. I am only too happy to oblige. Believe me, Roger—only too happy.

CLAUDE: Yes, Roger, yes. She is only too happy to oblige. And I am, too. Only too happy to oblige. There are times when I become weary of observation—when even the images in my mind become dull. An insistent yearning begins. My inner climate thickens. Something wishes to escape. A restless clamor makes itself felt. Perhaps if I just came near . . .

TINA: Let me lead you both . . .

(They execute a dance. Lights fade. All the women gather together)

LAURA: Being a woman is difficult.

ISOBEL: So much is known about us.

FRANCESCA: So much is expected of us.

TINA: Women are the shadows of men.

MELINDA: Men are always terrified of women.

LAURA: A woman inspires both trust and fear.

ISOBEL: Oh, how glorious it is to be a woman!

FRANCESCA: How secretive!

TINA: And how strange!

MELINDA: Feel our arms—how soft they are!

LAURA: Let us cling to our womanhood.

ISOBEL: We are part flower.

FRANCESCA: And part magic.

TINA: A man's wounds never heal as quickly as a woman's.

MELINDA: The burdens of guilt lie less heavily upon a woman than upon a man.

LAURA: A man always falls silent when we speak.

ISOBEL: Because he hears beyond our speech.

FRANCESCA: Let us vow to be women together.

TINA: For many centuries to come.

MELINDA: But let us acknowledge our enemy.

LAURA: Time.

ISOBEL: Time.

FRANCESCA: Time.

TINA: Time.

MELINDA: Time.

LAURA: Let us re-acknowledge our enemy.

ISOBEL: Time.

FRANCESCA: Time.

TINA: Time.

MELINDA: Time.

LAURA: Time.

(They move off)

JACOB: Will you play a death scene with me, Laura?

LAURA: Who will play the victim?

JACOB: I warn you—ask no questions.

LAURA: Will it be a heart-rending scene?

JACOB: It will be a scene of mixed emotions.

LAURA: Tell me how to begin.

JACOB: Sit down, Laura. Raise your arms in a beseeching gesture. Now, implore forgiveness.

LAURA: Dear God, forgive this sad, sad woman here. Yes, I have strayed, and have fallen upon other men. I, dear God, am surely the most inconstant of all women. But I am plagued by this need to injure my own man. What sustains me is the knowledge that the injury is, of itself, a call for help. Jacob, you would love me less if I did not injure you. I could not bear to lose your love. And so I beseech forgiveness. Will you forgive me?

JACOB: I will forgive you only if you promise to fall into another man's arms at once.

LAURA: I promise.

JACOB: Let the men come forward, then.

(All the men stand facing Laura, including Jacob)

LAURA: Broaden your shoulders, men. Stand up straight, and show yourselves. Little Laura is here! First, she'll strut for you. Next, she'll stand still for you so that you may appraise her enticing and dazzling body. Now she will show you the subtle motions of seduction. Are you watching, Jacob? Prefer, if you will, the inner elbow. You, there, Roger—touch my left shoulder—pure silk, wouldn't you say? Come close, Barnaby —the back of my neck has a special sweetness—won't you discover it? A bone for you, dear Claude. Right here, Claude, is a hip bone. Feel it very gently, Claude, very gently. And for you, Douglas, the curve of my belly. Place your head right here. The pressure must be delicate so that the shape of that exquisite curve is not disrupted. My breasts are for you, Sam. Place your head on my right breast—and place your hand on my left breast. Yours are the gestures of sanctity, Sam.

JACOB: There is an awkward logic to all this. I am moved by the spectacle of arms, hands, heads and lips upon the body of a woman. But I become ecstatic when the body happens to be Laura's. And yet, in that same instant of ecstasy, I become wracked with a rage that undoes me. The pain is physical —and quite logical.

LAURA: Now, go back, you men. We must discover even subtler places. The inner thigh. Who will place his lips on the inner thigh? You, Sam—come up. There, now. Like that. Who will place his hands on my buttocks? Douglas, you're the lucky one. Come close, Roger. You may nestle 'round my leg. And you may stroke and stroke . . . and stroke. Barnaby, put your arms around my waist. Encircle me. Grasp me tightly. Claude—I give you my lips. Don't be afraid, Claude. After all, no harm in a kiss.

JACOB: The time for dying comes nearer and nearer. Observe my death scene, Laura. First, death enters through my eyes. It moves slowly through my limbs. It makes its way carefully through my innards. It pauses to take effect. Now it spills into my blood stream. Oh, what a rush of death! Like a fierce gust of wind! Soon I will be drenched in death. Consider well this death scene, Laura. I grapple with it, but only passively. Paralysis of feeling now sets in. And with it comes something incredibly delicious. Pleasure inundates me. It steals softly through my paralyzed limbs. It lingers in unexpected places . . . it flows. It moves. It runs over me. Laura . . . Laura . . . I . . . am . . . dying . . .

(All the women now come forward and surround Jacob. They grasp him, feel him, devour him with their hands. The men are doing similar things with Laura. Abruptly all action ceases. Blackout. When lights return couples are once more together, dancing as when play started. Claude stands to side. Then he beckons to Sam)

CLAUDE: Hello, Sam.

SAM: Hello, Claude.

CLAUDE: Would you care to dance?

SAM: No, thank you.

CLAUDE: Have I offended you?

SAM: No.

CLAUDE: Well, what is it, Sam?

SAM: I'm in pain.

CLAUDE: Where?

SAM: All over.

CLAUDE: When did it start?

SAM: I don't remember.

CLAUDE: Can you describe the pain?

SAM: Vaguely.

CLAUDE: Describe it vaguely, then.

SAM: What do you think of Isobel?

CLAUDE: I'd rather not say. Does she cause you pain?

SAM: All women cause me pain.

CLAUDE: Are you sure you don't want to dance?

SAM: Absolutely.

CLAUDE: I've not offended you, have I?

SAM: No.

CLAUDE: Well, go on. Why do all women cause you pain?

SAM: Walking on the beach one night, a young child came upon two shadows. They were the shadows of two women. The child explored further. He saw that the shadows were two women in a fierce embrace. The child ran from what he saw. But the image continued to haunt him. It haunts him still. On the beach, that night, the pain began. I cannot make it stop.

CLAUDE: How can I help you?

SAM: Never tell Isobel.

CLAUDE: Never tell Isobel.

SAM: Never tell Isobel.

EVERYONE:

(Chants) Never tell Isobel.

(The chanting gets louder. Some mad music starts. The couples reunite. Claude leads them in the chant. He then turns to audience and motions it to chant "Never tell Isobel." The chant becomes a song)

EVERYBODY: *(Singing)* Never tell Isobel!

(As everybody is singing the lights dim and the play is over)

Burton Cohen

THE GREAT AMERICAN CHEESE SANDWICH

Burton Cohen

Though a New York City boy with a wide range of experience, Burton Cohen tries in his work to go beyond the ostentation of city life to focus on the basic problems of the American family. *The Great American Cheese Sandwich* presents these problems in a satirical manner, while affirming the virtues of family life.

Mr. Cohen's plays draw from the complex realm of human interaction he has observed while teaching, designing textiles, and owning a circus (a form of theatre he does not recommend for the faint of heart). His work penetrates to the drama and the innermost core of family ties. His experiences as an Off-Off-Broadway actor have given him a fresh perspective on presenting emotions in theatrical terms.

Mr. Cohen is a graduate of City College, where he received his Bachelor and Master Degrees in Art. His teaching experience in New York led to the publication of his first children's book, *Nelson Makes a Face*.

As this book goes to press, Mr. Cohen reports that a new play, *The Pickle*, has been commissioned for performance by the Actors Theatre of Louisville, and that an adaptation of the gothic thrillers of Louisa May Alcott, *The Sweet Revenge of Louisa*, was given a reading performance in New York City.

The Great American Cheese Sandwich and its companion piece, *Jackie Lantern's Hallowe'en Revenge*, another one act play with the same set of characters, comprise a full evening of theatre.

Characters:

MOTHER
FATHER
BETSY, *their daughter, late teens*
TOM, *their son, early twenties*
MR. WIGGINS

NOTE: *The play is to be performed in a stylized, exaggerated manner. The characters tend toward the raucous. It is almost as if they are all hard of hearing. They talk at each other with a great deal of heartiness, but there is a curious lack of contact among them.*

Scene:

An All-American farmhouse kitchen. A kitchen table and chairs, stage center.

FATHER: *(At table)* I am sitting here beside my very good friend the Great American Cheese Sandwich. We've known each other for years—American and me. We've fought the good wars and caroused about town. We've been high as a kite together and lower than low. We've had many a yock and many a sob. When things get rough I've always known American'd be there when needed—no if's, and's or but's. If the coal was running low in the mines or the moose were hiding out in the swamps when I got home there he'd be, lying on the table waiting for me. I'd press his bread gently and watch the mustard ooze down his crusts. I'd run my fingers over the tips of his lettuce—what more could you ask from a friend? While all them pinko freakies out there were—

MOTHER: *(Off)* Father! Help me drag the corn into the house!

FATHER: Excuse me, please.

(He exits)

MOTHER: *(Off)* Now mind you don't bump the hens!

FATHER: *(Off)* Yes, Mother.

MOTHER: *(Off)* Just a little bit more now. Just ease it into the crib there! Now pull up the sides and put on the nightlight. It's too late for a bath now—way past its bedtime.

FATHER: Good night, li'l feller.

MOTHER: Hush now and let's be off before you wake it.

(Mother and Father come into the kitchen. She is wearing a housedress)

MOTHER: I thought I'd nigh unto faint, what with harnessing the pigs and rolling the eggs!

FATHER: I sure wish I could've helped you, Mother, but I just got back from staking the fields and plowing the oats. I was settin' a spell with my good friend American.

MOTHER: He sure looks restful today, don't he?

FATHER: Like a babe in a manger, Mother.

MOTHER: How many years has it been now?

FATHER: Too many to count.

MOTHER: And they've been good years, too, haven't they Father?

FATHER: The best.

MOTHER: Well, I can remember when we first settled here some thirty years ago. The wolves was bangin' down the doors and the winds was whistlin' through our socks, but Old American pulled us through.

FATHER: And he hasn't changed a bit, has he, Mother?

MOTHER: Changed! Why that old American Cheese Sandwich ain't never gonna change. He'll just always set there glowin' bright orange when ya need him.

(The lights dim. A spotlight hits her. To audience)

Change! Why I don't know what I'd do without Old American. Pull your chairs a little closer to the fire and I'll tell y'all about the night I had my first born . . . I have two, ya know. Big Tom, as handsome and strapping a son as you'd want, and Little Betsy, as sweet and petite and ginger n'spicey as you could ask fer in the age of a sow.

Times was real tough then. The winters would freeze the hay to your fork and the summers would roast the hogs in the troughs! It was an especially cold winter and I was just about ready to pop with Big Tom.

It was a long way to the doctor and we knew he could never make it to us in the waist-deep snow, so we decided to hitch the team and go to him.

Well, after battenin' the barn we packed a mess of American Cheese Sandwiches and set out.

The sun was low in the West and the wind was whippin' us without mercy. No sooner had we gone half a mile when it began to hail. The stones were as big as horse teeth and they were beatin' on us and the team like unto make you cry.

Dad laid the stick to the ponies but they couldn't move in the drifts. He called to them—"Halloo, there," and "Gee! Gee! Ya lazy varmints!" He beat 'em and hollered at 'em, but it was no go. We were stuck there and Big Tom was gettin' mighty impatient inside me. He was like to doin' a war dance in there. Pretty soon he wouldn't take "no" for an answer. He wanted out more than a hen in a den full of foxes!

There was nothin' to do but let him have his way. Well now, a blizzard ain't exactly the perfect place for birthin' a baby. What with the hail peltin' us, the wind whippin' us, the team ready to drop—things were mighty inappropriate, if ya know what I mean. Well, just when we thought the situation couldn't get worse, over the hill come a pack of the wildest mangiest wolves you could ever want to see in the life of a prairie squirrel.

As luck would have it—we had nothin' to defend ourselves with. It seems in the rush of gettin' out, Pa forgot his gun—and we didn't even have a knife. "All is lost!" I said to Pa.

FATHER: Now never you mind, I've got a plan.

MOTHER: He said to me.

FATHER: Hand me two of them American Cheese Sandwiches.

MOTHER: Them wolves don't eat sandwiches, Pa.

FATHER: Never mind, just give them to me.

MOTHER: Better make it fast, Pa. Little Tom is thrashin' like a bobcat in a barrel of nettles.

FATHER: You just lie down in the wagon.

MOTHER: *(To audience)* Well, he slides two of them slices of cheese out of the sandwiches and flattens the edges with his fingers so they're real fine. Then he holds them both high in the air so the cold winds can get at 'em. Well, the air was so cold it froze them two slices of cheese into razor sharp knives.

When the wolves was upon us, Pa just kept slashin' wildly till we were surrounded by a score of dead wolves. The rest high-tailed it back over the hill. Lickety-split! Pa, still using his two cheese slice knives, skins the wolves and makes a warm fur shelter over me and the soon to appear Tom.

Well, to make a long story short, when Tom finally did pop, there in our cozy wolf tent, along with his ration of mother's milk, we also let him have *(A big finish)* you guessed it *(The lights come up)* . . . a big fat American Cheese Sandwich!

FATHER: Which is probably why Tom is such a strapping fine boy today.

MOTHER: He sure is, Pa, and a credit to us all.

FATHER: Haven't seen the boy for hours. Where'd he go?

MOTHER: Don't rightly know. He was up early this morning and seeding the turnips, then he did the rest of his chores—dappling the cows and such, then I lost track of him.

FATHER: Maybe he's up in his room studyin' up his school books.

MOTHER: *(Shouting upstairs)* Tom! You up there studyin' up?

TOM: *(Off, shouts back)* Sure am, ma'am!

FATHER: Never wastes a second, that Tom . . . and where's Little Betsy?

MOTHER: Well, she high-tailed it out of here after sloshin' the chicks. Real eager she was, too. I expect she's down by Cherry's Department Store pickin' out a prom dress for this Saturday night. She's real sweet on that Willie Jones . . . you know, the pharmacist's boy . . . and there ain't no better time for showin' off how pretty you are than on high school prom night. She's probably pickin' out some frilly, fluffy thing that'll show off her figure.

FATHER: Well, that accounts for the two young'uns. Now how about you?

MOTHER: What d'ya mean, Pa?

FATHER: I've noticed that you've been lookin' mighty peckish lately. You ain't been grindin' the millet as fine and some of the starch has gone out of your aprons.

MOTHER: Well, I could never fool you, Pa. It's true.

FATHER: What's on your mind, my little hickory pie?

MOTHER: It's the State Fair next week.

FATHER: Why, you've been looking forward to that all year. Real determined to win a ribbon you were, too.

MOTHER: That's just it. I'm real sleepless about it.

FATHER: Why, woman?

MOTHER: I was countin' on takin' a prize with my corncob jelly but the corncobs is all sour this year.

FATHER: Well, then make something else.

MOTHER: I can't. Everything else is taken up. Millicent Walker does the Hog Foot Pie. Theresa Fenwick does the Slippery Elm Pickles. Helen Wilks will bake her light-as-air Chocolate and Green Pea Cake and Old Lady Scroggs will take the honors with her Macaroon 'n Marshmallow Finger Rolls. There ain't nothin' else.

FATHER: Dang blast, if you're not right!

MOTHER: I tell you, it's got me climbin' the walls, Pa.

FATHER: Now hold on there. I don't want you to go gettin' sick about it.

MOTHER: Well, it's makin' me sick. I'm like unto bein' at my wit's end!

FATHER: There's gotta be a way out of this, Ma.

MOTHER: There ain't! There just ain't!

BETSY: *(Off)* Hello! I'm back!

MOTHER: Well, come on in here and let's see what you bought, daughter.

BETSY: *(Off)* Now just hold on a few moments and I'll slip into it.

FATHER: Well, hurry, girl. It's not every day I get to see my little girl in her prom dress.

BETSY: *(Off)* Just a little bit now . . . a few more snaps. Here I come!

(She enters dressed in a typical white prom dress. She also is over eight months pregnant)

MOTHER: Well, aren't you somethin'!

FATHER: Why, you're prettier'n a field of thugweed to a hungry goat.

BETSY: *(Breathless)* Thank you! Thank you! You don't think it's a little young?

MOTHER: Just listen to her, Pa! Well, how old do you think you are? You're only eighteen, child! If that ain't young then I don't know what is.

BETSY: I mean some of the girls are wearing off-the-shoulder dresses with their hair up.

FATHER: There'll be none of that for you, young lady. We brought you up to be decent! Your hair is staying on your shoulders where it belongs—and real petite it is, too. Why, when you go marching up on that stage to get your graduation paper all them fellers will be bowled over by your clean, sweet, All-American, farm fresh, one hundred percent, milkfed, peaches 'n cream girlishness—*(Harder)* and that's how we planned it—*(Grindingly)* and that's how it is!

MOTHER: Have you heard from Willie Jones, honey?

BETSY: I sure did.

MOTHER: Is he takin' you to the prom?

BETSY: He sure is and his father is letting him use the Chevrolet.

MOTHER: Well, ain't that real nice of him. Why do you suppose he's doin' it?

BETSY: I don't rightly know.

MOTHER: You don't suppose it's because he would like to see his son hitchin' with some sweet young farm girl who's burstin' with vitality?

BETSY: *(Eagerly)* Do you really think that's the reason, ma'am?

MOTHER: Well, why else? And a lot worse you could do, too. His father's sure to take him into the medicine business —a likely candidate for husbandhood, I'd say.

BETSY: Don't you think you're rushing things, Ma? After all we're just going to a silly old prom together.

MOTHER: Well, how do you think it starts? First you lark a little bit, then you do some spoonin'—nothin' too familiar, mind you—somethin' by the light of the silvery moon, then he pecks you on the cheek and you try not to blush, then after a while, if he behaves like a gentleman, you can let him put his arm around you.

BETSY: *(Giggling shyly)* Oh, Ma!

MOTHER: Now we gotta be realistic, girl! Once he's got his arm around you, well, you're as good as hitched.

FATHER: Aren't you rushing things a little, Ma?

MOTHER: That's how we did it, isn't it?

FATHER: I couldn't rightly say I was so head over heels for you. It just happened, that's all I know.

BETSY: I just think that's so sweet!

MOTHER: Well, that's how it's gonna happen to you, honey, you'll see. Someday you'll be walkin' down that aisle all sweet and dreamy like a little field flower and your Daddy and me'll be as proud as two popinjays. Why, just thinkin' about it gets me all teary.

BETSY: Oh, Ma, it sounds wonderful! Do you think it'll really happen to me that way?

MOTHER: Why sure, honey—*(Slyly)*—if you play your cards right!

BETSY: I sure hope Willie likes it.

MOTHER: Why do you think he won't?

BETSY: It's hard to tell what a man will or won't like. Most of the time they don't notice anything.

FATHER: Well, I sure like it, honey.

BETSY: But you're my father. You don't count.

MOTHER: Well, why don't we get your big brother down here and see what he says.

BETSY: Oh, all he knows is football, the big lug.

MOTHER: He's a man ain't he, and that's what we want—a man's opinion—so let's call him.

BETSY: Oh, okay. We can try it.

MOTHER: Tom! Oh, Tom, honey!

TOM: *(Off)* Yes, ma'am!

MOTHER: Leave your books for a minute and come down here.

TOM: *(Off)* Alright, I'll be right down.

MOTHER: You'll see, Tom'll be honest and present the male point of view.

(Tom enters. He is a big clean cut All-American type. He also is dressed in women's clothes)

TOM: Hi, folks!

MOTHER: You're going to ruin your eyes studyin' all them hours, son.

TOM: It's the only way I can keep my scholarship and stay on the team, ma'am.

FATHER: How's the practice goin', son?

TOM: We're all a little stiff but we should be in shape for the opening game, Dad.

FATHER: You just keep at it, son, and you'll wind up an All-American.

TOM: *(Modestly)* Oh, I don't know about that but I'm sure going to try. What did you want me for?

MOTHER: We wanted your opinion about how your sister looks, son.

TOM: What do you mean, Mom?

BETSY: *(Playfully)* See, I told you! The big lug only sees footballs and goalposts.

MOTHER: Can't you see your sister has a new prom dress? We wanted the man's point of view.

TOM: *(Manly and shy)* Well, I don't know about these things. She looks good to me.

BETSY: *(Hitting him playfully)* Ya big dope! Is that all you have to say about a dress I spent all afternoon picking out?

TOM: It looks pretty to me, sis.

BETSY: How do you think Willie Jones is going to like it?

TOM: Well, if he says he doesn't I'll bust him one in the nose.

BETSY: Oh, he's too shy to say that. I sort of hope he'll be kind of bowled over with me and think about popping the question.

TOM: Well, gee! I don't know anything about popping questions. I don't know what to say.

BETSY: *(Playfully taking his arm and punching it)* See, I told you he'd be useless. All you know about is scrimmages and touchdowns.

TOM: Well, I've gotta stay in shape for the season and coach tells us to keep our minds clear.

FATHER: . . . and right he is too, son.

TOM: Coach says, "All a fellow needs is a clear head and a clear field."

MOTHER: A good thinker, that coach.

TOM: Coach says, "Don't let the little things get you down and the big things will keep you up."

BETSY: He sounds real wise, Tom.

TOM: Coach says, "A little lift in the morning will keep you flying all day."

MOTHER: Well, I'm sure glad you are under the influence of such a fine man, Tom.

TOM: All the fellows listen real hard when coach talks to them. He's turning us into "go-getters."

FATHER: My, my!

TOM: He doesn't want us to "drag our tails."

MOTHER: I should say not.

TOM: Coach says, "A little cheer in your heart will keep them cheering in the stands."

FATHER: Good sentiments, all of 'em, boy!

TOM: Coach asked me over to his house tonight while his wife is away to discuss strategies.

MOTHER: Well, I'm glad to see he's takin' a personal interest in you, son.

TOM: He told me he's sure I'll go far.

FATHER: "All-American" here we come!

TOM: (*The lights dim. A spotlight hits him*) Well, if I don't it won't be because I haven't tried.

(*To audience, stepping forward*)

There's nothing I like better than a good game of football. The feel of the pigskin tucked under your arm, it's like . . . well, it's like . . . a little baby nestling there—so little and round. You make your run through the field with all the fellows grabbing at you—just you and that little baby . . . trying to protect it and yourself from all them big guys grabbing at you. There's nothing like it.

I like the roughness and the toughness—the banging around you have to take. You've got this thing . . . that they want—all eyes are on you—they want what you've got. They throw their bodies . . . at . . . you—the crushing of shoulders, the knocking of hips—it makes you feel all . . . well . . . all . . . manly.

I can't tell you really how good it feels—just you and the other guys—the scrimmages together, the passes, the touchdowns—

(*Slowly bending over as if to pass a football through his legs. Gently and coquettishly*)

—signals on . . . one, six, two, eight!

(*In a trance, slowly rising*)

Do you think that I look good in beige?

(*The lights come up. He steps back*)

FATHER: Well, all this lollygagging is getting us nowhere. Your mom and me have a real serious problem.

BETSY: What's that, Daddy?

MOTHER: It's the corncobs, honey. They've gone sour and I can't make my jelly for the State Fair.

BETSY: (*Horrified*) Oh, that *is* trouble, Mom!

FATHER: Does anyone have any suggestions?

TOM: Well, I don't know anything about these things, Dad.

BETSY: (*Hitting him on his arm*) Ya big lug! Will you get your mind on something besides football! This is big trouble! We've just got to come up with an answer.

MOTHER: I didn't want to worry any of you, but it's just

been on my mind for the longest time. I-I don't know what . . . I'm . . .

(She breaks down, sobbing uncontrollably)

FATHER: There, there, honey, we'll find a way. Sometimes things get rough but we've got to muddle through. After all, we've got us, don't we, gang?

BETSY and TOM: You bet, Dad.

FATHER: What's a family fer if not to pull together during a catastrophe?

(The lights dim. A spotlight hits him. To audience)

God knows, that's the truth—and we've certainly had enough catastrophes around here—the twisters, the floods, the leaky plumbing. It's enough to make a body heave in his grave—even if he ain't in it yet.

And what've you got to fight it all with? A pair of overalls and two calloused hands. The sweat of your brow and the straining hearts of a pair of roans . . . and of course that somethin' extra that pulls ya through—Old American Cheese.

(Very enthusiastic)

Would you like to hear about the great flood? Sure, ya would! Jes' lean back in your seats and I'll tell you all about it.

(Like a pitchman)

It was durin' the spring thaw. The sun grew so hot that it made all the snow on the mountaintops come rushin' down. Down the water come tumblin'—thrashin' against the flood gates and flailin' against the gushers. What wasn't burblin' was sloshin.' There was water everywhere. It filled the corrals and overflowed the canals. The sheep were floatin' in the meadows and even the eagles was movin' on to higher ground.

MOTHER: What are we gonna do?

FATHER: Says Ma to me.

MOTHER: The young'uns are doin' the backstroke in the nursery.

FATHER: We gotta evacuate the house, Ma!

MOTHER: Where to?

FATHER: The roof! *(Shouting)* Grab your pitiful possessions! *(All climb on table)* We clambered to the top of the house, the young'uns a bawlin' and the hens droppin' eggs all over outta fear. I, of course, grabbed my faithful friend Old American Cheese. When we got to the roof Ma says to me.

MOTHER: We seem to be in a fix, Pa.

FATHER: "Now don't you worry, Ma," says I, "I have a plan."

MOTHER: Do it, Pa. Do yer plan!

FATHER: Well, naturally it involved Old American, as if you couldn't guess. Luckily, I had the wits to grab all of it we had in the house. As I told you before the sun was real hot and I pushed and pulled and molded that cheese with my bare hands. It took a long time, but by sunset I had made us an American Cheese Boat—a sloop it was—and we all climbed aboard and sailed all the way to Seattle where things were drier and we were able to munch on the rudder for a little nourishment.

(As the lights come up, they all climb down)

BETSY: How old was I, Pa?

FATHER: Too young to know up from down, honey.

BETSY: Things were sure old-fashioned and exciting then. Nothing ever happens to me now.

MOTHER: You've gotta make things happen to ya, honey.

TOM: That's what coach says, too, Betsy. "If you just keep standing still, you never know how long you'll still be standing!"

BETSY: Well, I sure feel like *I'm* standing still.

(The lights dim. A spotlight hits her. She steps forward)

Oh, when will something happen to me? *(Slowly, trance-like)* I do everything that your supposed to—I cross my legs at the ankles. I get the Basic Seven . . . and chew them thirty-two times. I'm full of "personality" . . . *(She hikes dress to knees and bestrides a chair, back to front. Pause. A new deep raunchy voice)* They call me Shanghai Lil . . . When I was twelve they snatched me into a black coupé and threw me in a cage on a Chinese junk. They slit my feet so I couldn't run away and then the men had at me! Lord knows, I could handle the entire crew even then. Not a whimper out of my sly little mouth. One, two, three . . . bang, bang, bang! I was a pro even then. By the time we docked, I had organized the boat into a first class opium ring. We covered the territory from Mei Loon to Kai Soong. Once established on the mainlands, I spread my favors amongst the Mandarins and the Cantonese . . . *(Slowly, bitingly hard)* . . . the more they wanted . . . the less I gave 'em! Soon I gave nothing myself but had my "girls" do it for me. And quite a bunch they were, too. Jade Ass Hannah . . . Mother of Pearl . . . A Thousand Eggs Evelyn

... All "good" girls, and if they weren't good, well ... *(Taking a long puff on an imaginary cigarette and blowing it high in the air)* ... they never got very far.

As you might've guessed my downfall was a man—a low-down wharf rat—but *quite a man!* A swindling, lying, cheating, stealing swine, but I was crazy about him, the big lug! I won't bore you with the details—just one day he was gone along with my money, the girls, the opium, in short everything I'd built up ... and now I ... *(She rises, starting to "come to")* ... I ... just wish ... that ... *(Her voice is lighter and demure again)*

I ... I'm a ... big hit at the prom.

(The lights come up)

MOTHER: *(Hugging Betsy)* Now don't you worry, honey. Yer just so petite and pretty everyone will fall head over heels fer you.

BETSY: It's you that I'm really worried about, Mom. What will you do if you can't make your corncob jelly for the State Fair? What will we all do? Not to have anything in the State Fair is a catastrophe!

MOTHER: Well, it sure is the hog's knees, daughter, but I don't have the answer.

TOM: Coach says, "If you don't know the answer ya gotta re-listen to the question."

MOTHER: Well, maybe coach can "re-listen to the question," but I'm stumped.

FATHER: Now there's an idea! Why don't we call up coach? Maybe he can help us.

BETSY: Oh, that's terrific! Let's do it. You call, Tom.

TOM: Well, I don't know. Coach is a busy man.

BETSY: *(Shouting)* Oh, do it! Do it, Tom!

FATHER: *(Quietly and seriously)* It's fer yer mother, son.

TOM: In that case I'll just have to.

BETSY: Oh, wonderful.

(All gather around telephone as Tom dials and spot hits him. A long pause)

TOM: It's ringing. *(Shyly)* Hello ... Hello, Mrs. Entweiler, this is Tom from the team. Can I speak with coach? Well, I'm just fine, fine. Thank you kindly, yessir, ma'am. Oh, they're all fine, too, thank you, ma'am. Yes, she's fine ... and he's fine ... and she is, too ... we're all just fine ... *(Pause)* We just have a little catastrophe and we thought coach might be able to help us. Is he there? Oh, thank you kindly, ma'am. *(To the others)* She's going to get him. He's scrimmaging. *(Brightly)* Hello, coach, sir. This is Tom from the team. My family is all around me . . . Well, they're just fine . . . He says "hello" to everyone . . . Well, sir, we have this little catastrophe that we're trying to work out here and we thought you might be able to advise us. It seems that Mom's corncobs are all turned sour and she can't make her corncob jelly for the State Fair . . . *(Pause)* Yes, sir, it sure is serious stuff. Could you advise us what to do? You can! Wonderful! *(All crowd closer to telephone excitedly. Tom is carefully repeating what Coach says)* "The answer lies on your own doorstep . . . It's all there right in your own backyard . . . Look for the silver lining . . . and . . . and what, sir? I didn't catch the last one . . . *(Pause)* . . . and wait . . . till . . . the . . . sun shines, Nellie." Well, thank you kindly, sir. Well, I'm sure it will be . . . and what was that . . . Well, yes . . . Well . . . *(Very coyly and insinuatingly)* . . . you know I do . . . Bye.

(He hangs up. The lights come up)

FATHER: God, what a mind that man has!

BETSY: *(In awe)* You bet!

MOTHER: But what're we supposed to do, Pa?

FATHER: Well, I don't rightly know, but I know it's good advice . . . and I'm from Missouri.

BETSY: I think it's perfectly clear. We're supposed to wait till the sun shines, Nellie.

TOM: I have to agree. It is very clear. We'll do that.

MOTHER: What? What're we doin'?

FATHER: We're doin' what the coach says, Ma. We'll "Wait till the sun shines, Nellie."

MOTHER: Well, okay!

(All sit motionless, waiting—long silent pause)

MOTHER: *(Loudly)* Who's Nellie?

FATHER: Well, I don't rightly think I believe I know.

MOTHER: *(Pause)* What is she gonna do when she gets here?

FATHER: *(Patiently)* We'll have to wait and see.

MOTHER: *(Pause)* Can she cook?

TOM: I sure hope so, ma'am. I'm getting a little hungry.

FATHER: Have a hunk of Old American, son.

TOM: I don't mind if I do. *(Helping himself. Munching)* Gets better every time I taste it.

FATHER: What's good is good.

TOM: That sure is the truth.

BETSY: *(Slowly and thoughtfully)* What's . . . good . . . is . . . good.

FATHER: Well, that's what I just said, honey.

BETSY: What's . . . good . . . is . . . good. Why, *that's it!*

FATHER: What, dear?

BETSY: That's the answer!

FATHER: Well, that's always the answer, dear . . . To what?

BETSY: To Mom's problem.

MOTHER: How so, honey?

BETSY: The coach says the answer is in our own backyard, right?

TOM: That's what he said.

BETSY: And it's on our own doorstep, right?

TOM: Yep, that, too.

BETSY: And Old American always helped us out in the past.

FATHER: You bet.

BETSY: And it's always good, right?

FATHER: Sure is.

BETSY: Then we'll make . . .

TOM: *(Interrupting)* I think I know!

BETSY: You're right!

MOTHER: Right about what, daughter?

BETSY: About how we'll win that prize at the State Fair.

FATHER: Well, let's hear it, honey.

BETSY: *(Loud and triumphant)* We'll make American Cheese Sandwich Jelly!

FATHER: Well, ain't that somethin'! The answer was right under our noses.

MOTHER: It sounds real good, honey.

(There is a loud knock on the door)

MOTHER: Who could that be?

TOM: I'll get it, ma'am. *(He goes. Off)* Well, you sure may. Come right in. *(He returns with Mr. Wiggins)* This is my Mom, Dad and Sis. This is Mr. Wiggins, the photographer.

MOTHER: How nice. What can we do for you, Mr. Wiggins?

MR. WIGGINS: I'm here to take your picture as the winners of the State Fair Jellies, Preserves, Condiments and Other Edibles Contest.

MOTHER: But we ain't made it yet. How can we be the winners?

MR. WIGGINS: Why waste time?

FATHER: Well, that's sure true.

MOTHER: I don't know if I like this.

MR. WIGGINS: Why?

MOTHER: I like to struggle a little bit first.

MR. WIGGINS: Why bother? A winner is a winner.

FATHER: The man has a point, Ma.

MOTHER: It don't seem right.

MR. WIGGINS: Nonsense! What's right is right.

TOM: Why you sound just like coach.

MR. WIGGINS: I have done some end running and forward middle passing in my time.

TOM: I thought so.

FATHER: I think we should listen to the man, Ma.

BETSY: I do, too, Mom. He's obviously a good sort.

MR. WIGGINS: Oh, I am . . . and I'm sent from the State Fair, so I must know what I'm talking about.

MOTHER: Oh, I don't doubt that you do, but somethin' is holding me back from takin' the photo and I cain't put my finger on it.

FATHER: Now don't be so stubborn, Ma.

MOTHER: I'm not bein' stubborn. I jes' cain't, I say!

MR. WIGGINS: I'm a busy man. I have other photos to take . . . the prize winning crab grass . . . the prize winning boll-weevil . . . etcetera . . . all important stuff!

MOTHER: I don't mean to hold you up, Mr. Wiggins. I cain't help it.

FATHER: Maybe you could come back later, after all the others?

MR. WIGGINS: I'm going to have to. I can't waste time on temperament. I hope you'll be ready when I get back!

(He exits)

FATHER: Well, what in thunder is wrong with you, Ma? Here is a man who is all set to name us as the winner and take our picture jes' as pretty as a June Bug and you skedaddle up the works!

MOTHER: I know! I know, Pa. I feel simply terrible, but I don't rightly know why. I don't mind bein' named the winner—Lord knows, the jelly is good—even though it ain't been made yet. It's the dang photo—I jes' cain't let 'em take it of us!

BETSY: Should I redo my hair, Ma? Would that help?

MOTHER: No, it ain't that, daughter.

FATHER: You wanna change yer apron, Ma?

MOTHER: No! What's good enough fer the horses is good enough fer the hogs!

FATHER: Well, then what is it?

TOM: Is my face dirty, Ma? Should I scrub up?

MOTHER: No. It ain't exactly that.

FATHER: Well, woman, yer enough to try the patience of an ol' milky cow.

MOTHER: Get offa me, alla ya! I'm tryin'. I'm tryin'! There's jes' somethin' in the way.

(The lights dim. Spotlight hits her. She walks forward. To audience)

Have you ever felt like someone's starin' ya in the back and ya turn around and they ain't no one there? Well, that's how I feel. Actually, I've been feelin' that way fer quite some time. I couldn't even tell ya since when. Maybe it's since little Betsy come home from that summer camp speakin' Chinese. I mean, how do you learn Chinese at the Lake Wahkoogah Camp fer little Indian Maidens? It's a might too enterprisin', if ya know what I mean. Wouldn't it unnerve ya? It sure did me—though no one else seemed ta care.

Maybe this feelin' goes back to the time I found Tom sleepin' with a football crammed in his pajama bottoms and I wakes him up and says, "Tom, why you got that thing in there?" and he says, "Don't stop me, I'm going for a touchdown," and he drifts right off to sleep again. Now wouldn't that make the curlers pop yer hairnet?

Now there's somethin' I'm tryin' ta tell ya. I don't know what it is, but I'm sure tryin' ta tell it. It's there jes' as sure as that ol' scarecrow is out there freezin' the blood in them blackbirds. There's somethin' here freezin' my blood. *(Pause)* Well, I said my piece . . . at least, I think I said it . . . Well, I said somethin' . . . there's no denyin' that . . . somethin's been said here . . . whatever it is.

(The lights come up)

FATHER: Ma, I think I got the answer to why ya don't want the picture took.

MOTHER: *(Relieved)* I knew I could depend on you, Pa. Tell me quick.

BETSY: Yes. What is it, Dad?

FATHER: Well, now, this is a family photo, ain't it?

MOTHER: *(Impatient)* Yeah! Yeah!

FATHER: And who's the family? Name 'em.

TOM: Well, there's you and Mom and Betsy and me.

FAMILY: And . . .

MOTHER: *(Growing more impatient)* And! *And who?*

FATHER: Well, I'm surprised at you all. Yer gonna hurt his feelin's.

MOTHER: Who? Who's feelin's?

FATHER: Well, Old American's feelin's—that's who! Ain't he been a member of our family as far back as you could remember?

TOM: You sure are right, Dad. You're gettin' as good as coach.

BETSY: You've got a point there, Dad. Is that it, Ma? Is that what's troubling you?

MOTHER: *(Perplexed, dazed)* Well, I don't know . . . I guess so.

FATHER: Of course it is, honey! We couldn't take a family photo without Old American bein' in it. No wonder ya felt funny about it.

MOTHER: *(Scratching her head)* Yeah! No wonder!?

(A loud knock at the door. Tom goes to answer it)

TOM: I'll get it.

(He returns with Mr. Wiggins)

MR. WIGGINS: You folks ready yet?

FATHER: We sure are, Mr. Wiggins.

MR. WIGGINS: Well, now you winners just arrange yourselves for the big photo while I get my camera.

(He exits)

FATHER: Now, Ma, you set in front holdin' Old American on a plate . . .

TOM: . . . and you sit beside her, Pa.

BETSY: . . . and you should hold the other side of the plate.

FATHER: Well, if you think so.

BETSY: I sure do, and Tom and I will stand behind you.

(Mr. Wiggins returns with a large camera on a tripod)

MR. WIGGINS: Well, that's right pretty. *(He sets camera*

downstage center with his back to audience. From under the cloth)
You folks ready?

BETSY: We sure are.

MR. WIGGINS: Okay . . . One . . . Two . . .

MOTHER: *(Slightly hysterical)* Stop! I cain't! I cain't. Somethin's still not right!

FATHER: What in tarnation is wrong with you, Ma?

MOTHER: *(Shouting)* I don't know! *(Emphatically)* I . . . do . . . not . . . KNOW!

MR. WIGGINS: *(Out from cloth)* You people sure are time wasters!

BETSY: *(Emphatically)* Well, *I* know! And pretty dumb we are not to think of it. Of course you're upset. You've got a brand new hat upstairs and here we are taking a photo for the whole world to see and you don't even have it on! Just hold on, Mr. Wiggins, and I'll go and get it.

(She goes hurriedly off)

FATHER: Is that it, Ma? Is that the fly in your ointment?

MOTHER: *(Calmer. Still perplexed)* Well, I don't know. I guess so. Maybe that's it.

MR. WIGGINS: I certainly hope so. I've got to get home and whittle.

(Betsy returns with an outrageous straw picture hat covered with flowers, cherries, etc. She plunks it on Ma's head)

BETSY: Now! That makes everything perfect.

FATHER: *(Controlling himself)* Is that it, Ma?

MOTHER:

(Intimidated and with little conviction)
Yeah! Sure! That's it. That's just about it.

MR. WIGGINS: It's about time. *(He goes back under cloth)* Now . . . One . . . and two . . . and . . .

(The phone starts to ring madly. It is somehow loud and insistent)
Oh, for God's sake, what now!

BETSY: Don't anybody move! I'll get it. *(She rushes to phone)* Hello! *(She listens for a long time, obviously growing angrier and angrier. Livid with rage, she shouts into the phone)* Chung chow kow soong lang loong kai fooom! Oh so mahng ping tik toll feng so weng wing poong tang la feng boh soh ka lai mang feng lik teng to! *(She slams down the receiver. Controlling herself)* It was someone from summer camp.

(She returns to place in posed group, straightening herself)

MR. WIGGINS: Now, once and for all! Everybody look at the birdie and all together . . . one, two, three . . .
(All smile in unison and say:)
ALL: Cheese!
(Large flash of camera)

Curtain

John Bartholomew Tucker

GOOD NEIGHBORS

John Bartholomew Tucker

John Bartholomew Tucker makes his playwriting debut in print in this volume with his satire *Good Neighbors*. In Mr. Tucker's play a pair of adulterous neighbors appear to live out the soap opera plots of the television fantasies they watch and which employ them—the woman as an actress, the man as a director. It is as if they are entrapped by the tube that feeds them. *Good Neighbors* is the second of four short plays about love which were performed on the bill *What Are You Doing For Lunch Today?* at the New Shandol Theatre in New York in 1980. The other three plays rounding out the evening are *The Fifth Anniversary, . . . and a Happy New Year* and *Gather Ye Rosebuds*.

Mr. Tucker is well known to New Yorkers as a television host for *A.M. New York* (for which he won an Emmy). During his illustrative career in the media he has been in front of the camera on such shows as *Treasure Island* and *Candid Camera*, and his distinctive voice is familiar as the spokesman on commercials for Jell-O, Fotomat, and Kraft.

A stage performer as well, Mr. Tucker has appeared in productions of *The Last of the Red Hot Lovers, The Male Animal, Who's Afraid of Virginia Woolf, Harvey, The Four Poster,* and *The Seven Year Itch*.

Characters:

ANN
BILL

Scene:

A living room somewhere in Westchester County, outside New York—probably one of the River Towns. It is extremely well-furnished in a modern way.

At rise, we discover Ann Wells, a woman in her early thirties. The first thing one notices about Ann is her beauty. She possesses a simple, wholesome, charming, pure beauty.

As a matter of fact, she looks as pure as the driven snow—and, like the snow, she is about to drift.

At the moment, she is scurrying about, arranging a buffet luncheon for two on the coffee table—all the while watching a small portable television that sits on a table with its back to us. Apparently, a soap opera is playing, although it is difficult for us to hear it.

It is obvious that Ann has a very bad cold—sustained sniffles and several sneezes are testament to that.

A doorbell rings offstage. Ann gasps slightly, stands for a quiet second as if readying herself for something important, then hurries off to answer the door. She speaks in a loud urgent whisper.

ANN: I'm coming . . . I'm coming.
(The doorbell rings again)
I'm coming . . .
(We hear her open the door, off)
Bill? Where are you? Bill?
(We notice that a door on the other side of the room, leading directly from the outside into the living room, is trying to open, but a chain holds it. An arm reaches in, desperately trying to unhook the chain. The doorbell rings again. Ann rushes back into the room)
Bill? . . . Bill?
(The doorbell rings a third time, and the door being held by the chain is rushed at several times in a violent manner)
Bill . . . is that you?

(Bill's voice is heard)

BILL: Ann, open the door. For God's sake, open the door!

ANN: *(Unlatching the chain)* I'm sorry. The doorbell only rings in the front—and I didn't think you'd be coming in this way.

BILL: Don't talk so much. Just let me get in. Fast!

(Bill enters on his hands and knees. It must be autumn outside because he brings in quite a few leaves as he crawls. Several minutes from now, when he finally stands up, we will see that he is a pretty decent looking man of about forty who sports a handsome moustache in the latest style and is given to wearing horn-rimmed glasses, corduroy jackets and grey flannels. At the moment, though, he is rather out of breath, extremely nervous, and still on his hands and knees)

BILL: That crazy Hannigan dog—they ought to keep it tied up! He was sniffing at me the whole way. Half-way across the lawn he started to growl. Scared the hell out of me!

(He sneezes)

ANN: *(Giggles with amusement)* But what are you doing on your hands and knees—and why the side door? I thought you planned to walk straight across the front yard—just the way you would if Jim were home.

(She sneezes)

BILL: I thought about it all morning. Someone might have seen Jim leave today. Then they might see me walking over and notice if I stayed for a while. The whole *neighborhood* would get suspicious.

ANN: I don't think so.

BILL: So I crawled behind the stone wall the whole way. With that crazy Hannigan dog sniffing at me.

ANN: But what if someone saw you crawling behind the wall with a dog sniffing at you? Wouldn't that look more suspicious than if you'd just walked over here and knocked on the door?

BILL: No one saw me except the Hannigan dog. *(A bashful chuckle)* And he won't talk.

ANN: Still, I think it would have been . . .

BILL: WAIT . . . get down! Someone will see you. We can't be too careful.

(He gestures violently to get her down. For a moment, they are on hands and knees, facing each other, very close; and it is easy to tell

that they want to kiss. Their eyes are locked. Suddenly, they begin to crawl toward each other)

ANN: Oh, Bill . . .

BILL: Oh, Annnn . . . *(They almost embrace)* WAIT! First things first. We mustn't be seen together. We've got to close the shutters. *(As she starts to stand)* NO . . . stay down!
(He begins to crawl around on all fours beneath the windows, reaching up to close interior shutters. Ann follows his lead)

ANN: I can't believe that we're alone together. I just can't believe it.

BILL: Neither can I. *(They are crawling on all fours very quickly now)* I've thought about this for months—years.

ANN: When you slipped me that note on Sunday my heart stopped.

BILL: I debated about it for weeks.

ANN: You're shy.

BILL: I'm a coward. I figured if I told you, and then you told Jim, I could always deny it. But if I wrote it, and you showed it to Jim, he could kill me.

ANN: Why *did* you write it then?

BILL: I don't know. The impetuosities of passion. "Wrong no man, and write no woman." Now I'm doing both —simultaneously.
(They have, by now, closed all but one of the shutters. They slither up separate sides of the last one and close it together)

ANN: You're impetuous. I like that.

BILL: You're wonderful. I love that.

ANN: Oh, Bill! After all those cocktail parties, and Sunday brunches where we've been in the same room together, pretending we didn't really notice each other. Finally, here we are alone.

BILL: It's wonderful. Wonderful!
(They embrace slowly, shyly, sweetly)

ANN: *(As they part)* I feel that something fresh and bright and new has entered my mind, and my body, and my heart, and my soul.

BILL: That's *beautiful.*

ANN: *(A girlish giggle)* It's from yesterday's script where I told Doctor Bob that I was in love with his son.

BILL: *Actresses.*

ANN: *Directors.*

BILL: Directors don't quote lines from yesterday's script.

ANN: You do, too.

BILL: But not yesterday's soap opera. With us, it's Shakespeare, Congreve, Marlowe and Moliere.

ANN: It's the same thing. Jim quotes both kinds.

BILL: *Ahhhh—*

ANN: What's the matter?

BILL: Whenever one of us mentions his name, I feel guilty.

ANN: I know. So do I. But we mustn't. We really mustn't. We just can't help it. This is something that . . . Oh, Bill—
(She runs to him and throws her arms around him. They embrace. Then she sneezes, a small sneeze. They pay no attention to it and continue to embrace. Then he sneezes—violently. Still in his arms)
You have a cold, too?

BILL: *(He makes light of it. This cold will certainly be no problem)* Got it last night.

ANN: Fever?

BILL: A little, I think.

ANN: Chills?

BILL: Once in a while.

ANN: Cramps?

BILL: Well . . . yes, every once in a while.

ANN: *(Delighted)* We've caught the same bug. The cramps are the worst part, aren't they?

BILL: They're terrible. Crawling across the yard behind the wall, I thought I'd die. And every time my stomach growled, Hannigan's demented dog would growl—But I didn't want to tell you any of that.

ANN: Why?

BILL: I mean . . . to write a love note to your next door neighbor, to arrange a secret meeting in her living room, to hold her in your arms, to feel your heart pounding with passion . . . and then to spend the time telling her how . . . AGGHHHH!

(He doubles over)

ANN: Oh, you poor thing!

BILL: I'll be all right—But see what I mean? I'm not talking about how soft your lips look, and how I'm longing to kiss them—I'm talking about my virus.

ANN: It doesn't matter. We're here, together. And now nothing can—AGGHHHH!

BILL: I know, I know. It's awful.

ANN: It comes so suddenly.

BILL: Maybe a little Pepto Bismol?

ANN: No, no, I'm all right. So what if we have a few pains, or aches, or fever—

BILL: Don't you have *chills,* too?

ANN: —Or chills, too. I want my arms around you. I want you.

BILL: And I want you, too.

(They embrace with passion, almost knocking each other over. Each sneezes slightly)

ANN: Oh, Bill, Oh, Bill! *(She grabs his hand and starts to pull him)* Let's go up to the bedroom.

BILL: *(He resists)* Good Lord, no!

ANN: Why not?

BILL: That's not a place . . . for this. That's a place where men get shot. Men very much like me. In fact, men exactly like me.

ANN: No one's going to shoot you.

BILL: I couldn't. I just couldn't. That's where you and Jim sleep. That's where you and Jim . . . I mean, I just couldn't. I'd be impotent for the rest of my life.

ANN: Then why not here? If we're not careful we'll talk away the whole afternoon.

BILL: All right. Here.

(They stand for a moment and then rush at each other)

ANN: Anyway, it's the proper room. It's the room where you gave me the note on Sunday, and the room where I called you at your office on Monday.

(It's not a very ballet-like scene that ensues. It's hurried, rushed, awkward, with great urgency, and all thumbs on both their parts. Murmurs of "I'm so glad you did that on Sunday," "So am I, I couldn't wait," "I couldn't sleep at all last night," "Neither could I," and other things we can't quite understand as she unbuttons and pulls off his shirt, and he unbuttons and pulls off her blouse. It ends with him in a T-shirt and her in a bra—and a mighty shiver and sneeze from both)

ANN: Look at us—trembling with anticipated ecstasy!

BILL: Actually, I'm having a slight chill.

ANN: Me, too.

BILL: Well . . . ?

ANN: Yes . . .

(They have at each other again; this time they attack the raiments below the belt—the same wisps of phrases are heard along with some breathy groans, and sneeze here and there. But it doesn't work as well on the slacks as it did on the shirt and blouse. It's very awkward, and ends as a kind of combination dance and wrestling match. They finally fall to the floor)

BILL: I think it might work better if we did it ourselves.

ANN: Yes—

BILL: Actually, I usually take off my shoes first.

ANN: So do I.

(They're both grinning wildly as they run madly about taking off shoes, socks and slacks)

ANN: I never thought I'd be in the middle of my living room taking off my clothes. It's exciting. Jim would never do anything like this. Never!

BILL: Neither would Helen.

ANN: Who's that?

BILL: Helen. My wife.

ANN: Oh? I thought you said Helen.

BILL: I did. Helen.

ANN: *(Really pronouncing it)* H-Elen?

BILL: Yes—H-Elen.

ANN: And all these years I thought her name was E-llen. You know, without the H.

BILL: No, it's with an H. Always has been. *(He shudders —still dashing about)* Oh, God—what a time to catch a virus. I can't believe it. Bad timing *again*.

(Ann is shivering and laughing simultaneously)
What's so funny?

ANN: *(Acute laugh)* We got sick at the same time. Isn't that romantic?

BILL: *(A burst of emotion)* That's another thing I love about you. Your sense of humor.

ANN: I'm glad you said that. I've always thought I had a good sense of humor. But I never get cast in any comedies. *(She has run to him and is tickling him on the ribs. He jumps up and down, laughing like a schoolboy)* Maybe that's because I work on Soaps. Casting directors have a prejudice when it comes to Soap actresses.

BILL: That's probably true.

(The tickling, jumping and chortling continues, then suddenly

there's a pause. He's wearing only T-shirt and shorts, and she's wearing only bra and bikini. This is it)

Well . . . ?

ANN: Yes . . . ?

BILL: Well . . . ?

ANN: Just . . . let me check the TV. I want to make sure Jim's on today's show. He's supposed to come on about halfway through. His big scene. Right after the operation.

BILL: Who's being operated on?

ANN: Old Doc Colton.

BILL: I thought he had an operation just three months ago.

ANN: He did, but Doctor Bishop caught him drinking again last week and—

BILL: Who's Doctor Bishop?

ANN: That's Jim.

BILL: Oh—

ANN: —He caught him drinking again and warned him it might kill him, but Old Doc Colton didn't listen. He got drunk on Tuesday's show and crashed his car. Jim—Doctor Bishop—is operating on him today. Jim doesn't know that old Doc Colton has been having an affair with young Missy Bishop, his only daughter.

BILL: My God, Young Missy Bishop is seventeen and old Doc Colton is in his sixties!

ANN: I know—And so does old Doc Colton. That's why he's drinking. *(We don't see the front of the television, but by now she has it on)* There's Jim now. He's coming out of the operating room and smiling. The operation must have been a success. Oh, no—*(She lunges at the television set and turns the audio dial before the volume comes on)* I'm turning off the sound. I couldn't stand to hear Jim talking. Not with me like this.

BILL: *(Crossing his hands over his groin)* I know what you mean.

ANN: Oh, have I hurt your feelings? I'm sorry.

BILL: No, no. I'd probably feel the same way if Helen were on a Soap instead of a crazy fund raiser for Channel 13.

ANN: Jim is smiling and rubbing his hands. The operation must have gone very well.

BILL: On the other hand, maybe he found out about old Doc and Missy, his only daughter, and he's glad the patient died.

ANN: No, no—he's giving the O.K. sign to old Doc Colton's niece Mona—that's the one *he's* having an affair with. They're writing her out of the show at the end of the month—another car crash. Leslie is furious.

BILL: Who's Leslie?

ANN: Leslie Burdick. She plays Mona.

BILL: *(Peering more intently at the television set)* I might have worked with her once at the Cleveland Playhouse.

ANN: I didn't know you ever worked at the Cleveland Playhouse.

BILL: Years ago. I directed Shelley Berman in *Othello*. He played Iago. Brilliant.

ANN: What did Leslie play?

BILL: I don't remember. Maybe I didn't work with her. She's probably too young.

ANN: *(Looking at television again)* He's looking into the camera. Oh, my God, he's looking right *at* me!

BILL: They're just fading to black, that's all.

ANN: No, he's looking. He's accusing! *(To television set)* Jim—Jim, I'm sorry! I don't want to hurt you. It's just that Bill and I—

BILL: For God's sake, don't mention *my* name—

ANN: It's just that Bill and I . . . we can't help it. We just can't help it.

BILL: He's *looking* at you over Mona's shoulder, and now he's kissing her. Why should you feel guilty if he doesn't?

ANN: But that's acting. This is . . . this is . . . ah, good, commercial break. There's Frieda Rappaport. She gets all the I'm-cute-as-hell-but-I-love-to-get-on-the-floor-and-scrub-it-commercials. You'd think they'd cast someone else once in a while. Anyone else. I've been up for seventeen in the last six months and haven't even had a call-back.

BILL: I don't know anything about the world of commercials. The closest I ever came was when they asked me to direct the Eastern Airlines commercials. That was when they had Orson Welles as spokesman. Naturally, they wanted a classically-trained director. I told them it would be an honor and a privilege to direct Mr. Welles in anything—anything *except* a commercial. They suddenly got defensive and picked another director.

(He sneezes)

ANN: Frieda Rappaport, the "Queen of Commercials," wouldn't understand what you're talking about.

BILL: I know. Agghhhh . . . !

ANN: Oh—you poor thing! *(She sneezes)* But we're losing the moment.

BILL: I know. Just let me sit on the couch for a minute. I'll be all right.

ANN: And let's not look at the television anymore. It's ruined the whole mood. *(She's playful)* Bill . . .

BILL: *(He sneezes and shudders from a violent chill)* Yes?

ANN: May I join you on the sofa? *(She sneezes)* But let's get under the Afghan. I think I'm getting another chill, too. *(Still playful)* Just a little one though.

BILL: Me, too. *(Not very playful. In fact, a little desperate)* And mine's just a little one, too.

(She has taken the Afghan from the edge of the sofa. She opens it and snuggles in next to him, spreading the blanket over the two of them)

ANN: There. That feels better, doesn't it? Warm as toast. You give off so much animal heat.

BILL: I think it's probably my fever.

ANN: No, it's you—the two of us together.

BILL: I think it's my fever.

ANN: You're shaking.

BILL: I know. So are you.

ANN: I know. Isn't it wonderful just to lie here in each other's arms, shaking.

BILL: Oh, yes . . .

ANN: Bill? When did you first notice me?

BILL: The first time I saw you. You waved and said, "Welcome to the neighborhood."

ANN: Is *that* what I said? Nothing witty or anything?

BILL: I thought it was just the perfect thing to say.

ANN: Somehow I don't really recall ever seeing Ellen for the first time.

BILL: *H-E*len. I know. A lot of people say that.

ANN: When did you first . . . care?

BILL: During that winter the Armstrongs and the Smeltzers kept having those Sunday Brunches—just before all four of them ran off to Spain together.

ANN: For me it was the Warners' egg nog party four years ago.

BILL: I remember that. We kept bumping into each other by the egg nog bowl. *(Ann laughs)* And now . . . here we are. *(They embrace. Bill sneezes. Ann sneezes. During the following few speeches, they remain in each other's arms and try to continue the conversation as if nothing were wrong, but they both begin to shake, and their rattling voices are painful indications that the chills have returned)*

ANN: I should keep a diary. Today's entry would make wonderful reading someday. The trouble is—most days don't.

BILL: I know. That's why people don't . . . *(The fever, the chills are too fierce to overcome)* Aaaagggghhhhhh!

ANN: Me, to . . . AAAAHHHHHH GGGGGGHHHH! Ah, . . . Ah, . . . Ah, . . .

(During her chill, she slowly starts to pull on her slacks)

BILL: Maybe some consommé. I fed that to the whole cast up in Boston last spring. I didn't get sick at all *then*. I had to wait until *now*. *(He sits and begins to pull on his trousers)* You're getting dressed, huh?

ANN: Hmmm? I guess so. So are you.

BILL: Oh?—I didn't notice. It's just like that time on the bus.

ANN: What time?

BILL: That time on the Greyhound bus near Providence, Rhode Island.

ANN: What are you talking about?

BILL: My bad timing. I've been plagued with bad timing all my life! But the Greyhound bus was the worst! There was snow in New York and Philadelphia, so we had to land in Boston. And they couldn't get us on a train, so they put us on a bus to New York. And who was I sitting beside in the back but Sarah Fairchild herself. At first I thought it was Faye Dunaway, but it was Sarah Fairchild. And I said a few dumb things like how much I liked her pictures, and how I couldn't help but admire her wonderful body, particularly so after having seen her in *Cry of the Damned* where she'd had that big nude scene in Shepherd Strudwick's apartment, and how I'd always thought that she would be wonderful in Chekhov or Ibsen, and how I'd love to direct her on the stage . . . when all of a sudden, she leaned over and whispered into my ear, "Why don't you stop talking and get under my coat?" And I said, "Right here on a Greyhound bus?" and she said, "Why

not? It's dark. Who'll notice?!! . . . and anyway, *who cares?"*
. . . I forgot to mention that she was a little high on
something . . . and just then . . . Just as I got under that big
coat with THE Sarah Fairchild . . . just as I felt her moist, full
lips on my ear lobe, her fingers flitting down my ribs . . . just
then . . . FOR THE FIRST TIME IN THE HISTORY OF
MASS TRANSPORTATION . . . some idiot stood up in front
and tried to *HI-JACK A GREYHOUND BUS!* I couldn't believe
it.

ANN: What happened?

BILL: Nothing. She screamed, along with everybody else.
And that was it.

ANN: I mean with the hi-jacker.

BILL: He only hi-jacked it about a half mile off the road.
He wanted a ride home. He should've been shot. But by then
it was all over. Bad timing. Look at today. I'm damned!

ANN: *(The phone rings. She picks it up)* Hello? Oh, hello, Mrs.
Hannigan. How are you?
(At hearing the name, Bill begins to dress at breakneck speed)
What? No . . . no, I *didn't* see him crawling behind the stone
wall . . . and . . . and your dog was *barking* at him? Well . . .
as a matter of fact, he's right here now. We're having . . . tea.
Why don't you join us? No? Well, all right . . . another time
then . . . Bye.

BILL: She saw me?

ANN: Uh-huh . . . and she thought she knew why you
were crawling.

BILL: But you never explained.

ANN: Why bother? Who could?
*(They look at each other for a moment and then begin genuinely to
laugh loudly together)*

BILL: I know.

ANN: "Dear Diary . . . Guess what happened to me today?
Absolutely nothing."
*(They laugh some more. Then suddenly, he reaches out and holds
her hands in his)*

BILL: We can't end it like this. We just can't.

ANN: No, no . . . we can't. This is only the beginning.

BILL: *Yes,* only the *beginning.*

ANN: It's probably just a forty-eight hour virus anyway.

BILL: Well . . . seventy-two hours . . .

ANN: At the *most,* seventy-two.

BILL: *(Excited—afresh)* Next Monday then? Monday afternoon?

ANN: Yes, Monday. *(Happily, passionately, they embrace. Then she pulls away)* No, wait. Monday is my painting class, and we're meeting here.

BILL: *(The momentum is building now)* Then Tuesday?

ANN: Yes. Oh, yes. *Tuesday. (They embrace. She pulls away a second time)* Oh, I'm sorry, I'm sorry. Tuesday's my group.

BILL: Group?

ANN: Therapy.

BILL: Oh—

ANN: But Wednesday. *(Even more passion) Yes—Wednesday.*

BILL: I can't. Parents day at school.

ANN: Thursday and Friday, I'll be working.

BILL: How about the week *after* next.

ANN: *(She embraces him)* Yes—the week after next. *Yes.*

BILL: Wait a minute . . . I'm forgetting . . . I'm on the Town Council now . . .

ANN: . . . And that's the week for the Library auction . . .

BILL: Then comes Halloween . . .

ANN: . . . And Thanksgiving.

BILL: The whole holiday season is always . . Let's make it . . . *(With renewed passion) January. The first week in January.*

ANN: *(Even more intensely than before) Yes. January.*

BILL: No, wait. I'm forgetting. Joe Papp. Rehearsals.

ANN: February?

BILL: Yes, *February.*

(He embraces her)

ANN: Ah—*February.*

(The curtain begins to fall)

The only trouble with February is . . . No, . . . I'll just ignore it. *Oh, Bill—this is only the beginning.*

BILL:

(A final embrace)

Yes. Only the beginning.

The Curtain Falls

Thomas Gibbons

THE EXHIBITION
(Scenes from the life of John Merrick)

SOURCES: Sir Frederick Treves, *The Elephant Man and Other Reminiscences* (Cassell and Co., 1923) and *The Cradle of the Deep* (E. P. Dutton, 1911). For biographical information on Frederick Treves, Ashley Montagu's *The Elephant Man* (1971).

Thomas Gibbons

Unlike Bernard Pomerance's *The Elephant Man,* the Broadway success dealing with the same subject and populated by twenty characters, Thomas Gibbons' first play *The Exhibition,* employs just two characters to relate in dramatic terms the tortured life of John Merrick. What could have resulted in a static duologue instead, in the creative hands of Mr. Gibbons has developed into a tense and compelling dramatic mosaic. Although *The Exhibition* and *The Elephant Man* share the same topic, they are vastly different in approach and construction as well as in length.

A grotesquely deformed Victorian sideshow freak, John Merrick possessed features so severely distorted that he was described as the figure of a man with the characteristics of an elephant. Inwardly, he had an acute intelligence and romantic imagination, but outwardly he was a monstrous abomination, revealed in twisted, distorted flesh. He was indeed a creature without human hope until a British surgeon, Dr. Frederick Treves, discovered Merrick and made an attempt to reclaim him for the human race. Treves became his rescuer, friend and confidant, taking him away from the tawdry Victorian sideshows and placing him in a private room in the London Hospital.

Gibbons questions whether Merrick was really the inhuman monster he was perceived to be. He also seeks to find an explanation for Merrick's misery. Does Merrick exist to test the humanity around him? And was his life destined to be one long and harrowing "exhibition?" Drawing from fully documented material, Gibbons has made *The Exhibition* more than an historical drama about an ill-fated man. As one critic observed, "In his hands, it has become a poem which tears at the heart."

Thomas Gibbons was born in Philadelphia, Pennsylvania, in 1954, and graduated from Villanova University in 1976. He became interested in the subject of his drama after reading Treves' *The Elephant Man and Other Reminiscences.* Originally published in 1923, the year of Treves' death, it was republished in 1971 by Ashley Montagu in his book, *The Elephant Man.* In the autumn of 1976 the author journeyed to London in pursuit of further research. "I saw the skeleton of John Merrick, the mask which he wore, and the model of St. Philip's Church which he built. These, and a few other objects, are on display in the Medical College Museum of the

London Hospital. The Librarian of the College is something of an expert on the case of the Elephant Man and he showed me a pamphlet entitled *The Life and Adventures of Joseph Carey Merrick, the Great Freak of Nature! Half a Man and Half an Elephant.* This document purports to be the autobiography of John Merrick (there is some confusion over his name). Although I doubt that Merrick himself wrote it, the pamphlet is a fascinating work. Merrick's first and last words in the play, and a few other passages, are direct quotations from this 'autobiography.'"

The first version of Mr. Gibbons' play was written for a playwriting seminar at Villanova and subsequently came to the attention of The Philadelphia Company where it was presented as a staged reading in April, 1977. The play was given a full-scale production in March, 1979, and was greeted in the Philadelphia press as "a searching, moral drama that reverberates with universal meanings." During this period the play was performed under its original title of *The Elephant Man*, but to avoid confusion with the Pomerance work, the author retitled it *The Exhibition*. It was presented again for an extended engagement in October of that same year.

Characters:

SIR FREDERICK TREVES
JOHN MERRICK, *the Elephant Man.*

Scene One:

The history.

Scene Two:

A garden on the grounds of the London Hospital. Early 1887.

Scene Three:

Merrick's room in the Hospital, November, 1889.

Scene Four:

1923.

Scene One:

Dark empty stage.

Lights come up. The Elephant Man stands in center of stage. He wears a dark cloak-like garment extending to the floor. On his right hand is a glove; the left is bare. His head is covered by a black yachting cap from which hangs a white cloth mask: a hole for the left eye. In his left hand he carries a wooden walking stick.

Silence.

ELEPHANT MAN: *(A recitation)* I first saw the light on the fifth of August, 1860. I was born in Lee Street, Wharf Street,

Leicester. The deformity which I am now exhibiting was caused by my mother being frightened by an elephant; my mother was going along the street when a procession of animals were passing by, there was a terrible crush of people to see them, and unfortunately she was pushed under the elephant's feet, which frightened her very much: this occurring during a time of pregnancy was the cause of my deformity.

(Lights fade.

Lights come up downstage right. Treves sits on a bench reading from a leatherbound journal. He is seventy years old)

TREVES: This is how it began. It was a November afternoon in 1884. A late hour. Pale, dwindling autumn light. *(Quietly)* I was just thirty years old, so full of confidence. *(Pause)* I happened to pass by a vacant greengrocer's, on the Whitechapel road.

(He reads from the journal)

"The whole of the front of the shop, with the exception of the door, was hidden by a hanging sheet of canvas on which was the announcement that the Elephant Man was to be seen within and that the price of admission was twopence. Painted on the canvas in primitive colors was a life-size portrait of the Elephant Man. This very crude production depicted a frightful creature that could only have been possible in a nightmare. It was the figure of a man with the characteristics of an elephant."

(He pauses, obscurely disturbed; continues)

"The transfiguration was not far advanced. There was still more of the man than of the beast. This fact—that it was still human—was the most repellent attribute of the creature. There was nothing about it of the pitiableness of the misshapened or the deformed, nothing of the grotesqueness of the freak, but merely—*(Turns page)*—the loathsome insinuation of a man being changed into an animal. Some palm trees in the background of the picture suggested a jungle and might have led the imaginative to assume that it was in this wild that the perverted object had roamed."

(He lowers the journal, closes his eyes)

The exhibition was closed. I sent a boy round to find the showman. After a while he came; reeking of liquor. "I should like to see this Elephant Man," I said. "A shilling for a private showing, sir." I gave it. We entered. Cold, damp. On a shelf, some old tins, a few shriveled potatoes. At the end of the shop was a curtain. (*Gestures*) He pulled it back . . .

(*He reads*)

"The showman pulled back the curtain and revealed a bent figure crouching on a stool and covered by a brown blanket. In front of it, on a tripod, was a large brick heated by a Bunsen burner. Over this the creature was huddled to warm itself. It never moved when the curtain was drawn back."

(*He pauses, turns the page*)

"Outside the sun was shining and one could hear the footsteps of the passers-by, a tune whistled by a boy and the companionable hum of traffic in the road." (*Quietly, not reading*) Innocuous sunlight. Hiding *him* all the while.

(*Pause. He reads*)

"The showman—speaking as if to a dog—called out harshly: 'Stand up!' The thing arose slowly and let the blanket that covered its head and back fall to the ground. There stood revealed the most disgusting specimen of humanity that I have ever seen."

(*He stops again. Lights come up on the Elephant Man upstage left*)

"The most striking feature about him was his enormous and misshapened head." (*He shapes the deformities with precise gestures*) "From the brow there projected a huge bony mass like a loaf, while from the back of the skull hung a bag of spongy, fungus-looking skin. On the top of the skull, a few lank hairs. The osseous growth on the forehead almost occluded one eye. From the upper jaw there projected another mass of bone. The nose was merely a lump of flesh." (*With growing agitation*) "The face was no more capable of expression than a block of gnarled wood. The right arm was of enormous size and shapeless. The hand was large and clumsy—a fin or paddle rather than a hand. From the chest hung a bag of the same repulsive flesh . . . like a dewlap suspended from the neck of a lizard—"

(*He lowers the journal, distraught*)

ELEPHANT MAN: My deformity was not perceived much at birth, but began to develop itself when at the age of five years. I went to school like other children, until I was about eleven or twelve years of age, when the greatest misfortune of my life occurred, namely—the death of my mother . . . (*Dwindling*) Peace to her, she was a good mother to me . . .

(He fades back into the darkness)

TREVES: *(Composed now, places journal on bench)* From the showman, I learnt nothing about the Elephant Man except that he was English, and that his name was John Merrick. As at the time of my discovery of the Elephant Man I was the Lecturer on Anatomy at the Medical College. I was anxious to examine him in detail and to prepare an account of his abnormalities. Therefore, I arranged for him to come to my room at the college, where I exhibited him to the Pathological Society of London. *(Pause)* After an interesting discussion the meeting was adjourned. I returned him in a cab to the place of exhibition, and assumed that I had seen the last of him. *(Pause; quietly)* The next day I found that the shop was empty. The show had been closed by the police. He had vanished, completely.

(Silence)

Two years passed. One day I was summoned by the police to the Liverpool Street Station. In a waiting room there, surrounded by a curious mob, I found Merrick, exhausted and starving. *(With astonishment)* He had given the police a calling card.

(The card is in the journal. He holds it up)

My card. I'd given it to him at that first meeting. Two years before.

(Lights come up on the Elephant Man, huddled on the floor. With his left hand he extends the card)

ELEPHANT MAN: *(Weakly)* The measurement round the head is thirty-six inches, there is a large substance of flesh at the back as large as a breakfast cup, while the face is such a sight that no one could describe it. The right hand measures twelve inches round the wrist and five inches round one of the fingers. The feet and legs are covered with thick lumpy skin, also the body, like that of an elephant . . .

(Lights fade)

TREVES: I drove him at once to the hospital and installed him in an isolation ward in the attic. *(Pause)* I realized that a place must be found for him, and made inquiries. From the Royal Hospital for Incurables: no. From the British Home for Incurables: no. Not even if someone were to pay for him. *(Pause)* What choice did I have? It was clear that he had no place to go. I decided to keep him at the hospital. This was irregular; the hospital was not a refuge for incurables; but I would not abandon him a second time. The chairman of the committee wrote to the *Times* to appeal for funds.

(He unfolds a faded newspaper clipping and reads)

"Sir—I am authorized to ask your powerful assistance in bringing to the notice of the public the following most exceptional case. There is now in a little room off one of our attic wards a man named John Merrick"—and so on and so on to the appeal. *(Reads)* "The Master of the Temple on Advent Sunday preached an eloquent sermon on the subject of our Master's answer to the question, 'Who did sin, this man or his parents, that he was born blind?' showing how one of the Creator's objects in permitting men to be born to a life of hopeless and miserable disability was that the works of God should be manifested in evoking the sympathy and kindly aid of those on whom such a heavy cross is not laid."

(He places the clipping in the journal)

Our faith in the generosity of the English public was not misplaced. In a week enough money was forthcoming to maintain Merrick for life without any charge upon the hospital funds. *(Pause)* Thus the Elephant Man came to live at the London Hospital.

(Lights come up on the Elephant Man, standing at center of stage. Upstage, slightly left, is a life-size poster of the Elephant Man: a crude exaggerated depiction, garishly colored. Hanging in front of the poster is a curtain—as Treves describes it, "a red tablecloth suspended from a cord by a few rings."

Downstage, to the left, a small table on which stands a detailed model of St. Philip's Church in London. Next to it, a candle and extinguisher

Silence)

ELEPHANT MAN: I've just been out walking in the garden. Alone. Treves allowed me to go. What an adventure! It's a moonless night . . . of course. Otherwise it would not have been permitted. *(Pause)* I went down to the hedge and listened to the people passing by in the street. Courting couples. *(Elegiac)* Women's laughter, their soft voices! *(Quietly)* Prostitutes from Whitechapel. I have no illusions about them. Having lived there for a time. *(Pause)* Actually . . . I remember little about that time in my life. The gaslight shining through the window. The people. When he showed me, he turned the lamps down. The only light was supplied by a single candle, flickering at my feet. To heighten the effect.

(*Strident showman's voice*) Ask yourselves, ladies and gentlemen: Where does he come from? (*Quietly*) Gazing at me in the mysterious light. (*Showman's voice*) You're a mystery, Merrick! (*Muses*) He said that to me quite often. A mystery. I could not speak very well then. I answered him rarely.

(He lapses into silence, takes a few shuffling steps)

It was not what I expected. To be out in the garden, alone. Treves used to send a nurse with me. That's over now, I suppose. Not that there was anything. He never sent the same nurse. No chance for . . . attachments to develop. As if they would. No. Anything that happens, will happen only —(*Touches mask*)—within me. (*Pause*) But one needs a presence to build on. Sometimes, walking in the garden with the nurse at my side, it almost seems . . . If I forget certain facts: that this is a hospital, that she is a trained nurse, that I wear this . . . (*Touches mask*) In the end there are too many things to be forgotten.

(Silence. Suddenly, muted churchbells pealing. He moves to the table at left, points to the model with his walking stick)

I am not without my recreations. I built this model with my left hand alone. St. Philip's Church. I can see it from my window. (*Hesitantly*) There's a game I play . . .

(He lights the candle, kneels behind the table. Extending the candle across the table, he slowly raises it up over the model)

Once I saw the sun rise like this over St. Philip's. God's fire, hanging over his house. (*Pause. Somber*) I was lying in the street. In a state of utter exhaustion. It was the end. Mud-covered, too tired to feel the indignity any longer, the humiliation. I had lost whatever humanity I possessed. No longer thought it precious, no longer cared. (*Pause*) Then the sun rose. A flame over the spire. I went in and lay down in one of the pews. It was dark. Quiet. I must have slept. A noise awakened me: two priests attending to their duties. (*His voice quickens*) I hid in a dark alcove. Watching. Soon people began to come in. They did not see me. They knelt and prayed. I heard voices whispering somewhere. Telling of terrible deeds, terrible thoughts. The sins of man. One by one they went to their confessions. And were forgiven.

(Silence. He extinguishes the candle. Lights come up instantly on Treves, downstage right)

TREVES: (*Rapid, unemotional*) My life, now, soon to end, after seventy years: the essentials. Born 1853, educated in London.

1875, house surgeon at the London Hospital. Assistant surgeon four years later, full surgeon by 1884. Lecturer in Anatomy, Lecturer in Surgery until 1897. In 1898, resigned to devote full time to private practice. In 1900 appointed Surgeon Extraordinary to Queen Victoria. 1901, Knight Commander of the Victorian Order. In 1902, I saved Edward the Seventh; created a Baronet, promoted to Grand Commander of the Order. Retired in 1908. Married in 1877; by my wife Anne—two daughters; one dead. Why was he born into such pain? (*Pause. Quietly*) To never touch, or be touched. To know yourself hideous, malformed, a thing that scalds vision . . . (*Perplexed*) And yet . . . I find a beauty in that. A beauty that blinds. Am I wrong? To see beauty in him?

    (*Lights fade slowly. Silence. Lights come up on the Elephant Man*)
    ELEPHANT MAN: People seem to think that I do not understand their feelings when they first see me. Their horror, their . . . outrage. But there was a time when I first saw myself, first saw my face, and had to accept the fact that this was *me*. Of course I could see the arms, legs, the rest. And of course I touched myself. Felt myself. But touch is deceiving. And perhaps I used—(*Holds up gloved hand*)—the wrong hand. I thought I was human. I took it on faith. But I could not see the face. I always assumed the face was normal; the face at least, I thought. (*Pause*) But that ended the first time I found a mirror. I was thirteen, I believe. Placed in a workhouse to labor at some useless, forgotten task. My peculiar virginity was that I had never in my short life encountered a mirror. People always withheld them from me, or hid them in my presence. One day, though . . . *I saw*. (*Pause*) It was late. Most of the men had gone home. I remained behind for the night . . . I always waited for night to fall before venturing into the streets. I passed by the foreman's room. He was gone. The door was ajar. No one looking. I was alone. A small room: clothes, a bed, trunks. I lit a candle, began to search for the mirror I knew he must have, that everyone had but me. (*With growing agitation*) I threw clothes aside—not here, not here! I had to know. In the back, a curtain. He'll be back soon. I grabbed it—
    (*He grasps curtain hanging in front of poster*)
    Draw it aside!
    (*Pulls curtain aside, sees the garish, cruel, portrait. Stricken*)
    Light! The mirror burst into light! All around me was light

And I saw—*I saw!* Gnarled head. Bone exploding out over
the eye. The face . . . the twisted body *My* body, *mine.* Me.
All—
> *(In anguish he collapses. Silence. His hands cover the mask. Long
> pause. Finally he lowers his hands. He draws up his legs, encircles
> them with his arms, places his head against his knees. Pause.
> Quietly)*

Treves does not allow mirrors here. It does not matter. I
have seen it. It is burned in my brain. *(Pause. Bleak)* The
doctors tell me my head is growing heavier and heavier. The
progress of the disease. For quite a while now I have found it
impossible to sleep in a normal position. It sinks into the
pillow; it bends on the stalk. They tell me its weight might
dislocate my neck. Instantaneous death. *(Pause)* Sometimes, at
night, in bed, I think I feel the bone growing. Blossoming
farther out of its proper shape. The skull becoming ever
more convoluted. *(Pause. Whispers)* Must I grow more monstrous?
> *(Silence. He huddles on floor. Lights fade very slowly.*
>
> *Lights come up on Treves)*

TREVES: Some notes I took, after I'd seen him, that first
time; what I sensed in him at first glimpse. *(Lifts journal, reads)*
"He had no past to look back upon and no future to look
forward to. At the age of twenty he was a creature without
hope. There was nothing in front of him but a vista of
caravans creeping along a road, of rows of glaring show tents
and of circles of staring eyes . . ." *(Lowers journal. Quietly,
self-mocking for a moment)* That's what I delivered him from.
(Urgently) But there was so much more that I wanted to give to
him: the world in all its joy and beauty . . . I wanted him to
get accustomed to his fellowmen, to become a human being
himself and to be admitted to the communion of his kind.
(Pause. Very seriously) I wanted to . . . reclaim him for the
human race.
> *(Silence. Slow fading of lights)*

Scene Two:

*A small garden on the grounds of the London Hospital. Early
1887. Lights come up to reveal the Elephant Man sitting on a
bench, center stage.*

Twilight. Silence.

TREVES: (*Calling, off*) John!

(*The Elephant Man looks around but does not answer. Treves enters at right*)

TREVES: Hello, John.

ELEPHANT MAN: Hello, Doctor.

TREVES: May I see your left arm, please? (*The Elephant Man extends his arm. Treves rolls up the sleeve, examines*) John, do you like living here at the hospital?

ELEPHANT MAN: Yes. (*Gratefully*) I am happy . . . every hour of the day.

TREVES: I'm glad. (*Examines, touches the arm clinically*) Very good. No sign of diseased tissue. Quite flawless. (*Rolls down the sleeve*) Thank you, John. (*Pause*) I have a surprise for you. You have visitors.

ELEPHANT MAN: (*Apprehensive*) Who?

TREVES: I've invited some people to meet you.

ELEPHANT MAN: Please . . . send them away.

TREVES: Now, John, they're rather eager to make your acquaintance.

ELEPHANT MAN: I would rather not see anyone.

TREVES: I think the company would do you some good. (*Pause*) You need to become accustomed to people. No one here wants to harm you.

(*Pause. The Elephant Man indicates the garden with his left hand*)

ELEPHANT MAN: What do you see here, Doctor?

TREVES: (*Puzzled*) Nothing. (*Smiles*) A garden.

ELEPHANT MAN: I see . . . a circus. (*Pause*) I was told once that my mother, while bearing me . . . had something happen to her. (*Simply*) That she went to a circus and was knocked down by an elephant. (*Muses*) I see the creature, sometimes, in my dreams. Standing over her in triumph, trumpeting into the night. The image of the elephant entered her and passed into her womb. (*Intensely*) How frightened she must have been! As she lay on the ground, the lights, the noise, the hue of the circus passed through her senses and into mine. (*Pause*) My original memories are of the circus.

TREVES: (*Patiently, as if to a child*) We used to believe that was possible—to be impressed in the womb. There is a poetry to it. But we know now it is not the true explanation.

ELEPHANT MAN: It *is* very strange, for, you see, mother was so beautiful.

TREVES: (*Gently*) I'm sure she was, John.
(*Pause*)

ELEPHANT MAN: (*Hesitantly*) Doctor . . . when I am next moved, can I go to a blind asylum? (*Softly*) They would know only the sound of my voice. Strange things might happen there . . . wonderful things. (*Touches mask*) I could burn this. (*Quickly*) Or to a lighthouse? I saw a photograph of the Eddystone lighthouse once. I could stay there. John Merrick, keeper of the Eddystone lighthouse. (*Excited, pointing*) Sea captains would rejoice: There's Merrick's light! Thank God for Merrick!

TREVES: You won't be moved again, John. You have a home here. The people of London have opened their hearts to you. (*Pause; gently*) This is your home now.
(*Pause*)

ELEPHANT MAN: (*Wondering*) A home? A place of peace. (*Timidly*) Have I found that?

TREVES: (*Finds himself moved by this*) A whole new life is opening for you, my friend.

ELEPHANT MAN: (*Quiet, rapid*) In Whitechapel they came in carriages to see me. Gaslight through the window. Carriages passing back and forth outside. Rattling away across the cobblestones. They kept moving me on, never let me rest. Always carriages, trains, movement.

TREVES: (*Consoling*) That's all over now, John. Why dwell on it? Everything has changed. (*Pause*) Let me bring your visitors here.

ELEPHANT MAN: Who are they?

TREVES: Friends of mine. I've told them about you. They want to be your friends.

ELEPHANT MAN: The showman was my friend.
(*Pause*)

TREVES: John, listen to me. I know what your life has been like, and I understand your feelings. You have been given nothing but hardship and cruelty. I want to show you that there is kindness, too, and pleasure. People can give you these. Later on I'll bring my wife to see you. And our little girls. Would you like that?

ELEPHANT MAN: (*Softly*) Once, I remember . . . I saw a woman with a child in her arms. How easily it rested there! (*Pause*) No child would ever come to me.
(*Pause*)

TREVES: You mustn't keep your visitors waiting. I'll bring them here.

(*He turns to go*)

ELEPHANT MAN: (*Puts his hands to his eyes*) There is a tangible force emitted by the eyes. And I can feel it. (*Treves, halted by this, turns back*) As I stood there in the small circle of light . . . displaying myself . . . I would register the various pressures and sort them out. Children's stares were timid and wondering. Not hard to bear. Men were different. Their eyes bored into me, brutal and hard. (*Pause*) But women's eyes were worse—oh, much the worst! Such absolute horror. (*Angrily*) Cast him out, I can't look at him, throw him out, into the trash-heap, into the night! (*Pause. Quietly*) Sometimes, when they had gone, I would gaze at my body. Amazed that I wasn't bleeding from a hundred wounds.

(*A long pause. Treves is silent. The Elephant Man turns to him*) Send me to a blind asylum. Please!

TREVES: (*Gently*) John, to be accepted there . . . would mean nothing.

(*Pause*)

ELEPHANT MAN: Then bring them in, Doctor. It is not my place to deny them. I am supported on public funds.

(*Treves hesitates, then goes out right. Silence. It is quite dark now. Quietly*)

Home. Here? I would rather it be the blind asylum. Does Treves comprehend this: This love of the deformed for the blind? (*Pause. He spreads his hands to the garden*) This is your home. Can I believe that? (*Pause*) Now he will have them in at me. As before. But how can I say to *him*: You are diminished in my eyes. You are . . . disfigured.

(*Silence. He looks round the garden*)

We traveled across Europe in a wagon which had painted on one side, in red letters: The Great Freak of Nature; on the other, Half a Man and Half an Elephant. When we came to a town the showman would pull up the wagon and hire a few men to erect our tent. From the inside of the wagon I would listen to them shout as they hauled on the ropes. And watch the tent rise up, again. At dusk he would set torches round the tent. The people would gather. And I sat inside, waiting for the exhibition to begin.

(*Silence. He sits without moving in the garden. Suddenly, upstage right, a door opens; a shaft of light shoots across the stage and strikes him)*

Scene Three:

November, 1889.
Darkness.

TREVES: *(Voice only)* "It was not until I came to know that Merrick was highly intelligent, that he possessed an acute sensibility, and—worse than all—a romantic imagination, that I realized the overwhelming tragedy of his life."
(Lights come up on Treves sitting on bench downstage right. The journal is open in his hands)
TREVES: *(In a reverie)* The sky above was the deepest blue . . . The sea within the reef was a wondrous green . . . The air was heavy with the smell of the sea . . . *(Pause)* In November of 1889, I arranged for Merrick to take a holiday in the country. He passed two weeks there in green seclusion.
(Pause. Muses)
I often ask myself: Was I as kind to him as I could have been? Perhaps I could have done more, something to —*(Falters)* Perhaps the kindest thing would have been to find some . . . woman, from Whitechapel, and bring her to his room one night; give her enough drink, and when she was insensible, unaware, bring him in from some dark corner and . . . let him. *(Pause)* Awful thought: to use a woman in that way. But at least he would have had some knowledge of the transactions of the flesh. Just one moment to last him for life! Did he want that? Oh, I saw his eyes when regal ladies came to visit. He was amorous, he would like to have been a lover . . . *(Pause)* Would he even have known what to do? The simple mechanics of the act? Once I saw him weep when a woman merely shook his hand. What did touch mean to him?
(Pause. He lifts the journal, reads)
"Merrick's case attracted much attention in the papers, with the result that he had a constant succession of visitors. The Merrick whom I had found shivering behind a rag of a curtain in an empty shop was now conversant with duchesses and countesses and ladies of high degree." *(Pause; quietly)* He became the pet of the nobility.

(Lights come up on the Elephant Man, seated in a chair at center stage. His cloak is new, of richer and more colorful material than the first; but around this he has wrapped a white bedsheet. In the intervening three years his head has grown considerably and is now hidden behind a larger mask. At upstage left there is a coat-stand, on which hangs a magnificent opera cape)

TREVES: *(Approaching him)* John. Some of your society friends are here.

ELEPHANT MAN: I will not see them.

TREVES: *(Concerned)* What's wrong? You have refused all of your visitors for the past three days.

ELEPHANT MAN: I will not see them.

TREVES: It is unhealthy to shut yourself away like this.

ELEPHANT MAN: Did you know, Doctor: on my birth certificate the space for my father's name is left blank. I've had to create myself. Manufacture a past. I'm like a character left unfinished by its author. Before he could give me my whole history he abandoned me. Or renounced his writing. Or died.

(Pause)

TREVES: What am I to say to your visitors? They are concerned about you.

(The Elephant Man stands)

ELEPHANT MAN: *(With deep yearning)* To walk alone the sweet bright earth . . . with no fear. To stand with no mask in the light of the sun. In the deep country . . .

TREVES: What happened there? What happened in the country?

ELEPHANT MAN: I stood in a field and watched the sun set through the dark trees. I said to myself: I am away from them now, away from all the eyes. *(Intensely)* If I could have died in that instant! *(Quietly)* But I could not end myself like that—a hateful thing dying off in a field.

(Pause)

TREVES: *(Gently, hands outstretched to room)* John . . . your place in the world is here.

ELEPHANT MAN: The showman wrote a speech for me once. A spiel. To be delivered the moment I let the cloak fall. *(He lets the sheet drop to the floor)* "I first saw the light on the fifth of August, 1860 . . ." When you brought me here I thought I'd found peace. You said: "People will grow accustomed to you." But the exhibition never ends. Their hatred grows heavier and heavier upon me.

TREVES: (*Distressed*) That's not true. No one hates you here. I took you away from the hatred.

ELEPHANT MAN: When dusk came to Whitechapel I would go to the window and look into the street. The women would stand beneath the gas lamps . . . the men drift in like dogs. And the sales would be made. All night long, the gleam of coins. (*Pause*) Once, a couple, drunk, stumbled into my shop . . . and began to consummate their bargain on the floor. I watched from behind the curtain. Appalled. The light was dim. All I could see was a grunting form thrusting like a locomotive. The mercenary grinding of flesh against flesh.

(*Pause*)

TREVES: (*Baffled, calming*) John . . . you must forget that time. Your life has changed since then. Completely. But you must put those days behind you. You only hurt yourself. (*Pause*) I know there seems to be no purpose in your suffering.

(*Pause*)

ELEPHANT MAN: Do you remember when you first found me, Doctor? (*Treves does not answer*) You exhibited me to the Pathological Society of London. And then sent me back to the exhibition.

(*Pause*)

TREVES: John—

ELEPHANT MAN: (*Interrupting*) You asked me to come to your room at the College. (*Pause*) I remember how astounded I was by this invitation. This intervention. You interviewed me for an hour. I was awed. And frightened. But how kind you were, how concerned. I could not speak very well then. I made very little sense. But you listened. You smiled and nodded. And then sent me away, thinking me an imbecile.

TREVES: (*Defensive*) I realize it is no excuse, but . . . you gave me no reason to believe otherwise. (*Quickly*) I know that is harsh.

ELEPHANT MAN: That same night I was back on exhibition.

(*Pause*)

TREVES: (*Quietly*) That is the great shame of my life. That I did not see . . .

ELEPHANT MAN: (*Oblivious*) With nothing to remember you by but your name printed on a few calling cards.
(He holds up several cards)
TREVES: Where did you get them?
ELEPHANT MAN: I took them from your desk that day.
TREVES: I went back to the greengrocer's the following day. The police had closed it up. There was no trace of you. (*Pause*) I did go back!
ELEPHANT MAN: Doctor Frederick Treves. (*Intensely*) How I treasured that name! (*Treves is silent*) I thought you were my saviour. At the exhibition that night I dropped my cloak proudly. (*Rages*) The buffoons gaped at me! (*Softly*) I felt like shouting at them, joyously: I have been saved. I am saved! (*He lets one of the cards fall to the floor*) Then the authorities closed the show down. We had to move on. This show's immoral, they said. Indecent. (*Lets a card fall*) Inhuman. (*Pause*) As if they knew what inhuman was. (*Pause*) Finally there was nowhere to go but the Continent. Then it was hard. We were foreigners, we starved. (*Lets card fall*) But I never lost my faith in you, Doctor. I was certain that Treves would come one glorious day. Out of a flaming sky. To take me away from it: the hunger, the crowds, all of it!
(He lapses into silence, stares at the cards in his hands. After a moment he lets another fall)
I waited for you, Doctor. Through all the wandering, all the exhibitions. I dropped my cloak a thousand times . . . saw ten thousand women turn away in disgust. We wandered on, all over the Continent, the days ran together, little towns strange languages. And I waited for you, Doctor. I knew that someone had been kind to me once. Had spoken to me. (*Lets a card fall*) I waited. (*Slowly*) For two years. (*Anguished*) Two years! (*Pause*) Finally, in Brussels, the showman abandoned me. I had become a burden to him. One night, as I slept, he stole the little I'd managed to save from our earnings . . . and left. When I awoke, no showman. No food, no money. Nothing left. (*He lets the last card fall and holds up his empty hands*) And still there was no Treves.
(Silence. Treves takes a few steps toward him, stops)
TREVES: (*Shaken, quietly*) John. Haven't I helped you? Perhaps, once, I was mistaken . . . (*He spreads his hands*) But surely this is better than what you had. (*The Elephant Man regards him silently. Imploring*) John!

(The Elephant Man moves to the coatstand upstage left, and drapes the opera cape around his shoulders. Treves walks slowly back to the bench downstage right. A silence)

TREVES: Merrick loved to imagine himself a dandy and a young man about town. The Elephant Man became, in the seclusion of his chamber, the young spark, the Piccadilly exquisite. The rake, the gentleman of London. *(Pause)* He invented for himself a second life, and entertained me for hours with tales of amorous conquests, triumphs at the gambling tables, hectic revelries that lasted until dawn. The pursuits of a young aristocrat. All the while sitting furled in his opera cape, a gift from visitors. He told me of a life of pleasure, indulgence, sin. *(Quietly)* And I assisted him in this illusion. I assented.

(The Elephant Man comes downstage, resplendent in his cape. On his ungloved left hand he wears several large rings. He grasps a silver walking stick)

ELEPHANT MAN: *(Grandly)* Good evening, Dr. Treves.

TREVES: *(Bowing)* Good evening, John.

ELEPHANT MAN: *(Extends his left hand)* I purchased a new ring this morning.

TREVES: It is very beautiful.

ELEPHANT MAN: Thank you. To adorn myself . . . is all I have left to me now. *(Pause)* I have been out walking along the river. Reliving old memories.

TREVES: *(Smiling)* Yes, that can be very pleasant.

ELEPHANT MAN: The people I've known . . . the moments I have had. I led a life of such privilege and light. The graces of civilization. *(With deep sadness)* But all that is closed to me now. For me there can be no more friendship, music . . . touch.

TREVES: *(Disturbed by the sadness in this)* Why no more, John?

(Pause)

ELEPHANT MAN: Something happened to me . . . a long time ago. When my life was so different. Something I have never told anyone. But I would like to tell you, Doctor.

TREVES: Yes. I will listen.

ELEPHANT MAN: I was not always like this. Not always— *(Indicates his body)*—this ruin. *(Pause)* I lived for many years in society.

TREVES: Society, yes.

ELEPHANT MAN: Yet all that time haunted by a question: Was there nothing that went deeper, to the very core of my life? Nothing but that barren journey through society? I was attracted to waste and emptiness. Loneliness fascinated me. I wanted to burn away all desire for love, all the need to touch. (*Pause*) One night I walked alone through the streets of London. I went down to the river and looked out across the water . . . at the lights of society. No voice spoke to me, no hand touched me. I felt, for the first time, the enormous beauty . . . of being apart from my own kind.

(Pause)

That was the beginning of the Great Experiment of Solitude. I ended all contact with others. Became, in my heart, a creature of ice. Seeking to create . . . endless loneliness. (*Pause*) I wanted to record the agony of a figure lost in an empty landscape. I knew that the figure in the landscape would be my own. That I would have to create in the midst of emptiness. Inhabit the emptiness without . . . dissolving into it.

(Pause. He sits; no longer addressing Treves; lost in a private pain)

I was dying in the desert of my own making but I *would not* cry for help. I made of my destruction a test of human kindness. If love existed, I would be saved. From myself, from my own silence. (*Pause*) But perhaps there exists a race of souls who never find love on this earth. The blame is not theirs. Love is not infinite. Someone must settle for solitude. (*With profound pain*) I made of my life . . . a wasteland.

(Silence. In the darkness Treves sits listening. After a moment the Elephant Man begins again to speak, in a new voice: rapid and flat, almost a chant)

One night I awoke in the grip of a strange fever. I went to the mirror and looked at my face. The skin had grown thick and rough, like the hide of a beast; it twisted into such a sight no one could describe. I raised my hand that was no longer a hand, a fin or paddle rather than a hand.

I went into the street. A storm had begun; the rain thundered down on me. I ran through the streets crying for help. The sounds from my throat were awkward and without meaning. The city was empty. All life had vanished. I stumbled down to the river and collapsed on the bank. My flesh was burning, I could feel the rending of my bones.

I dragged myself to the water and tried to drink. In a flash of lightning I saw that the river had gone dry. The city had become a famished desert of stone. I lay on my back with my mouth gaping to the rain, and I watched as my body became, finally, inhuman. Then a voice spoke to me—no, not spoke, but made itself known, like a voice in a dream: Your loneliness is a crime. You have withdrawn from humanity. The mark of your solitude has been set upon you. Take up the mask and cover your face. You are an outcast now in the eyes of men. (*Anguished*) A monster that will never find love or peace, a freak no human will ever touch! You will spend your life in a place of exhibition! Exhibition—

(He falls to the floor, convulses. Treves crosses the stage, tears the cape from the Elephant Man, flings it away)

TREVES: John—what you say is not true! You are none of these things. No one is such an outcast. No one is such a monster. (*Intensely*) In every man, no matter how different —at some level, there is belonging.

ELEPHANT MAN: (*Screams*) At what level do I belong? Where can I say to men: I am like you, I am one of you?

TREVES: You are human. You have a soul, that I have seen. (*Spreads his hands*) In this place you are not strange. To *me*, not strange.

ELEPHANT MAN: (*Desperately*) Frederick! You have taken me into this hospital, into your life. Yet . . . to admit me so far . . . but no further—

TREVES: But—I have given you . . .

(The Elephant Man kneels painfully before him, reaches out his left hand)

ELEPHANT MAN: (*Pleading*) If someone would *touch* me, I'd be human . . . for a moment. Please! The way a father does touch his son.

(Silence, as Treves comprehends what is being asked of him. The Elephant Man grasps his hand, brings it toward his face. With his right hand he begins to remove the mask. But at the last instant Treves pulls his hand away—and immediately realizes what he has done: his failure)

TREVES: (*Shocked, quietly*) I cannot.

(The Elephant Man lowers his mask; sinks back, turns away. Silence. Treves starts to speak, says nothing)

ELEPHANT MAN: (*Softly*) I am sorry . . .
(*Pause*)
TREVES: (*Faltering*) John. I am . . your friend. (*With great difficulty*) Forgive me.
(*Pause*)
ELEPHANT MAN: (*Quietly*) Give me your hand, Doctor. (*Pause. Treves hesitates*) Don't worry. Your hand.
(*Treves extends his hand. The Elephant man begins to remove the rings from his left hand and place them in Treves' hand*)
TREVES: (*Tries to pull his hand away*) What are you doing?
ELEPHANT MAN: (*Giving him the rings*) They gave me rings and walking sticks, diamond stickpins and pretty photographs to surround myself with. They said to me: "John, take them, you can be like us, you can be one of us." And I took them. (*He releases Treves' hand*) My last showman stole everything I owned. But I give these to you.
(*Silence. Treves turns away, takes a few steps*)
TREVES: (*To himself, an intense whisper*) Should I have turned you away that day? (*He looks at the rings in his hand. Pause. Quietly*) I think I shall go home now. It is late. Anne will worry.
ELEPHANT MAN: Yes. Go home, Doctor. Go home to your wife and children.
(*Silence. Treves holds out the rings*)
TREVES: These are not mine. Take them.
(*Silence. The Elephant Man does not take them. Treves places them quietly on the floor next to him. Pause*)
Goodnight, John.
(*There is no answer. He hesitates, then goes out right. Silence. With his walking stick the Elephant Man sweeps the rings across the stage. Pause*)
ELEPHANT MAN: (*Quietly, remote, a recitation*) When I was fifteen I went into the infirmary at Leicester, where I remained for two or three years, when I had to undergo an operation on my face, having three or four ounces of flesh cut away; so thought I, I'll get my living by being exhibited about the country.

Scene Four:

1923
Lights come up slowly. Treves sits on the bench downstage right.
Also on the bench are his journal, the walking stick and mask of the
Elephant Man.
A pale cold light.

TREVES: (*Quietly*) Exhibition: exhibit . . . exhibitor. (*Pause*)
Did I ever help him?

(Silence. He stares at the ground)

I did quite a lot of traveling after I retired. That was in
1908. (*Softly*) He had been dead a long time by then. (*Slight
pause*) The first place I went to was Europe. I knew he had
been there. He often took great pleasure in describing to me
the scenes he remembered. A street in Paris; a tiny village
somewhere; a landscape glimpsed from a moving cart . . .
Fragments. Was I trying to retrace his wanderings . . . that
long trail of humiliation? (*Pause*) In every city, each town or
village we paused in, I wondered: Did they stop here? Was the
exhibition held here? I looked into the eyes of the people.
Had they been in the audience? Paid to see him, long ago?
Did they remember him? I could not bring myself to ask. One
night it occurred to me: What an unholy pilgrimage this had
become. I had brought the exhibition with me. The exhibition was in me, in the image of him that I carried. I was the
exhibition.

(He falls silent again)

After that I went on, in a fever of wandering. I fled to lands
he had never seen. Where the question "Was the exhibition
here?" could not possibly be asked. Searching . . . (*Genuinely
uncertain*) For what? All I found was a world emptied of his
presence. (*Calmly*) Finally I came . . . to a place of the heart's
silence, that I have never left.

*(He pauses for a moment. When he speaks his voice is tranquil,
and he extends a hand as if to touch what he describes)*

The sky above was the deepest blue, while upon the reef
the surf broke in a line of white. The sea within the reef was a
wondrous green . . . In the distance, where the small cliff
ended, there came a beach, curved like a sickle, with palms
and impenetrable trees along the rim of the strand. The air
was heavy with the smell of the sea, while upon the ear there
fell no sound except that of the surf on the reef.

(Pause. His calm vanishes. He stares briefly at the ground. With self-contempt)

No people. I just wanted to escape them. To be alone. After a lifetime of human flesh, its palsies, tumours, wounds . . . I wanted, finally, the health of earth. The calm of the tides. The silence of stones.

(He falls into a reverie, then picks up the journal and begins to read)

"Some six months after Merrick's return from the country he was found dead in bed. This was in April 1890. He was lying on his back as if asleep, and had evidently died suddenly and without a struggle. The method of his death was peculiar. He often said to me that he wished he could lie down to sleep . . . —*(A long silence)*—'like other people.' I think on this last night he must, with some determination, have made the experiment. The head must have fallen backwards and caused a dislocation of the neck."

(He closes the journal, puts it aside. He takes up the mask)

I took his mask and walking stick from him. Without realizing, for years afterward, how much I had lost that day. *(Pause)* Did I help him? I truly believed that I could help him. *(Pause; a beginning of anguish)* Why do the failures outweigh the victories? I saved a king once. Edward the Seventh, on the eve of his coronation, fell gravely ill. I diagnosed acute appendicitis and operated on him successfully in Buckingham Palace. Beneath my hands—for me to save, to preserve —lay the embodiment of a society. Of the Empire. And I did save. His gratitude made me a Baronet. But for Merrick's pain, what operation was there? What mere operation? *(Pause)* Did I help him? Anne tries to comfort me: "Remember the thousands you have helped, have cured; have solaced when there was no cure." Yes. But I could not help *him*. Or do anything more, really, than stand guard over him in his solitude. *(Angrily)* It is not enough! *(Quietly, a realization)* I should have been . . . the keeper of his peace.

(Ponders this. After a moment he holds up the mask)

Once, after he died . . . I wore his mask for a moment, secretly. Trying to see what he saw.

(Pause. He dons the mask in silence, in a gesture oddly formal, ceremonious. He stares ahead, does not speak; a new and strange figure. After a few moments he removes the mask. He is changed, a torment deep within has been released, yet his first words are quiet)

His skeleton stands, now, in the college museum. In a small room it shares with a few other exhibits. (*Pause*) I stood there, in the darkness, in the silence . . . and looked at the skull. (*Carefully*) The left side is smooth and polished. But on the right the bone seems to go berserk. Becomes gnarled, twisted, creviced. Leaps outward, folds inward in intricate and useless filigree. The mouth gapes open, teeth pointing in every direction. Utterly useless. (*Pause. With great pain*) I looked into the sockets that his eyes peered from, thirty-three years ago . . . and tried to remember the intelligence imprisoned there. The mind that perceived. But all I could see was an endless stream of tears welling from that darkness. I tried to imagine words spluttering from that blasted mouth. But all I could hear was an endless shriek of agony.

(*Pause. He slips the mask over the handle of the walking stick*)

This is the question that haunts me now: Why did people turn away when they saw him? Could it have been, truly, that he was so hideous? Or did they see in him, without realizing it, a blinding beauty? A beauty so rare and radical that it must walk cloaked and masked?

(*Pause. He closes his eyes*)

Why was he born into such pain?

(*He stops again*)

When he first came we knew the answer. Our appeal: "One of the Creator's objects in permitting men to be born to a life of hopeless and miserable disability was that the works of God should be manifested in evoking the sympathy and kindly aid of those on whom such a heavy cross is not laid." (*Pause*) Am *I* the manifestation of God's mercy? His love—does it touch only through human hands? (*Self-hatred*) Where is the evidence of love? That I let him inch into my life? Watched him beg, and still not give? Why—that I could not touch him, why? In my deepest self, what deformity?

(*He lifts the mask and walking stick into the air. Despairing*)

To the question of his birth: is this the only answer? For us?

(*He thrusts the walking stick into the ground. It leans at a slight angle, the mask staring out. He falls silent, exhausted, stares at the mask. Long silence. Weakly*)

It was an afternoon in late November. London autumn, cold and dull. Leaves scraped through the streets and were crushed under the wheels of carriages. I was walking down Whitechapel road, returning to the hospital. I stopped by a poster on which was the announcement that—(*Tenderly*)—the Elephant Man was to be seen within. (*Pause*) When he stood up, and dropped his cloak . . . I knew that all I had been taught, and any skills I possessed . . . were useless. (*Pause*) Something in me, now, is extinct, I will not feel it again.

(He sits in silence; aged, dying)

Slow fading of lights

Michael Snelgrove

DEFINITELY
ERIC GEDDIS

Michael Snelgrove

Michael Snelgrove's long association with the Maidenhead Players at Maidenhead, Berkshire, England, achieved fruition when their production of his play *Definitely Eric Geddis* was selected for the finals of the All-England Festival in 1979. The play came within one point of being chosen as the national championship winner.

The British *Amateur Stage* describes the play as "An amusing satirical romp sending up the modern world of marketing —in which with the right package the slick advertising executive can sell anything. The Eric of the title decides to put this to the test by persuading an ambitious advertising man to 'sell' him, a typical, very ordinary and unexceptional individual, as a 'superstar.' The gullible public, ever ready for the latest sensation, accept the myth, but soon Eric realises any possibility of his future happiness must depend on its destruction and his return to normality and sanity."

Mr. Snelgrove was born in 1952 at Maidenhead, educated at the Maidenhead Grammar School and St. Catherine's College, Cambridge, where he studied English literature. He taught at Hampshire College until 1979, and now is Lecturer in English at Langley College, Berkshire.

Other plays by Mr. Snelgrove premiered by The Maidenhead Players are *Belladonna*, written for an all-women cast in 1977, and *Hidden Meanings* in 1980.

Married and now residing in Bracknell, Berkshire, Mr. Snelgrove is currently summoning up the energy to write a full-length play.

Definitely Eric Geddis is dedicated to The Maidenhead Players.

Characters:

Simple settings on a bare stage represent:

An office.
The Boardroom.
A tube train in the rush hour.
A radio studio.
A television studio.
A quayside.
A car.
A pub.

Scene One:

The lights come up on the office. Rodney Sanderson, fortyish, trendy, is working at his desk. After a few moments we hear an altercation from the outer office.

MAUREEN: Not that one! Please, not that one!
ERIC: Unhand me! I warn you, young lady . .

RODNEY: What the hell?

(The door bursts open to reveal what appears to be a mobile rubber plant. It sways in the doorway)

RODNEY: What in God's name are you doing, Maureen?

(The rubber plant totters in. Maureen follows it)

MAUREEN: It's not me, Mr. Sanderson. It's somebody called . . .

ERIC: *(A disembodied voice wafting from behind the plant)* Eric Geddis.

RODNEY: What?

ERIC: *Eric Geddis!*

RODNEY: Well, what, pray, are you doing with my plant?

MAUREEN: I tried to stop him, Mr. Sanderson, really I did . . .

ERIC: I'm holding it hostage.

RODNEY: Hostage? What are you talking about?

ERIC: Either you see me or the plant gets it. Smash. On the floor.

RODNEY: That's blackmail!

ERIC: Blackmail's a dirty word. I prefer to call it persuasion.

RODNEY: Look, Mr. . . . ?

ERIC: Geddis.

RODNEY: Geddis. Let's be reasonable about this, shall we? You put the plant down and we'll have a nice little chat, all right?

ERIC: Do you promise?

RODNEY: What?

ERIC: *Do you promise?*

RODNEY: Of course.

ERIC: No tricks?

RODNEY: Trust me.

(Eric lowers the plant and puts it on the floor)

RODNEY: *(Stepping in front of it)* Right. Out!

ERIC: What?

RODNEY: Out!

ERIC: You promised!

RODNEY: Meaningless. It's a hard world, Geddis, and I'm a very busy man. Shut the door on your way out.

ERIC: Thank you.

RODNEY: For what?

ERIC: For my first lesson in the realities of the advertising world. *(He produces an aerosol from his pocket)*

RODNEY: Oh no, not the ammonia! Not my eyes, please!

ERIC: Don't be daft; Mr. Greenfinger's Instant Weed Kill-er. I understand from the adverts that it's very effective even at long range. You listen to what I've got to say or the plant gets it right between the nodules. Right?

RODNEY: You're a hard man.

ERIC: It's a hard world.

RODNEY: Look, I'll be honest with you. That plant was given to me by an old and very dear aunt of mine who passed away recently, and frankly . . .

ERIC: Tell me, how long do you have to work in advertis-ing before you can't tell what the truth is any more?

RODNEY: What do you mean, exactly?

ERIC: I mean that this plant was given to you two Christ-masses ago by Sir Guthrie Miles, the Chairman of your Board. I mean that every time he's got you in mind for a promotion he asks you how it's doing. It's a kind of test, I suppose. I mean that if anything happened to it he might think twice about giving you that seat on the Board that you're driving yourself to an early grave to get. That's what I mean. Exactly.

RODNEY: You've done your homework. What do you want?

ERIC: I work in a factory, Mr. Sanderson. It makes lawn mowers. Clipitclose lawn mowers.

RODNEY: We handle that account.

ERIC: I know. One morning, as I clocked in for the twenty-third tax week of my nineteenth tax year at Clipitclose, I thought how nice it'd be to have money and to be famous. That's what set me off, I suppose.

RODNEY: Do you mind if I sit down? (*He sits*)

ERIC: It struck me that Fame is a very fickle mistress who only smiles upon the gifted and fortunate. By lunchtime —Doreen had given me cheese and chutney again—I'd decided that this was unfair. Why, I thought, shouldn't everybody else have a chance? Why not the average man in the street? The totally ordinary, untalented bloke?

RODNEY: Obviously because people aren't interested in them.

ERIC: But that's stupid. Because it seems to me that people are mostly interested in themselves, right? Number one.

RODNEY: I suppose so.

ERIC: Course they are. And if they're interested in themselves why wouldn't they be interested in one of their own kind?

RODNEY: Gracie Fields?

ERIC: You miss the point. She could sing and dance a bit. I want to be famous for having no talent at all.

RODNEY: That's ridiculous! You've got to do something!

ERIC: Why?

RODNEY: You can't get money for doing nothing.

ERIC: Try telling that to the hereditary peerage.

RODNEY: That's different. That's tradition.

ERIC: By the afternoon tea break I'd decided that what I'd thought of wasn't so original after all. It's happening all the time. I mean, look at all the rubbish that people sell just by putting it in the right sort of box and advertising it. Falls apart before you get it home sometimes. And films—look at them. You go to the pictures and see the trailer for next week's film and it looks smashing. So you go along to see it and find out that very often it's not worth watching. And what does it do? It makes millions of quid for somebody just because of the advertising, see? By the end of supper—cod's roe on toast—I thought, if they can do it for John Travolta they can do it for me.

RODNEY: Let me get this straight: you want me to run an advertising campaign to promote you?

ERIC: As a product, yes. As an ordinary bloke. I'm very untalented.

RODNEY: You're mad. Do you know how much a campaign costs? I'd be laughed out of the business, finance-wise.

ERIC: I haven't got much to offer. I'm not much of a talker—this must be the first time that I've put together more than six words for about ten years—I'm not much to look at, I don't have many ideas, I don't have any, what do they call it in the papers?—Charisma. Not much to go on, is there?

RODNEY: I wouldn't dare.

ERIC: Think of the professional challenge. You'd be selling something that you *knew* was rubbish. What a boost to your powers of persuasion. To sell a boring, tedious, worthless product to the unsuspecting public.

RODNEY: You're too late. We already handle the Liberal Party.

ERIC: I suppose that's a joke. I forgot to mention that I

haven't got a sense of humour and have voted Liberal man and boy.

RODNEY: I should have thought one disproved the other. So this isn't all a big joke, then?

ERIC: Not at all. I'm in deadly earnest.

RODNEY: You know, I've half a mind to give it a try. Just to see if it can be done.

ERIC: Half a mind isn't enough. I'm relying on you.

RODNEY: No, what am I saying? How would I get it past the Board?

ERIC: You'll think of something. After all, that's what the Head of Creative Thinking's for, isn't it?

(The lights go down on the office)

Scene Two:

The lights come up on the Boardroom. There is a long table with seven chairs at which sit Daphne, Emily and Sir Guthrie. A telephone is beside him on the table.

DAPHNE: Rodney's late.

SIR GUTHRIE: Something must have come up.

(Rodney enters)

You're late, Rodney.

RODNEY: Sorry, Sir Guthrie. Something came up.

DAPHNE: As long as you've come up with some ideas.

SIR GUTHRIE: I can speak for myself, thank you, Daphne. I'm sure that I needn't remind you, Rodney, that there's a spare seat up for grabs on the Board. But what we want are results, Rodney. Results pure and simple.

DAPHNE: Our clients are getting restless. May it be minuted, Mr. Chairman, that I deplore this unnecessary delay? I've had my doubts about the viability of the Creative Thinking Department for some time.

RODNEY: We all know that. And we all know that you'd like to incorporate us into your department.

SIR GUTHRIE: Do we have to? What have you got for us, Rodney? It'd better be good because I don't mind telling you that I've had my eye on young Clive Eggleton in Media Planning for some time. Good directorship material.

RODNEY: The thing is, ladies and gentlemen, is that I've got a new concept.

EMILY: A concept! I love concepts!

SIR GUTHRIE: Miss Woodbender. If you could restrain yourself just for a few moments?

EMILY: I'm so sorry. It's my artistic streak, you see.

SIR GUTHRIE: Quite so. Carry on, Rodney

RODNEY: If it works—and I say if . . .

DAPHNE: Well, if you haven't got the courage of your own convictions . . .

SIR GUTHRIE: Daphne!

RODNEY: If it works it'll put us light years ahead of other agencies, concept-wise.

EMILY: This is so exciting!

SIR GUTHRIE: Another interruption from you, Miss Woodbender, and you'll be back designing posters for superabsorbent nappies.

RODNEY: What I propose is that we create a market for a product.

DAPHNE: How devastatingly original! And what do you think this agency has been doing for the last forty-seven years?

RODNEY: If I could finish? We create a market for a product that doesn't yet exist.

SIR GUTHRIE: I sense impending disaster. (*Reaching for the telephone*) What's young Eggleton's number?

RODNEY: For example: we create widespread public interest in a name. Say, purely at random, Eric Geddis.

EMILY: Eric Geddis.

RODNEY: Thank you, Emily. We saturate the public with the name: posters, radio, TV—the works.

DAPHNE: Lunatic thinking, not creative. He's gone mad!

SIR GUTHRIE: But what's the point? The public can't buy a name. We don't get any percentage from a name!

RODNEY: We do things in reverse. We build an image, an ethos, around the name. We make sure that everybody knows it but can't buy anything to do with it. Imagine the curiosity, the frustration. So, instead of a firm coming to us with a product to sell, we go to the highest bidder with a ready made market concept and a name. It's very simple. He knows that there's a market, he supplies the product, we lease him, the Name, and everybody's happy.

EMILY: Brilliant! I can see it now.

RODNEY: Then, at the right moment we show our man to

the public and—here's the real selling point—the man behind the Name that we've built up with so much mystery turns
out to be ordinary. Absolutely normal. The public are encouraged to think that such a vaunted celebrity is as depress-
ingly average as they are and they buy the product in vast
amounts out of gratitude and a strong sense of image
identification.

SIR GUTHRIE: Childishly simple but quite brilliant.

DAPHNE: There's something that you seem to have over-
looked, dear Rodney.

RODNEY: Which is?

DAPHNE: Where exactly do we find an Eric Geddis?

RODNEY: He's sitting in my office now.

DAPHNE: How clever you are, Rodney!

SIR GUTHRIE: At one stroke we take control of the market
instead of having to grovel to clients.

DAPHNE: There must be a catch.

SIR GUTHRIE: Shall we take a vote on it? Those in favour?
(*He raises his hand*)

(*Emily raises her hand*)

SIR GUTHRIE: Those against? (*Daphne raises hers*) Carried.
How do you see the campaign shaping up, Rodney?

RODNEY: I thought to start with—and this is right off the
cuff of course—we'd use the tantalizing approach. You know
the kind of thing: posters that give nothing away, hints
designed to mystify and intrigue; tease them, don't
enlighten . . .

(*The lights go down on the Boardroom*)

Scene Three:

*The lights come up on a tube train full of people. Two girls are
talking.*

1ST GIRL: If that dirty old man touches me up again I'm
pulling the cord.

2ND GIRL: Cynthia, what's "Geddis?"

1ST GIRL: I don't know. Look, do you mind?

MAN: Sorry. Hand slipped.

2ND GIRL: Only on that poster over the door it just says
"Geddis."

1ST GIRL: I hate the tube. It's always the same in the rush hour. Why is London full of middle-aged sex maniacs?

2ND GIRL: I've never heard of "Geddis," have you?

1ST GIRL: Must be something.

2ND GIRL: New film, is it?

1ST GIRL: Might be a group. Sounds like a group.

2ND GIRL: No, hold on. I'm sure that I've heard of a perfume called "Geddis."

1ST GIRL: No, that's jeans, isn't it?

2ND GIRL: Isn't it that film?

1ST GIRL: What, the one about the stunt man?

2ND GIRL: No. Cigarette, is it? "Geddis?" "Geddis?"

1ST GIRL: I don't know what it is really.

2ND GIRL: Nor me.

(The First Girl glares at the man in the bowler)

MAN: Sorry.

(The lights go down on the tube)

Scene Four:

The lights come up on the office. Rodney and Eric are seated at the desk. Emily holds the design layouts.

RODNEY: It's working, Eric. Fifteen percent increase in public interest.

ERIC: What now?

RODNEY: That's where Miss Woodbender here comes in. What have you got for us, Emily?

EMILY: I've got the roughs here. (*She produces the designs*) A photograph of Mr. Geddis: half profile, silhouetted. Underneath: "Geddis—going places."

ERIC: People might think I was a suitcase.

EMILY: If that doesn't increase response my name's not Emily Waldorf.

RODNEY: Your name's *not* Emily Waldorf.

EMILY: So it's not. I get carried away. It's the . . .

RODNEY: Artistic streak in you, yes.

EMILY: I would have been Emily Waldorf if I could have got that nice man in accounts to propose to me in 1948.

RODNEY: Well done, Emily. Get it distributed as soon as you can, will you?

EMILY: Wilco.

(Emily goes)

RODNEY: Well, Eric. Time for training.

ERIC: Training?

RODNEY: Certainly. We can't show you as you are. I mean, you're average but not average enough.

ERIC: Thank you.

RODNEY: Don't mention it. I've got somebody to knock the smooth edges off you.

(Pamela enters)

RODNEY: Ah, Pamela! Do what you can with him, will you?

PAMELA: Your own teeth, Mr. Geddis?

ERIC: Man and boy.

PAMELA: You must learn to use them.

ERIC: I've always chewed my food very thoroughly.

PAMELA: Your smile, your smile, Mr. Geddis.

ERIC: I told him. I've got no sense of humour.

PAMELA: No matter. Smile all the time. Vacuously. People want to see a smile and they don't care what you're smiling at. It reassures them. Use all your teeth. *(Eric does. It looks awful)* Yes, perhaps we'd better tone it down a bit. *(Eric gradually loses the smile)* That's it! Hold it there! Now your walk: shoulders forward, slouch, drag your feet! *(Eric slopes about a bit)* Fabulous. Now your voice is far too interesting.

ERIC: I hadn't noticed.

PAMELA: Flatten your vowels. Speak in a monotone.

ERIC: What shall I say?

PAMELA: Try, "The quick red fox jumped over the rapidly running rabbits."

ERIC: Pardon?

PAMELA: Just say your name.

ERIC: Eric Geddis.

PAMELA: Flatter.

ERIC: Eric Geddis.

PAMELA: Better. Again.

ERIC: Eric Geddis.

PAMELA: Splendid. Now try the voice, the walk and the smile together.

ERIC: Bloody hell!

PAMELA: Voice!

ERIC: *(Shambling around, smiling self-consciously)* Eric Geddis. Eric Geddis. Eric Geddis.

RODNEY: Just the surname.

ERIC: Geddis. Geddis. Geddis.

RODNEY: Brilliant. I think we've got ourselves an image. Thank you, Pamela, darling. Watford Rep little knew what a treasure they were losing when they let you go.

(Pamela exits)

ERIC: I feel awful doing that.

RODNEY: *(Picking up the telephone and dialing)* You'll get used to it.

ERIC: Who are you 'phoning?

RODNEY: Commercial radio. Time for the next stage.

ERIC: Which is?

RODNEY: Jingles. You'll be a wow!

(The lights go down on the office)

Scene Five:

The lights come up on the Disc Jockey. He is sitting at a table on which are arranged records, a turntable, tape recorder, etc . . . He speaks into a microphone.

DJ: This is you know who, on you know what, broadcasting to you on you know how many metres. I love you and you love me, I am you and you are he as the walrus said. Fabulous sounds all day through from me to you so you'll never be blue. That true? You bet it's true and that's from me to you, too. I'll be back, Ricky Jack, picking a record from the rack right after this break. *(He pushes in a tape)*

(Eric's voice is heard)

ERIC: "Geddis. If you're going places, go with Geddis. Geddis makes sense, so go with Geddis. Geddis makes sense, so Geddis straight, all right?" *(Jingle:)* "Eric Geddis—a name to conjure with."

DJ: Eric who? Wish I knew: bet you do, too. I'm dying to know, I'm dying to go—with Geddis. Don't muzzle the puzzle: Eric who? I'm going with Geddis whoever you are, 'cos he's going far. Okay cats, it's the Boomtown Rats. *(He cues up a record)*

(The lights fade on the Disc Jockey)

Scene Six:

The lights come up on the office.

RODNEY: This is very encouraging, Eric. Latest computer analysis shows that despite complete public ignorance as to your identity over eighty-three point nine percent of the entire population want to get to know you. Fifty-seven point six percent would be prepared to spend money to do so. Twenty-two point ninety-nine percent of the female population think that you're the kind of man they'd like to marry. You're hot property, Eric.

ERIC: That's nice.

RODNEY: I can almost feel their grubby little fingers itching in their pockets. The Board are very pleased: we're almost ready to show you.

ERIC: At Whipsnade?

RODNEY: Come on, we're late.

(The lights go down on the office)

Scene Seven:

The lights come up on the Boardroom. Sir Guthrie, Daphne and Sam Smedley are seated at the table. Rodney enters and Eric follows.

SIR GUTHRIE: Ah, Rodney! and Eric! I can't tell you how much we've been looking forward to meeting you.

DAPHNE: Some of us anyway.

ERIC: Mutual, I'm sure.

SIR GUTHRIE: It's time to realize the asset, Mr. Geddis.

RODNEY: We've got a deal, Eric.

ERIC: Deal?

SIR GUTHRIE: We've sold you—or rather your name—to the highest bidder. Endorsements, Eric. Little idea of mine. You give your name to a product for a percentage. I'd like you to meet Mr. Sam Smedley.

SAM: This him, is it? He don't look much.

ERIC: Thank you.

RODNEY: That's the point. Eric, Mr. Smedley is Europe's largest manufacturer of cosmetics and surgical appliances.

SAM: Started off with a bucket of animal musk and a few bits of elastic in a shed in Halifax. Got where I am today through hard work, shrewdness and a complete insensitivity to peoples' feelings. I like what you represent, Mr. Geddis. The integrity of the working man. I'm prepared to put my money where my mouth is. Two hundred thousand for his name on my after-shave.

RODNEY: How about—off the top of my head—"Eric Geddis pour l'homme?"

SAM: Eyetalian, eh? Still, if you say so. You married, Eric?

ERIC: What's that got to do with you?

SAM: Wife's name?

ERIC: Doreen.

SAM: Half a million for your name on the after-shave and hers on my battery-operated ladies' razor.

RODNEY: Done.

ERIC: Now hold on . . .

SAM: I admire you, Mr. Sanderson. What you've got here is unique.

RODNEY: Or rather it isn't.

SAM: Exactly. I'm not slow to applaud ingenuity when I see it. To sell rubbish and create a market before you've got a product. Brilliant. Don't know why I didn't think of it myself. Must be getting old.

ERIC: I'm not sure about all this. Doreen's a very retiring creature, you know. She hates drawing attention to herself, quite the shrinking violet in fact. I'm sure she wouldn't appear on telly or anything like that . . .

(The lights go down on the Boardroom)

Scene Eight:

The lights come up on Doreen. She is in curlers and a dressing-gown and she is shaving her legs.

DOREEN: Eric did used to moan so about my legs. "Like getting into bed with two porcupines," he used to say. Not any more. Not since I started using the Smedley Comfishave Mark Two. Now he says my legs are as smooth as a baby's bottom. Why not buy one and please your man?

ERIC: *(Off: calling)* Doreen!

DOREEN: Eric looks forward to bedtime now. I wonder why? *(She winks)*
(The lights go down)

Scene Nine:

The lights come up on the Boardroom. Sir Guthrie, Sam, Eric and Emily are seated at the table.

SAM: Sales up thirty-two percent. You can't get to sleep at night for the buzzing of millions of Comfishaves. Men all over the country are afflicted with rashes through using my after-shave.

ERIC: Thus my claim to fame is assured.

(Doreen and Ralph enter)

SAM: I'm going to offer you both further contracts. Three years, million a year.

DOREEN: Each.

SAM: Done.

ERIC: Doreen!

DOREEN: Make the most of it, I say.

ERIC: And what's young Ralph doing here?

DOREEN: May I introduce Ralph, our little boy?

RALPH: I'm sixteen, Mum.

SIR GUTHRIE: Pleased to meet you, my boy.

DOREEN: I thought we might be able to use him.

RODNEY: The family image. I like it.

RALPH: Dad!

ERIC: Don't be difficult, son.

RODNEY: Emily, do some roughs. I'm going to book some airspace.

(Rodney and Emily exit)

DOREEN: Another two hundred thousand for Ralph.

SAM: You're on. I'll put his name on my Acne Remover: he looks as though he could use some of it himself.

RALPH: Do something, Dad.

ERIC: Could you leave us alone? I'd like to have a word with Ralph.

SIR GUTHRIE: Naturally. Doreen, I'd like a word about your forthcoming national tour.

DOREEN: All right, Sir Guthrie. You put him straight, Eric.

(Sam, Doreen and Sir Guthrie exit)

ERIC: What's the matter, son?

RALPH: It's Mum. She didn't ask me or nothing. Just dragged me along here without so much as a by your leave.

ERIC: It's a very good idea.

RALPH: It's daft.

ERIC: What is?

RALPH: All this. They're using you.

ERIC: It's my idea.

RALPH: That makes it worse. Look Dad, we're ordinary: nothing's going to change that. Mum's got all carried away.

ERIC: The money's good.

RALPH: I like just being ordinary. I can't go nowhere without being pointed at. I don't like it. I don't like what you're doing.

ERIC: Have you thought I might be doing it for you? I don't want you working in a lawn mower factory all your life like me.

RALPH: Perhaps I don't mind doing that. Perhaps I don't see anything wrong in it.

ERIC: If you say so.

RALPH: Every time I went round to Sheila's her Mum treated me like I was Prince Charles. I hate what you're doing: you're not like my Mum and Dad any more. I used to look up to you because you worked hard and didn't get much for it. Now look at you: you're earning money for doing nothing at all. It's dishonest!

ERIC: I'm sorry you see it like that.

RALPH: Can't you stop it? It's not too late. Tell them all to get lost.

ERIC: I couldn't stop it now, even if your mother would let me. Anyway, I'm quite enjoying it.

RALPH: I'm going away, Dad.

ERIC: Away?

RALPH: I've given up the apprenticeship. And Sheila.

ERIC: Where are you going?

RALPH: Don't know. And, I'm changing my name.

ERIC: Now listen, Ralph . . .

RALPH: No, you listen. You're not my Dad any more. You're Eric Geddis. You're a product, like washing powder. I can't get on with a product. I'm over sixteen and you can't stop me and there's no point in trying.

ERIC: I see.

RALPH: You'd better tell that friend of yours not to waste any time on my account. Perhaps I'll write in a couple of months.

ERIC: Look, son . . .

RALPH: It's no good, Dad! I've made up my mind, all right? So it's no good. Say goodbye to Mum for me. I don't suppose she's got time to listen but try anyway. I hope you enjoy yourselves. See you, Dad.

(Ralph exits)

ERIC: *(Looking after him)* Bye, son.

(The lights go down on the Boardroom)

Scene Ten:

The lights come up on the office. Doreen is sitting in front of a mirror having her hair done and her nails manicured.

HAIRDRESSER: Ever thought of a tint, Mrs. G.?

MANICURIST: What colour for the nails?

(Eric enters)

ERIC: Doreen.

DOREEN: Not now, dear, I'm busy.

ERIC: I'd better have a word with you.

DOREEN: Sir Guthrie's just finalised the details of my nationwide tour. Sixty-seven towns in six days. It's very exciting.

ERIC: It's about Ralph. I think we'd better have a word.

HAIRDRESSER: I think that a nice Titian red might suit, don't you, Mrs. G.?

DOREEN: I'm opening forty-two supermarkets in twenty-seven days. If I keep to the schedule Sir Guthrie says that I'll get into the Guinness Book of Records. Scarlet on the nails, I think, dear.

MANICURIST: Okay.

ERIC: Ralph told me to say goodbye to you.

DOREEN: I must say I'm very excited. We never got further than Margate for our holidays.

ERIC: He's gone, Doreen!

DOREEN: Titian red? Sounds lovely.

ERIC: Perhaps forever.

DOREEN: Won't be too bold, will it?

ERIC: We might never see our son again!

DOREEN: What about a nice discreet blonde?

ERIC: Doreen!

DOREEN: Oh, are you still here, Eric?

ERIC: I want to talk to you. *Now!*

DOREEN: There's no need to shout! I'm very busy, you know. What is it anyway?

ERIC: Ralph has . . .

(Rodney enters)

RODNEY: Come on. No time for gassing.

ERIC: What?

RODNEY: This is it! The big day! The day that we show you to the Press!

ERIC: What, now?

RODNEY: It's on your itinerary, if you'd bothered to read it. Page thirty-seven. "Press conference to coincide with the starting of the Eric Geddis Round the World Yacht Race."

ERIC: The what?

RODNEY: Didn't I tell you? Never mind, get your coat on.

ERIC: Doreen . . .

DOREEN: You run along like you're told. I'll see you in a fortnight when I get back from my Australasian tour.

ERIC: But . . .

RODNEY: Come on, Eric. They'll be all waiting down at Plymouth—The air taxi's on a meter you know. And don't worry. You'll be a wow.

DOREEN: Bye dear.

(Rodney bundles Eric out of the office)

Do you think I've got the face for a rich auburn?

(The lights go down on the office)

Scene Eleven:

The lights come up on a group of Journalists and the Commodore. The scene suggests a quayside with a cannon facing upstage.

Rodney enters.

RODNEY: Ladies and Gentlemen, if you please. Today is the day that you have all been waiting for. The day that the whole country has been waiting for. May I present to you for the first time the man of mystery himself, the face behind the unique after-shave, the one and only, Eric Geddis!

(Fanfare. A bright light is on Eric as he appears upstage. The Journalists applaud)

RODNEY: Eric will answer any questions, so, fire away.

1ST JOURNALIST: Julian Symes-Fitzwilliam, *Sunday Heavy.* Can you deny reports that you are, in fact, the brilliant philosopher Hans Schwarzbecker, founder of the Leipzig School of Logical Positivism?

ERIC: You what?

2ND JOURNALIST: *Women's Monthly*, Mr. Geddis. Your name has been romantically linked with Bianca Jagger, Britt Ekland and Fiona Richmond. Have you any comment?

ERIC: I'm not Superman.

2ND JOURNALIST: Which answers my next question.

3RD JOURNALIST: Craddock, *Daily Mammary.* What's your attitude to pornography?

ERIC: I always read your paper.

1ST JOURNALIST: Do you read modern novels?

ERIC: Only if they're in large print.

2ND JOURNALIST: What do you think of women and sex?

ERIC: They very often go together.

3RD JOURNALIST: Any thoughts on nudie models on page three, Eric?

ERIC: None that I can tell you about.

1ST JOURNALIST: Any thoughts of entering politics, Mr. Geddis?

ERIC: I haven't got a sense of humour. Can I start the race now?

(They part and Eric goes to the cannon)

I hereby declare the "Eric Geddis Round the World Yacht Race" open. God bless it and all who sail in it.

(He pulls the string and the cannon fires. Cheers and then "Oh")

COMMODORE: Scrub *Ocean Wanderer* from the race and call the lifeboat, will you?

(The lights go down on the quayside)

Scene Twelve:

The lights come up on a car in which Rodney is sitting. He has a telephone beside him.

RODNEY: Didn't I tell you? They loved you. Pity about

Ocean Wanderer but there's nothing the public likes more than a disaster. I've taken the liberty of setting up an Eric Geddis fund for the widows and dependents. Fantastic press, though —look what *The Mirror* says about you.

ERIC: Not just now.

RODNEY: This is going to do you a lot of good.

ERIC: Us, don't you mean?

RODNEY: Something wrong?

ERIC: No, no. Look, do you mind if I pop out on my own for a bit? I fancy a quiet drink.

RODNEY: Course. Go to the *Albion:* good pint there. Don't forget your three o'clock appointment.

ERIC: Right.

(Eric leaves and Rodney picks up the telephone. The lights go down on the car)

Scene Thirteen:

The lights come up on a table at which two attractive young women sit. The scene suggests a pub with music and background noise. Eric, drink in hand, approaches them.

ERIC: Do you mind if I sit here? There doesn't seem to be anywhere else.

1ST GIRL: Help youself.

(Eric sits)

2ND GIRL: Haven't seen you here before.

ERIC: I'm not much of a drinker. Somebody told me it was nice here.

1ST GIRL: Don't I know you?

ERIC: Don't think so.

2ND GIRL: You do look familiar.

ERIC: That's probably because I'm the famous Eric Geddis.

1ST GIRL: You're joking!

ERIC: Wish I was.

2ND GIRL: You were in the papers.

ERIC: Yes.

1ST GIRL: We're both great fans of yours.

ERIC: Can't think why. I haven't done anything.

2ND GIRL: But you're famous. That's enough surely?

ERIC: Can I trust you?

2ND GIRL: Of course you can.

ERIC: Well, on the quiet, I'm not really happy at all.

2ND GIRL: You must be mad!

ERIC: I wonder sometimes. You mustn't repeat what I'm going to tell you.

1ST GIRL: Of course we won't.

ERIC: Well, it's all a big con, all of it. I've never felt so miserable. My son hates me, my wife's gone off God knows where. I've got no privacy—this is the first time I've been allowed out by myself. I wonder if I've taken the right decision: I'm not the Eric Geddis I used to know and love. I can't seem to talk to people any more, that's why it's so nice to talk to you. You seem interested in what I've got to say and . . . am I boring you?

(There is an embarrassed pause. The girls seem to be looking around. Suddenly three Photographers leap out and start taking flash photographs. The girls leap onto Eric, smiling at the cameras, kissing him, etc.)

ERIC: What's going on?

PHOTOGRAPHER: Smile, Eric! Come on, girls, look as though you're enjoying it. Relax! Ruffle his hair!

(The photographic frenzy is over in a few seconds. The Girls stand up)

ERIC: What was all that about?

(Rodney enters)

RODNEY: Got everything you wanted, boys? If you hurry you should make the late editions.

(The Photographers exit)

Thanks girls. Cheques'll be in the post tomorrow.

(The Girls exit)

ERIC: You arranged all that!

RODNEY: Course I did. Got to show the public that you've got some sort of social life. That's what they want.

ERIC: My private life's my own!

RODNEY: Not any more: you gave all that up when you came into my office. Look, old son, in this game once the bandwagon's rolling you've got to keep pushing it along. Got to stay in the public eye.

ERIC: I feel more like spitting in it.

RODNEY: Now, now. Come on—time for your appointment.

ERIC: And I thought they were interested in me as a person.

RODNEY: Don't be so naïve.

ERIC: What appointment?

RODNEY: Autobiography, remember? Got to meet Emlyn Graves—the writer.

ERIC: I thought I was supposed to write the autobiography. You can't get somebody else to write it! That's a contradiction in terms.

RODNEY: Not in showbiz. No time, you see. Got to get it to the shops a.s.a.p. All right?

ERIC: If you say so.

RODNEY: That's the spirit.

(The lights go down on the pub)

Scene Fourteen:

In the darkness the sound of pounding typewriters is heard. The lights come up on a table at which sit Sid, Ron, Roger and Cassandra hammering away at their typewriters.
Rodney and Eric enter.

RODNEY: Eric, meet Emlyn Graves.

ERIC: Which one?

RODNEY: All of them.

ERIC: *All* of them?

RODNEY: Much quicker: get to the presses in no time. This is Sid: childhood and schooldays.

SID: How do?

RODNEY: Roger: early maturity and marriage.

ROGER: Nice to meet you, er . . . um . . .

RODNEY: Eric.

ROGER: Oh, yes, Eric.

RODNEY: Cassandra: proud fatherhood to brink of fame.

CASSANDRA: Super to meet you.

RODNEY: And Ron: superstardom.

RON: Afternoon.

ERIC: *(Pointing to Roger)* He didn't even know my name!

RODNEY: They get confused: they're doing this sort of thing all the time. Last week it was Lena Zavaroni and next week it's . . . what is next?

CASSANDRA: Don't know yet: we're waiting for a star to be born.

ERIC: But they've never met me. How can they write about my life?

RODNEY: They can do wonders, believe me. Look at this: "My early life was marred by the frequent brawls between my drunken mother and father and the periods when, for the slightest offence, I was locked in the coal shed of our grimy Bradford terraced house with only porridge to eat."

ERIC: That isn't true! It never happened!

ROGER: Neither did your unfortunate encounter with a drunken gipsy in a public lavatory in Leamington Spa, but it doesn't half make good reading.

ERIC: This is all lies! It's fiction!

RODNEY: And unlike most fiction it'll make a mint. Ninety-two pages, six pounds ninety-five in hardback, plus the film rights—we can't lose.

RON: And think of what a colourful past you're inheriting.

ERIC: It's dishonest!

RODNEY: It's good business. A stirring tale of derring don't to get the public's hearts fluttering and their hands in their pockets.

ERIC: I suppose I will be allowed to read it? Just so that I don't underestimate the importance of my own past, you understand?

RODNEY: I do believe that you're developing a neat line in irony, Eric. Keep it under control, though, won't you? There's nothing the public hates more than irony in their heroes—makes them feel insecure, bless their little leather wallets. For God's sake don't use it on TV tonight.

ERIC: TV?

RODNEY: I've got you onto one of those chat shows.

ERIC: But I've got nothing to say.

RODNEY: And you just go on and say it. They'll love you. You'll be a wow.

ERIC: You keep saying that.

(The lights go down)

Scene Fifteen:

Music. The lights come up on a television studio. The Interviewer enters and sits on one of the swing chairs placed center. The music fades.

INTERVIEWER: Good evening. My guest tonight is current-ly enjoying an extraordinary success, yet he remains at heart a mystery. His name is known up and down the country but the public at large know him only through a few public appear-ances, one of them in an extraordinary award-winning adver-tisement. For those of you who've not seen it, here it is.
(The lights go down on the Interviewer)

FILM

We find Eric splashing on after-shave. A lovely girl appears and flings her arms around him.
GIRL: Eric . . . oh, Eric!
Another girl approaches and another and another. They all but stifle him. His face appears above the melee.
ERIC: Geddis After-Shave and Talc: for the man who wouldn't normally get a look in.
(The lights come up on the Interviewer)
INTERVIEWER: Will you welcome, please, Eric Geddis?
(Music. The audience applauds as Eric enters and sits)
   Welcome. It's true to say, isn't it, that you have risen from total obscurity to a remarkable overnight success?
ERIC: Yes.
INTERVIEWER: Now we have the "Eric Geddis Range of Cosmetics," the "Eric Geddis Power Tool Collection" and the "Eric Geddis Lack-of-Action Man for the Average Boy."
ERIC: Yes.
INTERVIEWER: Has this extraordinary success changed you at all?
ERIC: Yes.
INTERVIEWER: It would be remarkable if it hadn't.
ERIC: Yes.
INTERVIEWER: You must be extraordinarily rich by now?
ERIC: Remarkably.
INTERVIEWER: Now I know that you're interested in using this wealth: for instance you've just announced the "Eric Geddis Very-Limited-Over Cricket Tournament."
ERIC: Yes.
INTERVIEWER: As you probably know cricket is one of my abiding passions: you must feel the same?
ERIC: No.
INTERVIEWER: Then why are you sponsoring it?

ERIC: My accountant told me to.

INTERVIEWER: Fascinating. You must have some very firm views about wealth?

ERIC: No.

INTERVIEWER: Don't you have any opinions about anything?

ERIC: Not so's you'd notice.

INTERVIEWER: None at all?

ERIC: I don't like chat talks.

(There is laughter from the audience. The Interviewer laughs as if it is a very funny joke)

INTERVIEWER: Could you tell us a funny story?

ERIC: I haven't got a sense of humour.

INTERVIEWER: Do you enjoy being rich, famous, powerful, everything that I'd give my back teeth to be?

ERIC: I'd keep your back teeth if I were you. Much more useful.

(More laughter from the audience)

INTERVIEWER: Tell me, are you a happy man?

ERIC: Not very.

INTERVIEWER: Moderately happy?

ERIC: Don't know.

INTERVIEWER: Would you say that you are quite uniquely boring?

ERIC: If you want me to.

INTERVIEWER: Extraordinary. Well, Eric, may I say what a pleasure it's been having you on my show tonight!

ERIC: If you must.

INTERVIEWER: It's been extraordinarily remarkable to meet you.

ERIC: Ditto, I'm sure.

INTERVIEWER: A fascinating and unique man. Those of you who'd like to know more might be interested to learn that a West End musical based on Eric's life and called, appropriately enough, "Eric!" opens next week. With over six hundred thousand pounds backing it promises to be a uniquely extraordinary and fascinating show.

ERIC: I didn't know that.

(The lights go down on the television studio)

Scene Sixteen:

The lights come up on Roddy, Binky and the Chorus rehearsing the "Eric Geddis Song." Dotty is facing them. They get into a hopeless tangle and Dotty intervenes.

DOTTY: How many times? How many times? Girls to the *left*, boys to the *right!* Deaf, are you? Okay, okay, you might be acting this guy's boring, stupid relatives but do you have to *be* stupid and boring? We open next week! *Next week!* Ha! I have never, *never* been involved in such a hopeless, dismal, third-rate white elephant guaranteed to flop before the first interval! Well, I wash my hands of it! I don't care!
(Aretha enters)
I don't . . . *(She sees Aretha)* . . . think I've ever heard better songs! *(She pretends to notice Aretha suddenly)* Aretha! Darling!

ARETHA: Dotty. How's it shaping up?

DOTTY: Marvellous! Fabulous! Just polishing a few details!

ARETHA: Yes. Herbie's in New York, finalising the Broadway deal.

DOTTY: Broadway?

ARETHA: Something wrong?

DOTTY: No, no . . . great! Broadway! Marvellous!

ARETHA: This show is very important to our organization. You're sure it'll be ready?

DOTTY: Darling, now would I let you down? It's . . . creative, you know?

ARETHA: I got a telegram from Herbie this morning. Perhaps you'd care to hear it *(She reads from the telegram)* "Six hundred thousand tosheroons" . . . oh, dear . . . "tied up in this one. Stop. Return on investment imperative. Stop. Forget the artyfarty stuff. Stop. Reverse charge. Stop. Menechim."

DOTTY: Believe in me.
(Eric and Rodney enter)

ARETHA: Mr. Geddis? Mr. Sanderson? Allow me to introduce myself. Aretha Goring, Personal Assistant to Herbert Menechim, your producer. *(Introducing Dotty)* Dotty Baldwin, reputed to be the best choreographer in town.

DOTTY: Charmed.

ARETHA: Dotty, ask Roddy and Binky to step over, will you?
(Dotty motions to Roddy and Binky to join them)
Mr. Geddis, Lord Menechim has got you two extremely promising, up and coming, young artistes to play you and your lovely wife Doreen. They didn't come cheaply, of course, but as Lord Menechim would say, if he were here, what's money where art's concerned?

ERIC: Quite so.

ARETHA: Art, schmart, as Herbie's old mother used to say with monotonous regularity.

DOTTY: It's going to be a wow.

ERIC: Where have I heard that before?

DOTTY: An all-time winner. Honestly.

ERIC: I'm not happy about the title.

ARETHA: The title! What's wrong with the title?

ERIC: Well . . . why the exclamation mark?

ARETHA: If you want a hit musical you must have an exclamation mark. What would you prefer: a semicolon?

ERIC: Integrity. That's what I want.

ARETHA: Mr. Geddis, don't interfere in what you don't understand, there's a dear little man.

(Roddy and Binky move up)
Ah! Now I want you to meet your stars; Roderick Wimpenny—you probably saw him in Lord Menechim's TV series about Attila the Hun. Roddy played Attila's son-in-law. The critics loved you, didn't they, Roddy?

RODDY: Yes, yes. I found it very hard to get *inside* a Hun. Most taxing.

ERIC: Weren't you the one who grunted a lot and got his hands chopped off in episode six?

DOTTY: And this is Binky Bartlett. Best tap dancer in the West End until she had to have the plastic hips.

BINKY: We've heard *so* much about you and your dear little wife. Where is she, by the way?

ERIC: Last I heard she was halfway over the Timor Sea on her way to open a hypermarket in Auckland. Look, Miss Goring, I don't want to seem ungrateful or anything, but they're just not like Doreen or me.

ARETHA: And why do you think Lord Menechim is paying them? To act! If you invest all that money you get acting! Show him, Dotty.

DOTTY: Ah! Oh . . . right. Oh, God!

(She organizes the Chorus)

RODNEY: For God's sake stop picking holes, Eric!

ERIC: Well, it's daft! I mean Doreen and me aren't Noel Coward and Gertrude bleeding Lawrence, are we?

DOTTY: All right everybody? Roddy and Binky's duet then into the finale, right? And TRY!

(They go into the routine. Eric, Rodney and Aretha watch for a while and then they exit. At the end of the routine the lights go down on the Chorus)

Scene Seventeen:

The lights come up on the Boardroom. Sir Guthrie, Rodney, Daphne, Eric and Emily sit round the table. There is a telephone beside Sir Guthrie.

SIR GUTHRIE: I must say, Rodney, things have really taken off. Next week we hit the States: coast to coast coverage. Consider yourself a director for life.

RODNEY: Very kind, Sir Guthrie.

DAPHNE: Aren't we all overreacting?

SIR GUTHRIE: Try to control your natural enmity, Daphne, there's a good girl.

ERIC: I think the whole thing's getting out of hand.

SIR GUTHRIE: Eric, my boy, the world's at your feet.

ERIC: To kick about as I please? Have any of you ever stopped to think what it means?

RODNEY: What it means, Eric, is that the dear old public is as stupid, if not stupider, as it ever was.

ERIC: Exactly. We've proved our point. Can't we stop now?

RODNEY: No way. It's gone too far: the consumers won't let us stop now. Consumption, like revolutions, has to be self-perpetuating otherwise the masses turn on the leaders so to speak. Face the facts of life: the public is looking for something to spend its money on. You, useless domestic appliances, teeth-rotting sweets, anything, it doesn't matter what. Withdraw that right from them and they start getting shirty. We're only supplying a need.

ERIC: A need that we created.

RODNEY: There all the time. That's what it's all about: creating and exploiting needs. You can't back out now: you're

up to your ears in franchises and contracts for five years
—minimum.

ERIC: It's all a cheat.

SIR GUTHRIE: A cheat that you wanted as far as I remember. You'll have to learn to live with it. Now then, we were about to discuss the setting up of the Eric Geddis Heart and Lung Research Foundation to be financed from the profits of the Geddis Dwarf Size Cigarette . . .

(Maureen enters with a piece of paper)

MAUREEN: You'd better read this. *(She gives Rodney the paper)*

RODNEY: Oh, my God! *(Reading through the paper)* They can't do this!

SIR GUTHRIE: What is it?

RODNEY: Those swines at McCunley, Dodson and Prendergast. They've launched a campaign of their own!

SIR GUTHRIE: Well?

RODNEY: They've got a new image. A new boy!

SIR GUTHRIE: We've nothing to worry about. He can't compete with Eric.

RODNEY: No? Listen to this *(He reads from the paper)* "Introducing Bernie Slater: not only way *below* average but also illiterate, deaf in one ear and positively ugly!"

SIR GUTHRIE: Oh, God! I sense disaster.

RODNEY: They can't go wrong. We're way behind them, image-wise.

DAPHNE: That's progress, Rodney. The average of today is the has-been of tomorrow. And you should know.

RODNEY: You're behind this, aren't you?

DAPHNE: Me, Rodney?

RODNEY: You couldn't stand to see me successful, could you? I wouldn't be surprised if you didn't give them this idea.

SIR GUTHRIE: Now hold on, Rodney. *(The telephone rings. He answers it)* Yes? Put him on. *(He speaks to the others in the room)* It's Sam Smedley. *(Speaking into the telephone)* Hello Sam, good to hear from you . . . now hold on, we've got a contract . . . "Slater splash on cologne: the subnormal fragrance?" Oh, really, Sam, it'll never catch on . . . Sam, Sam? He's cancelled his contract! *(He replaces the receiver)*

RODNEY: It will catch on, of course. They'll *all* cancel their contracts.

DAPHNE: You're over the hill, Rodney.

RODNEY: You wait, you bitch! You just wait.

EMILY: That's it then. It's all over. And such a *lovely* concept!

SIR GUTHRIE: Pity your directorship was never finalised on paper, Rodney.

RODNEY: Now wait a minute . . .

SIR GUTHRIE: There's no room for sentiment in the advertising world, old man. And Eric . . .

ERIC: I'm finished?

SIR GUTHRIE: That's the way it is. One thing . . .

ERIC: All my money was tied up in Geddis Enterprises and it's all gone?

SIR GUTHRIE: Sorry.

ERIC: Doreen's too?

SIR GUTHRIE: Afraid so.

ERIC: She will be disappointed

SIR GUTHRIE: It's a hard world, Mr. Geddis.

ERIC: How fleeting is man's glory. What would it be now? Tax week forty-seven? I've always enjoyed tax week forty-seven since it embraces Shrove Tuesday and Doreen makes a lovely pancake. Well, I'd better be off.

(Rodney starts crying)

SIR GUTHRIE: Stop crying and pull yourself together, Rodney. You've got some hard thinking to do before midday tomorrow. I want a new concept!

RODNEY: I'll kill you one day, Daphne!

SIR GUTHRIE: That's enough of that! Get to work.

ERIC: Bye all. By the way—I'd get something for that rubber plant if I were you: it's looking definitely seedy.

RODNEY: Is that supposed to be a joke?

ERIC: You know I've got . . .

RODNEY: No sense of humour? I wonder sometimes . .

ERIC: Thinking cap on!

(Eric exits. The lights go down on the Boardroom. There is a pause)

Scene Eighteen:

Music. The lights come up on Bernie, a thin sallow youth, who is staring despondently at a piece of paper.

BERNIE: Bernie . . . Bernie . . .

(Eric walks into light and stands by Bernie's side)
Mr. Geddis, I can't . . .

ERIC: *(Taking the paper from him)* Let's have a look, Bernie. Ah, yes: "Slater: for the man who smells something rotten."

BERNIE: What?

ERIC: Sorry, I forgot. *(He walks round to Bernie's other ear)* "Slater: for the man who smells something rotten."

BERNIE: What's that mean?

ERIC: Buggered if I know, Bernie. You just repeat it like they tell you, all right?

BERNIE: And then I'll be stinking rich like you told me?

ERIC: If you say it right and they like you you're halfway there already.

BERNIE: Cor!

ERIC: Thing is, Bernie, they're a bloody sight dafter than what you are: make the most of it while it lasts.

BERNIE: Pardon?

ERIC: Never mind.

BERNIE: I'm ever so grateful, Mr. Geddis.

ERIC: Forget it. One more thing—we never met, right? You don't know me.

BERNIE: Right.

ERIC: Best of luck. Expect I'll see you cleaning out the basins at Clipitclose again before the new tax year's very old.

BERNIE: Not me, Mr. Geddis.

ERIC: No, not you, Bernie. Not you, not me. Definitely not me. Bye.

(Eric exits)

BERNIE: "Slater: for the man who smells something rotten. Slater: for the man who . . . Slater: for . . . Slater . . . Slater . . . Slater . . ."

(Music swells up. The lights fade)

Israel Horovitz

THE FORMER ONE-ON-ONE BASKETBALL CHAMPION

Israel Horovitz

Israel Horovitz is one of the most prolific playwrights of his generation and one of the most widely produced. His plays have been translated into more than twenty languages and performed worldwide. His new play *The Former One-on-One Basketball Champion* is the seventh play of his to appear in this series; the last, in the 1979 edition, was *Hopscotch,* one of four plays in *The Quannapowitt Quartet,* a bill of short related works.

Mr. Horovitz won his first acclaim in 1968 with *The Indian Wants the Bronx,* a powerful and terrifying study of violence on a New York street. The Off-Broadway production with the explosive Al Pacino in the major role went on to striking success in other major American cities, at the 1968 Spoleto Festival (Italy), the World Theatre Festival in England (1969), and numerous other countries. The play won a 1968 Drama Desk-Vernon Rice Award and three Obies, as well as a commendation from *Newsweek* magazine citing the author as one of the three most original dramatists of the year; it was published in the 1969 volume of this series.

Israel Horovitz was born in Wakefield, Massachusetts in 1939. After completing his domestic studies, he traveled to London to study at the Royal Academy of Dramatic Art and in 1965 became the first American to be chosen as playwright-in-residence with Britain's Royal Shakespeare Company.

His first play, *The Comeback,* written when he was seventeen, was produced in Boston in 1960. In the following decade Mr. Horovitz's plays were performed throughout the world. Among them: *It's Called the Sugar Plum* (paired with *The Indian Wants the Bronx* on the New York stage); *The Death of Bernard the Believer; Rats; Morning* (originally titled *Chiaroscuro,* the play was first performed at the Spoleto Festival and later on the triple bill, *Morning, Noon and Night,* Henry Miller's Theatre, New York, 1968); *Trees; Acrobats* (introduced in *The Best Short Plays 1970); Line* (in *Best Short Plays of the World Theatre: 1968–1973); Leader;* and *The Honest-to-God Schnozzola* (winner of a 1969 Obie Award).

His other stage plays include *Shooting Gallery; Dr. Hero; Turnstile; The Primary English Class* (a 1976 Off-Broadway success with Diane Keaton as star); *The Reason We Eat;* and an adaptation of Eugene Ionesco's drama, *Man With Bags.* He has written for television as well; most recently, a dramatization of Herman Melville's *Bartleby, the Scrivener,* presented in 1978 by the Public Broadcasting Service. His screenplay for *The Strawberry Statement* won the *Prix de Jury* at the 1970 Cannes Film Festival.

A series of seven plays—three grouped under the program title *The Wakefield Plays* and four under the title *The Quannapowitt Quartet*—were produced in 1978 at The Actors Studio and the New York Shakespeare Festival respectively.

Other published works include: *First Season* (1968), a collection of plays; *Cappella* (1973), his first novel; and *Nobody Loves Me* (1975), a novella.

Twice the recipient of a Rockefeller Foundation Playwriting Fellowship, Mr. Horovitz also won a similar fellowship from the Creative Artists Program Service, funded by the New York State Council on the Arts. In 1972 he received an Award in Literature from the American Academy of Arts and Letters, and in 1973 he was honored with a National Endowment for the Arts Award.

Sharing his knowledge of his craft, Mr. Horovitz has taught playwriting at New York University and Brandeis University. He was a founding member of the Eugene O'Neill Memorial Theatre Foundation and is presently director of the Playwrights Unit of The Actors Studio, where his script *Park Your Car in the Harvard Yard* was read in May of 1980.

Other recent productions include: *The Great Labor Day Classic* (1979); *The Good Parts* (1980); *The Pig Bit* (1980); and *Compliments of the Author* (1981), an original film script.

An avid competitive runner for twenty-seven years, Mr. Horovitz put his running experience into *Sunday Runners in the Rain,* which explores the American phenomenon of marathon running and the motivations of various participants. A production at Joseph Papp's Public Theatre in 1980 received rave reviews. Mr. Horovitz's enthusiasm for running has led to his forthcoming marriage to Gillian Adams, the British marathoner.

In *The Former One-on-One Basketball Champion,* published here for the first time, Mr. Horovitz has drawn again upon his experience in sports. This poignant study reveals the professional and personal triumphs and tragedies of a former professional basketball player and his relationship to a teenage boy, whose life is connected to his own in an unexpected way. The boy is presented with an opportunity to even the score. The play had its first reading at The Actors Studio in May 1978. The world premiere took place at The Gloucester Stage Company, Gloucester, Massachusetts, where Mr. Horovitz is artistic director. The play was directed by Denny Blodget, with Adam Horovitz as Katz and Jay Blitzman as Allen. Subsequently the play was adapted and taped for *Earplay*, a division of National Public Radio.

The author dedicates his play: "For Matthew Horovitz, who taught me my first game."

Characters:

KATZ
ALLEN

Music.
Lights fade up to bright white.
Morning.
City playground basketball court, asphalt. A netless hoop, regulation height, angled upstage left. Backboard battered aluminum, stanchion thick aluminum pipe.
Chain-link fencing defines playing area: front open to auditorium.
A 14-year-old boy, Irving Katz, shooting baskets: some from way outside, some inside, all in rhythm with the music.
Katz wears jeans, leather sneakers, a T-shirt and sweatband around his forehead.
Irving "Sonny" Allen enters, watches Katz a moment, sits by the side of the court.
Allen is enormous, just under seven feet tall. He wears a powder blue gabardine suit with a white short-sleeved shirt, open at the collar, with the collar of his shirt spread over the collar of his suit jacket. Allen is forty years old, fair-skinned.
Katz continues to shoot, not acknowledging the entrance of the older man.
The music fades out, as the lights reach their ultimate brightness. We now hear the sound of Katz's movement and the basketball hitting the ground and backboard. Otherwise, silence.
Katz is first to speak.

KATZ: You a pervert?
ALLEN: Why? You lookin' for one?
(Katz continues to play. When he sinks an exceptional shot, he turns to Allen and smiles)
KATZ: I sunk ten of those in a row yesterday . .
ALLEN: I picked the wrong day, huh?
KATZ: Never can tell. Maybe I'll do twelve today . . .
(Shoots: misses)
ALLEN: That's one in a row . . .
KATZ: Gotta' start somewhere . . . right? *(Shoots: scores)*
Right!
ALLEN: Too much wrist.
KATZ: Huh?

ALLEN: Too much wrist. You're shooting like a girl.

KATZ: If you're a pervert, mister, I got some bad news: my father's due back here about five minutes ago. He's a cop. With a gun . . .

ALLEN: Gimme. *(Allen stands: holds out hands for ball. Katz throws it to him.* There. *(Shoots: scores)* See how my hand came down . . . sharp . . . but very little wrist. Straight lines —automatic.

KATZ: *(Rebounds, drives, shoots lay-up. He looks at Allen)* You got one in a row. Wanna' try for two? *(Throws ball to Allen, who shoots: scores)* Two-in-a-row. Three?

[*N.B. Adjust dialogue to hits and misses, i.e., "Ya' missed two in a row, Wanna' try for three?"*]

(Throws ball to Allen, who now moves from sidelines on to court, jumps: shoots one-hand push shot from above his head. Katz rebounds, dribbles out to center court) Check my wrist, okay? *(Katz shoots: scores)* That better?

ALLEN: Still too much. Try none.

KATZ: How can I shoot with no wrist? My hand's attached to my arm by my wrist. I've *gotta'* use wrist . . . *(Set to shoot again)* Watch *(Shoots: scores)* Better?

ALLEN: Sure. Now add in a *little* wrist.

KATZ: What are you? A coach or som'pin'? *Katz sets, shoots, looks at Allen)* Better?

ALLEN: Didn't it *feel* better?

KATZ: *(After a pause)* Yuh. Did. *(Looks at Allen)* You wanna' play a little one-on-one?

ALLEN: For real?

KATZ: Well, you'll hav'ta' spot me some, right? I mean, how tall are you? Six-seven?

ALLEN: Six-six.

KATZ: You ever play pro?

ALLEN: Me? *(Shoots)* Don't talk crazy?

KATZ: *(Rebounds: lays ball up and in)* Play to twenty-one, spot me ten.

ALLEN: Ten?

KATZ: Ten.

ALLEN: That's *all*?

KATZ: Nickel a point?

ALLEN: How old are you, anyway?

KATZ: Sixteen.

ALLEN: Fourteen?

KATZ: Yuh. You?

ALLEN: Oh, I dunno' . . . Fifty, sixty . . .

KATZ: Thirty-five?

ALLEN: Forty.

KATZ: My father's thirty-eight. You gotta' *see* it to believe it!

ALLEN: Good shape?

KATZ: Like an avocado.

ALLEN: Green?

KATZ: That, too . . .

ALLEN: Big seed in the middle?

KATZ: Probably . . .

ALLEN: He never shoots with you?

KATZ: My father? *(Shoots: scores)* You got kids?

ALLEN: Me? *(Shoots: scores)* How come you're not in school?

KATZ: Me? *(Shoots: scores)* You on unemployment?

ALLEN: You cut the day or what?

KATZ: *(Shoots: scores)* We keepin' score here?

ALLEN: Who goes first? Throw fingers . . . Okay?

KATZ: You crazy? I started three shots back. I'm leading, thirteen–zip.

ALLEN: I hit one!

KATZ: Wasn't your turn. I didn't miss yet. *(Shoots a short shot: scores)* Fourteen.

ALLEN: Time!

KATZ: *(Stops)* What's a' matter here?

ALLEN: *(Takes off his jacket)* I got a rep I gotta' protect here.

KATZ: You got keys? . . . A wallet? . . . Better watch your stuff, huh? Put it in your pants pocket.

ALLEN: It's just you and me . . .

KATZ: You never know . . .

ALLEN: I'll risk it . . .

KATZ: I wouldn't . . .

ALLEN: It's *my* stuff, huh?

KATZ: Okay, you rather be sorry than safe . . . that's your business. You ready?

ALLEN: Go.

(Katz dribbles towards basket, but Allen guards him. The difference in their height is comic. Each time Katz shoots the ball, Allen simply takes his hand and pushes it back into Katz's hands

Each time Katz leaps into the air, Allen simply shoves the basketball, thereby shoving Katz as well, to the ground. Possible to revive music and choreograph this section, fading music and dance in and out. At end of wordless section, Katz speaks)

KATZ: Hold it.

ALLEN: Som'pin' wrong?

KATZ: Just hold it!

ALLEN: You callin' time?

KATZ: *Time!*

ALLEN: What's'a'matter here? *(No reply)* Something wrong?

KATZ: You've got a sixteen inch advantage. I'm five-even.

ALLEN: But you're leading, fourteen-zip.

KATZ: I've got a pain in my chest.

ALLEN: You're too young for that.

KATZ: I've gotta' talk to my boys.

(Katz holds his fingers to his temples, playacting deep thought)

ALLEN: What are you doing?

KATZ: *Shhhh! (Pauses: talks to himself, smiling)* Right. Got it! *(Looks at Allen)* You ready?

ALLEN: *(Nods)* Mmmm.

KATZ: *(Yells)* Hey, look? Porno skywriting! *(Allen looks up. Katz bounds in for layup; hits)* Fifteen! *(Whoops with laughter)* Whoaaaa! *(Dribbles back out to center line)* Six to go. *(Grabs his chest)* Oh, wow!

ALLEN: What is it?

KATZ: I got some kinda' weird pain in my chest . . .

ALLEN: You kidding?

KATZ: Wow! It really hurts . . . *(Katz kneels down on ground)*

ALLEN: You kidding me?

KATZ: I've never had this before!

ALLEN: Are you kidding me or what?

KATZ: Ohh . . . wow! This is very scarey!

ALLEN: Just relax, now. Go easy . . .

(Allen moves to Katz, takes ball, turns, shoots, scores, turns to Katz again, smiles. Katz looks up slowly. He drops hand from chest)

KATZ: Nice.

ALLEN: Fifteen-one. My outs.

KATZ: *(Standing)* Really nice.

ALLEN: How's your chest?

KATZ: I called time', ya' know . . .

ALLEN: Not true.

KATZ: I did!

ALLEN: Didn't hear it.

KATZ: Maybe som'body else did! *(Looks around)* Just us . . .

ALLEN: You're gonna' hav'ta' take my word.

KATZ: No way! We'll throw fingers.

ALLEN: Uh uh.

KATZ: C'monnnn!

ALLEN: Fifteen-one.

KATZ: I'm five-even, you're six-six—sixteen inches over me—and you're playing shady.

ALLEN: *Me* playing shady? *Me* playing shady? *You're* the one's calling "Planes! Planes!" *You're* the one in coronary arrest! You ready or what?

KATZ: *(Stands, moves into position to guard Allen)* Go.

ALLEN: *(Nods)* 'Kay . . .

(Allen dribbles forward, bounding, driving on Katz, who flies backwards on contact, skidding backwards in sitting position to point offstage beyond audience's sightline. Allen shoots: scores. There is a long pause. Allen stands center-court, frozen, watching point at which Katz skidded offstage. Katz enters quietly. He walks to Allen, looks at him)

KATZ: We need a rule.

ALLEN: What kind of rule?

KATZ: Like 'no driving' . . .

ALLEN: No driving?

KATZ: No driving.

ALLEN: What kind of game are we playing if there's no driving?

KATZ: A no-driving game. We shoot from outside.

ALLEN: You kidding me?

KATZ: Mister, I've got my whole life ahead of me. I have no plan to end it here, with you driving up one side of my head and down the other . . . *(Pauses)* No driving.

ALLEN: What's your name?

KATZ: Irving.

ALLEN: Irving?

KATZ: Yuh. Irving. Som'pin' the matter with Irving?

ALLEN: How'd you get stuck with a name like Irving?

KATZ: What do you mean?

ALLEN: You *named* for somebody? Is that how?

KATZ:　My uncle. He was named Issac. He died and they named me for him.

ALLEN:　I thought your name was Irving?

KATZ:　It is. I don't understand it either . . .

ALLEN:　You're Jewish, huh?

KATZ:　Som'pin' the matter with Jewish?

ALLEN:　'Course not. You just don't see too many basketball players who're Jewish.

KATZ:　That's true.

ALLEN:　There was a guy played for the Celts, name of Finkel. He was a Catholic, but everybody figured, with a name like Finkel, he was Jewish. He had a big Jewish following . . . up in Boston. He never played much . . . More of a warmup center . . . third line. Nice guy, they say. The Celts were in a series and Heinsohn put him in towards the end of the game . . . Cowens and Havlicek were both out with injuries, Jo-Jo White was down with the flu. Somebody else was sick, too . . . I forget. Anyway, Heinsohn put Finkel in near the end of the game, tie score, about four minutes to go. First thing Finkel does is get fouled. They were playing the Knicks and Phil Jackson jumped on his back . . . *(Smiles)* Finkel was a big guy . . . Maybe six-eleven . . . *(Pauses)* You should have heard the roar when the announcer called his name. Every Jew ten towns around was cheerin' . . . It was funny . . . *(Smiles, remembering)* Anyway. Finkel goes up to the foul line and what does he do? He genuflects . . . *(Allen laughs)* You should'a' heard the groan from the Jews in the crowd! It was hilarious. *(Allen laughs: Katz does not)* Don't ya' get it?

KATZ:　Not really, no.

ALLEN:　They all thought he was Jewish until they saw him genuflect.

KATZ:　'S that dirty?

ALLEN:　Is what dirty?

KATZ:　That word.

ALLEN:　'Genuflect' means to cross yourself and kinda' kneel. Like this. *(He genuflects)*

KATZ:　Oh, right.

ALLEN:　You never heard the word?

KATZ:　I must have heard it and forgot.

ALLEN:　You ever hear of Finkel?

KATZ:　Sure. He signed four times for me.

ALLEN:　You have a big autograph collection?

KATZ: Yuh, I guess.

ALLEN: Have you got any old timers?

KATZ: Sure.

ALLEN: Like who?

KATZ: Cousey?

ALLEN: You've got Cousey?

KATZ: Yuh, I've got him on a series card from the '50's, and I've got him twice on index cards.

ALLEN: How'd you do that? He never signs.

KATZ: I sent away.

ALLEN: With a letter?

KATZ: Sure. They never sign, if you don't send a letter . . . *(Pauses)* You were a pro, right?

ALLEN: Me? Naw. I just followed the game, closely . . .

KATZ: You ever meet any players?

ALLEN: A few.

KATZ: You from Boston?

ALLEN: How so?

KATZ: You follow the Celts?

ALLEN: Sure. I did.

KATZ: Who's your all-time favorite Celt?

ALLEN: My all-time favorite? *(Pauses, smiles)* Cousey. Yours?

KATZ: Yuh. I guess. *(Pauses)* What's your name?

ALLEN: Same as your's.

KATZ: Irving?

ALLEN: Irving.

KATZ: You Jewish?

ALLEN: Un-uh. Baptist.

KATZ: Is that a Protestant?

ALLEN: Very much so, yuh.

KATZ: A Protestant Irving?

ALLEN: It's a fact.

KATZ: How the hell did you get stuck with a name like Irving?

ALLEN: I got screwed.

KATZ: Me, too.

ALLEN: If you could pick any name under the sun, what would you pick?

KATZ: Instead of Irving?

ALLEN: Mmmm.

KATZ: Instead of Irving . . . I would   pick   Irwin.

ALLEN: You're kidding!

KATZ: Yuh, I am. Lemme' think . . . I would pick . . . Kid.

ALLEN: Kid?

KATZ: Yuh, ya' know how in movies, there's always some-body who's just called "Kid" . . . Like "Who the hell could ever lift a Buick, barehanded?" and they answer, "Let Kid try . . ." And then somè really serious guy kinda' slithers over and lifts up the car . . . and his name is "Kid" . . .

ALLEN: What's your last name?

KATZ: Oh, right. I see what you mean.

ALLEN: Huh?

KATZ: Katz. Kid Katz. No good.

ALLEN: Sounds like a middleweight contender.

KATZ: Sure, in 1936. Kid Katz . . . knocked out in eleven seconds in the first round . . . *(Pauses)* Maybe it's best that a name just gets picked for you in the first place.

ALLEN: Sure it's best. You could spend your whole life just looking for a better name . . .

KATZ: What's your last name?

ALLEN: Mine? Allen.

KATZ: Irving Allen?

ALLEN: Yuh. Ridiculous, huh?

KATZ: Irving Allen's a good name . . . Sounds like a presi-dent. Or a pro.

ALLEN: Sounds like a *butler*.

KATZ: You never signed, did you?

ALLEN: *(After a long pause)* No. *(Stands: smiles)* What'a'we got goin' for a score here? Fifteen-one?

KATZ: Yuh.

ALLEN: No driving?

KATZ: No driving.

ALLEN: My outs?

KATZ: We'll throw fingers for it.

ALLEN: You kidding me? You think I'm a dope or som'pin'? It was definitely my outs!

KATZ: We've been stopped for about an hour now—right? It's not like a time-out. It's like a new half, with a tip-off.

ALLEN: You wanna' do a jump?

KATZ: Yuh, sure. Wait'll I get my brother.

ALLEN: Why? He tall?

KATZ: Naw, he's a shrimp like me, but he's got a car. *(Pauses)* I'll stand on the car. *(Pauses)* For the tip-off.

ALLEN: Okay, we'll throw fingers. Once?

KATZ: Two out'ta' three.

ALLEN: Call it: ev's or odds?

KATZ: Uhhh, odds. *(They throw fingers)*

ALLEN: Once, twice, three . . . shoot! Yours! Once, twice, three, shoot! Mine. Once, twice, three, shoot! *(Pauses. Katz laughs. Allen throws ball to him to take out from behind half-court line)* That should show you what a great guy I am. It was definitely my outs . . .

KATZ: You ready?

ALLEN: No more Mr. Niceguy.

KATZ: What's that s'pose'ta mean?

ALLEN: Just what you think. I've been laying back, watching your game. The way I figure it, you don't score another point on me . . . *(Pauses)* You've got nothin' from the left . .

KATZ: Oh, yuh?

ALLEN: Everything you've hit is from the right . . . Typical for a right-handed kid.

KATZ: Oh, yuh?

ALLEN: All I have to do is keep you down left, there's nothing to worry about.

KATZ: Uh huh . . . *(Suddenly, Katz bolts down left of the basket, dribbling the ball with his left hand. He leaps in the air and takes a left-handed jump shot. He hits.) [N.B. If he misses, Allen allows him to continue to take shots until he hits.] Right! (Katz turns to Allen and smiles)* Sixteen-zip, I believe.

ALLEN: One.

KATZ: Sixteen-one. *(Smiles)* I took it up, left-handed: I dropped it, left-handed.

ALLEN: Once.

KATZ: Whoaaa . . .

ALLEN: *Once! (Katz bolts down left again. Allen steals the ball from him, easily. He shoots: scores)* Sixteen-two, I believe? My outs . . .

KATZ: Hold it.

ALLEN: What's the matter?

KATZ: Just hold it.

ALLEN: What's the matter?

KATZ: Time.

ALLEN: Chest pains again?

(Katz runs his hand through his hair, pulling it up from in front of his eyes and tucks it behind his ear)

KATZ: Okay.

ALLEN: Ready?

KATZ: Yuh. Ready. I said I was.

(Allen dribbles the ball forward five feet, lunges to the left, stops suddenly, fakes to the right. Shoots: misses. Katz fades to the right and Allen moves easily in on the right, stops, sets, shoots, hits. [N.B. If he misses, he rebounds and hits a layup.] There is a pause. The ball rolls to a stop. Allen walks back to the half-court line and waits)

KATZ: What are you waiting for?

ALLEN: The ball.

KATZ: I'm supposed to get the ball for you?

ALLEN: Yuh. I hit, you get. When you hit, *I* got. Remember?

KATZ: That's a new one on *me.*

ALLEN: You want me to walk all the way back for the ball, I'll do it, okay?

KATZ: I'll get it. *(He does)* No problem. *(He aims ball at Allen)* No sweat. *(He tosses ball to Allen)* Let's go.

ALLEN: Ready?

KATZ: Ah, come on, will ya'?

ALLEN: Sixteen-three?

KATZ: Right, right.

ALLEN: You nervous?

KATZ: I don't get psyched out that easily, ya' know?

ALLEN: You look nervous.

KATZ: Why? Just 'cause my pantleg's wet?

ALLEN: You're really ready, huh?

KATZ: Go.

(Allen shoots from where he stands. Swish)

ALLEN: Four. *(Smiles)* Ready? *(Katz nods)* Me, too. *(Allen shoots again from where he stands. Swish again)* Five.

KATZ: Okay. Time.

ALLEN: What for?

KATZ: Makes no sense to call this a game if you're gonna' just stand there and swish 'em through.

ALLEN: Well, hell, man. If I can't drive and I can't shoot from outside, what's left? You don't want to play basketball . . . you want to play a game called "I Win."

KATZ: It just doesn't make any sense for me to just stand here and watch you just throw 'em through from there! Maybe you figure I should let you *stuff*???

ALLEN: No wonder you were playing by yourself.

KATZ: What's *that* supposed to mean?

ALLEN: A guaranteed win: you against you. You win. No wonder.

KATZ: I was M.V.P. on my team last year, ya' know.

ALLEN: I can imagine. Just *you* on the team . . . who else *could*'a been M.V.P.?

KATZ: We had twenty men on the squad.

ALLEN: Twenty?

KATZ: Twenty.

ALLEN: What was your scoring average.

KATZ: Same as yours: eighteen.

ALLEN: You know who I am, huh?

KATZ: Eighteen-a-game lifetime average . . . M.V.P. two series years in a row with Boston . . . pulled a hamstring in your rookie year that put you on options from Milwaukee . . . that's when Boston picked you up . . . pulled the same hamstring the last three years you played . . . your last season was about . . . let's see . . . ten years ago. As far as I know, you never signed for anybody, not even your own kids.

ALLEN: I don't have kids.

KATZ: Yes, you do. Two. A boy and a girl.

ALLEN: You got a computer up there instead of a brain?

KATZ: I remember things.

ALLEN: Their stepfather adopted them. I haven't seen either one of them in six years now . . . *(Smiles)* They live up in Canada . . . last I heard.

KATZ: *(After a long pause)* You're walkin' fine *now*. You plannin' a comeback?

ALLEN: I'm forty.

KATZ: Look at Havlicek.

ALLEN: There's only one of them every hundred years or so.

KATZ: If that's what you think, then it's true, I guess. I personally believe I could be playing still at forty . . .

ALLEN: What's your secret?

KATZ: Desire.

ALLEN: Oh.

KATZ: I don't plan to give it up.

ALLEN: Aren't you kinda' small? Not that I want to cramp your style, but you are kinda' small . . . for sixteen.

KATZ: Fourteen.

ALLEN: Oh.

KATZ: Yuh. I'm the smallest kid in my class.

ALLEN: Look at Calvin Murphy.

KATZ: Exactly.

ALLEN: I'm sorry I brought that up . . . about your being small. I don't know why I did that.

KATZ: How come you never signed?

ALLEN: I never liked the whole thing, ya' know? Kids down around my knees with pens and pictures. I never liked it. *(Pauses)* It used to make me think of death. *(There is no response. Katz waits for Allen to continue. He does)* I figured I could just drop dead, ya' know . . . and the kids would just want a *picture* of it . . . *(Pauses)* I didn't like them selling my autograph . . . you know . . . for money . . . at the card conventions and all . . .

KATZ: Nobody ever *had* yours to sell, 'cause you never signed.

ALLEN: How much do you figure it was worth?

KATZ: Your autograph?

ALLEN: Mmm.

KATZ: On an index card or a picture?

ALLEN: Either. Both.

KATZ: Now or then?

ALLEN: *(Pauses, thinks: laughs)* Then.

KATZ: Hmm. Let's'ee . . . I would have to say, given the fact that you never signed, fifteen, *definitely*, for a picture and probably ten for an index card. 'Course, if you signed a lot, that would bring it way down . . .

ALLEN: Fifteen? Times how many?

KATZ: Huh?

ALLEN: How many times before I brought the value down?

KATZ: Let's'ee . . . a thousand maybe. . .

ALLEN: Fifteen thousand . . . You know how much I've got in my wallet now?

KATZ: I've got a buck-fifty.

ALLEN: Me, too. Hmmm. Same name, same bank account.

KATZ: That's all you've got?

ALLEN: Yup.

KATZ: How about your restaurant in Rhode Island?

ALLEN: For crying out loud, Katz, you know everything!

KATZ: I read about it. Fried clams. I like fried clams a lot.

ALLEN: They're not kosher.

KATZ: You got something against Jews, or what?

ALLEN: It went pretty good, while I was still playing . . . and for a couple of years after. But then, you know how things are, I sort of lost my name . . . *(Pauses)* I lost my name and . . . well . . . people sort of took it out on my clams: stopped eating them.

KATZ: You go bankrupt?

ALLEN: Worse. It was like a poker game when you don't know how to quit losing . . . and you start signing I.O.U.'s . . . That's what I did . . . with everybody I knew . . . all my friends . . . I signed I.O.U.'s. *(Pauses)* I was pretty dumb.

KATZ: You borrow from players, too?

ALLEN: Sure.

KATZ: Anybody big?

ALLEN: That's the nature of my business, Katz .

KATZ: I mean big names.

ALLEN: Sure. Everybody.

KATZ: You pay 'em back?

ALLEN: *(After a pause)* No.

KATZ: Who runs the restaurant?

ALLEN: Some people. A family. They bought it for taxes. I had to give it over to the town. Portsmouth, Rhode Island. Near the bridge to Newport. *(Pauses)* Pretty.

KATZ: Jews?

ALLEN: Huh?

KATZ: The family who got it?

ALLEN: Naw, I don't . . . *(Smiles)* Yuh. I guess they were . . . are.

KATZ: *(After a pause)* My father used to have a restaurant. Cuban.

ALLEN: Your father's Cuban?

KATZ: The restaurant was· Cuban. Havana Sunrise Take-Out . . . that was the name of it . . . Havana Sunrise Take-Out.

ALLEN: Sounds awful.

KATZ: Awful? Awful's nothin'! This place was guaranteed death. The black beans were so old they were green. The plantains were so old, they were black. You know what we used to call the Hot Diced Beef? *(Pauses)* Chili-Cats. You know why?

ALLEN: You kidding me?

KATZ: Hey, listen, if I had eaten at my father's restaurant, I wouldn't be here to be leading you sixteen-four, and that's a fact.

ALLEN: Sixteen-five.

KATZ: Whatever.

ALLEN: What happened to the restaurant? Does he still have it?

KATZ: My father? Naw. Long gone. There's a Dunkin' Donuts there now . . .

ALLEN: Business no good?

KATZ: In what sense?

ALLEN: Did he fold up the restaurant . . . your father . . . 'cause business was slow?

KATZ: Nothin' like that. My father folded up *personally,* because he was shot six times in the face and neck by a kid I went to school with . . . He robbed the register of a hundred and sixty-five dollars. There was a thousand more in the cigar box under the counter.

ALLEN: *(After a pause)* Your father . . . he . . . died?

KATZ: Beyond any question of a doubt.

ALLEN: *(Quietly)* What happened to the kid?

KATZ: That was sixth grade. Seventh grade, he spent up state somewhere . . . in a correction school. They say he learned printing. He's back down here now for eighth grade.

ALLEN: Are you kidding?

KATZ: How come you always think I'm kidding? I'm not kidding.

ALLEN: Do you ever . . . see him?

KATZ: Naw. Never felt like it. No point.

ALLEN: My God! That's ridiculous.

(Pauses)

ALLEN: Don't you . . . you know . . . wanna' *get even?*

KATZ: Do I want to kill him? Is that what you mean?

ALLEN: Well, yuh.

KATZ: I don't know. *(Looks up at Allen)* Let's play ball, huh?

ALLEN: Sure. You take it out.

KATZ: You're just doing that 'counta' my father, right?

ALLEN: Naw . . . right. *(Nods)* That's why.

KATZ: I accept. There isn't too much I can do about my father, but maybe I can still pull this game out . . . *(Pauses)* You ready?

ALLEN: Sure.

(Katz dribbles downcourt, fakes to his right, rolls left, lays the ball up and in) Seventeen.

KATZ: You just let me have that?

ALLEN: Nope.

KATZ: It wouldn't'a mattered, anyhow. I would'a taken it . . .

(He dribbles to halfcourt line, looks at Allen, smiles, nods. He dribbles to position four steps in from halfcourt mark, jumps, shoots, hits. [N.B. If he misses, he goes in for rebound and layup.]) Eighteen. Three to go.

ALLEN: How long ago?

KATZ: I told you. Couple'a years now . . .

ALLEN: That's a rough break.

KATZ: Pulling a hamstring and sitting out three season's a rough break, too, huh?

ALLEN: I guess.

KATZ: *Sporting News* picked you as Rookie of the Year, twice, right? Counta' you didn't finish your first year.

ALLEN: I don't remember.

KATZ: Twice, I think . . .

ALLEN: Just once. You can only be a rookie once. They didn't count my first year, 'cause'a my injury. They counted my second year as my rookie year and named me number one.

KATZ: But they said you *would've* made number one, first year, if you didn't get injured, right?

ALLEN: You weren't even born then . . .

KATZ: I collect back issues . . .

ALLEN: That's amazing!

KATZ: I remember the game against the Knicks, when you scored forty-one . . . Best one-on-one player in the game . . . "The One-on-One Champion" . . . Right? None better . . .

ALLEN: Twenty years ago now . . .

KATZ: The thing that was amazing about your game was the number of assists you had . . .

ALLEN: I was lucky . . .

KATZ: More n' thirty assists . . . in one game . . . and . . .

ALLEN: Lucky . . .

KATZ: Fifty-one points . . .

ALLEN: I got hot.

KATZ: You were *great!* Why don't you say it? You were great

ALLEN: Don't talk dumb . . . *(There is a pause)* I played a good game . . . *(A second pause)* I worked hard at it. *(Smiles)* You couldn't have seen the game. You weren't born.

KATZ: I've got all your clippings . . . I saw that game, maybe twenty times, on a training film . . .

ALLEN: You go to basketball camp?

KATZ: At the 'Y' . . .

ALLEN: They used the film, huh?

KATZ: I borrowed it and played it over and over at home . . .

ALLEN: Sixteen millimeter?

KATZ: I borrowed a projector from my Sunday school . . . *(Pauses)* I was just a kid. *(Pauses)* Maybe it's 'cause we've got the same name. Maybe that's it. *(There is a long, hard stare between the two men. Neither smiles. Neither speaks. Katz throws the ball to Allen for a "touch", before he takes it out to resume play. It is done, wordlessly. Katz shoots from mid-court: scores)*

ALLEN: Nineteen. I'm gonna' give you one more, Irving, then I'm going to play hard, left-handed.

KATZ: Hey, listen. You play your game the way you wanna' play your game. No skin off my teeth, right? *(Throws ball to Allen)* Touch. *(Allen throws it back to Katz)* Ready? *(Allen nods. Katz dribbles past him, stops beneath the basket, looks at Allen, shrugs; shoots an easy layup, in)* No skin off my teeth.

ALLEN: Five, right?

KATZ: Right.

ALLEN: Let's go.

KATZ: Touch. *(Katz throws the ball to Allen for a touch and Allen returns it. Katz dribbles out, Allen steals the ball from him, turns, leaps, and drops a one-hand jumpshot: scores. Allen takes his own rebound and moves quickly back to the half-court line, bounding gracefully. It is at this point that we first see his grace and confidence: he is a professional player, clearly so. He throws the ball to Katz)*

ALLEN: Touch. *(Katz looks at him, but Allen interrupts)* Don't talk to me! Play!

(Katz returns the ball to Allen and gets himself set for Allen's attack. Allen shoots: scores)

KATZ: Hey!

ALLEN: Seven. *(He moves to half-court line)* Touch *(The ball goes to Katz and back to Allen, who bounds in half-way, leaps, sinks shot)* Ball!

(*Katz breaks into a smile. He tosses the ball back to Allen, thoroughly enjoying Allen's expertise*)

KATZ: Ready.

ALLEN: You sure? (*Allen drives straight at Katz, who is terrified. Allen stops, suddenly. Katz falls over, backwards. Katz looks up from the ground to see Allen slowly set, shoot, and drop another basket*) Eight. (*He throws the ball to Katz, who has risen from the ground*) Touch. (*Katz does*)

KATZ: (*Returning the ball*) I thought that you were going to let me win?

ALLEN: *Any*body can let you win. It takes me to score sixteen straight.

KATZ: You and what army?

(*Allen dribbles out, Katz comes forward. Allen headfakes, rolls left, Katz rolls right. Allen dribbles in for an easy shot*) Nine.

KATZ: Time.

ALLEN: You really want to play it chicken, Katz, play it chicken. No skin off *my* teeth.

KATZ: I just have to fix my hair. (*He brushes hair out of his eyes*) Okay. Ready.

ALLEN: (*Standing at half-court line: smiles*) Lefty. (*He takes one step, stops, shoots, scores*) Rebound.

(*Katz goes for the ball, but kicks it. The ball rolls to Allen's jacket. Katz gets the ball, sits on ground next to jacket*)

KATZ: Time. I've gotta' sit down. (*He leans on Allen's jacket*) What the hell is *this*?

ALLEN: Nothing.

(*Both Katz and Allen are shaken*)

KATZ: C'mon, will ya'! What're'ya' doin' with this? Huh?

ALLEN: I'm just carrying it . . . for a friend. . .

KATZ: You've got great friends . . . (*Katz takes a pistol, .32 calibre, from Allen's jacket pocket*) It's loaded?

ALLEN: (*Nods*) Careful with that.

KATZ: Why? You 'fraid I'll hurt'cha'?

ALLEN: No. I'm afraid you'll hurt yourself.

(*Katz aims the pistol in opposite direction from Allen and fires a shot*)

KATZ: Wow!

ALLEN: *What the hell are you doin'*???

(*Allen takes a step toward Katz, who turns and aims the pistol at him*)

KATZ: Back up! . . .

ALLEN: Irving, what are you doing?

KATZ: What are *you* doing?

ALLEN: I was just walking up to the bridge . . .

KATZ: You planned to shoot the bridge? How come?

ALLEN: I was giving myself a choice.

KATZ: Oh. Right. A choice. Jump or . . .

(Katz puts gun back in Allen's coat pocket. The two men face one another. There is a long pause)

ALLEN: You don't know what it feels like to owe money all around . . . I owe more money than I'll make in ten lifetimes . . .

KATZ: Money, huh? That's it?

ALLEN: I'm finished, Irving. I'm walking around dead. The day the game threw me out, I was dead. I've just been walking around since then . . . making a fool of myself to everybody. No family left . . . no friends . . . just me inside my skin. Maybe a circus would have me, huh?

KATZ: So, it's not the money? It's the walking around dead?

ALLEN: You're a kid. You wouldn't understand . . .

KATZ: Boy, it's all through your family, isn't it?

ALLEN: What d'ya' mean?

KATZ: What do ya' mean "What do ya' mean?" *(Smiles: pauses)* Supposing we just stop lying now, huh?

ALLEN: I wasn't sure you knew.

KATZ: What did you think? I was a dope or something? You think I never looked at'm??? You think I'd really let'm walk around *my* streets . . . *my* neighborhood . . . and I was never even gonna' take a little peek?

ALLEN: I shouldn't have come here.

KATZ: Canada? What kinda' crap is *that*?

ALLEN: When they first got married . . . his mother and her new husband . . . that's where they lived.

KATZ: I don't get it. You figure I haven't been put through enough? You figure it's okay to just come around here . . . play a little one-on-one with me . . . for *what*? Can't be to find out what I know, 'cause he's already been tried and found guilty! The law's done exactly what the law's gonna' do Your son killed my father and my father's buried deader than a doornail and your son's probably playin' stickball right this minute . . . feeling' no pain and no regrets right?

ALLEN: Right.

KATZ: You see him?

ALLEN: Bobby? Yuh. I saw him.

KATZ: When?

ALLEN: 'Bout an hour ago now . . .

KATZ: And before that?

ALLEN: Six years.

KATZ: You like him?

ALLEN: I hate him, Irving. I've never met a kid I hated so much in all my life. The worst is, I see my mother and father's faces on'm . . . and that's the truth of it: that's the worst.

KATZ: He looks just like you. Spitting image.

ALLEN: What I came to do is to offer you the chance to get even.

KATZ: *(Flashes gun)* With this?

ALLEN: *(Nods)* Mmmm.

KATZ: You want me to kill your son?

ALLEN: Me.

KATZ: Huh?

ALLEN: I want you to kill *me*. Father for father.

KATZ: *(After a pause)* Too late. *(Smiles)* You're already dead. *(Pauses)* I got a different plan . . .

ALLEN: Give it to me, then . . .

KATZ: Stay back. *(Aims gun at Allen, who pauses)* What the hell am I doing? That's what you're after! *(Points gun at himself)* Stay back or I'll shoot myself. *(Looks up at Allen)* I don't *want* to shoot myself! *(Aims gun at sky; fires five rounds)* Empty. *(Drops gun)* You ready to play?

ALLEN: I . . .

KATZ: That was a question.

ALLEN: I . . .

KATZ: *(Screams) That . . . was . . . a . . . question!!!*

ALLEN: *(Nods)* Mmmm.

KATZ: Then let's go, old man. Let's hit it.

(Katz moves to the halfcourt line and faces Allen) I've been holding back on you a little, Mr. Allen, 'count 'a I didn't actually know if you knew. You knew. No reason to hold back any more, is there?

ALLEN: Irving, you've got to understand why I looked you up . . .

KATZ: You playin' ball, or what?

ALLEN: If I had money, I would give it to you . . . all of it . . .

KATZ: *(Throws ball to Allen)* Touch!

ALLEN: *(Throwing back ball, reflexively)* You got'ta' understand that when I saw Bobby last, he was eight. That's all: eight! *(Katz dribbles past Allen and scores)*

KATZ: Nineteen. Two to go . . .

ALLEN: His mother let us both down . . . I was on the road . . . I don't blame her, but . . .

KATZ: You're pathetic . . . *(Allen looks at him)* Touch! *(Allen catches the ball)* I use'ta' have dreams about you . . . I use'ta see you playin' in my dreams. I'd be down in the front seats . . . of the press row, or sittin' on the floor behind the backboard with the *special* kids . . . ya' know . . . kids like Bobby . . . that kind of thing. *(Motions for ball: Allen throws it to him, reflexively)* I once paid ten dollars for one of your cancelled checks, you know that?

ALLEN: Once I knew I was going to . . . you know . . . end it . . . I wanted to offer you the chance . . . to even things up.

KATZ: I sold it two years later for fifteen. It wouldn't be worth a dime now, you know that? Not a dime . . .

ALLEN: I wanted to bring him here with me . . . Bobby . . . so that he could look at you, face to face, man to man, and tell you he was sorry . . .

KATZ: *(Screams)* But he's *not* sorry, you asshole! *He's not sorry!* Do you think he is??? Huh??? HUH??? Do you? Do you??? *Do . . . YOU???*

ALLEN: *(After a pause)* No.

KATZ: I want to play now. I want to finish this game now. I don't want any more talk now. Do you get me?

ALLEN: Irving, you're fourteen . . .

KATZ: I'm *nine*teen! Nineteen, and two to go! Are you ready?

ALLEN: No!

KATZ: Well, *get* ready!

ALLEN: All my life, they treated me like a sideshow freak . . .

KATZ: I bought your old check for ten bucks—what does that make *me?*

ALLEN: Then they toss you out like ashes . . . You scatter . . . You blow around . . . You disappear. I don't want to disappear.

KATZ: Too late for that Mr. Allen . . . I couldn't get a nickel for your autograph now. Nobody would know who you were . . . Too late . . .

(Katz dribbles ball up-court. Allen screams)

ALLEN: No!

(Katz fakes to the left and dribbles right. Allen dives after the ball and falls. Katz looks at the fallen older man and smiles. He stops and watches a moment as Allen weeps, then he drives in to the basket, up and in: scores. Allen stops weeping and faces him)

KATZ: *(Cooly walking to half-court line)* One to go, Mr. Allen. Just one. *(Throws ball to Allen)* Touch.

(Allen catches the ball and stands: his attitude changed, icey. He throws the ball back to Katz, fast and hard)

ALLEN: Come on.

KATZ: I'm comin', pop . . .

(Katz dribbles out: Allen moves in to guard him. Katz fights bravely, but Allen steals the ball, turns, drives, scores)

ALLEN: Nine?

KATZ: Yuh. Twenty to nine . . .

ALLEN: *(Moves to half-court. He throws ball to Katz)* Touch. *(Katz throws it back to Allen, nods. Allen drives, scores. Katz is perspiring)* Ten. *(Throws ball to Katz)* Touch. *(Katz returns ball. Allen moves out, drives, scores)* Eleven . . . Touch . . . *(Allen lopes back to half-court and waits for Katz to throw ball to him. As soon as Katz does, Allen takes it out, leaps, scores)* Twelve . . . *(Allen dribbles to half-court, smiles; throws ball to Katz, who throws it back and nods. Allen dribbles out to Katz, who dives in hard for ball. Allen lifts ball, Katz flies on to his stomach on the ground. Allen waits for Katz to rise and dive for ball again. Katz does. Allen again raises ball, allowing Katz to fall again. Allen walks to basket, dribbling ball slowly in front of him, scores. Katz is weeping. Allen moves to half-court line, Katz rises, faces Allen)*

KATZ: Thirteen . . .

ALLEN: Touch. *(Throws ball to Katz, who whips it straight back to Allen, who takes one step forward, leaps up, shoots a one-hand push shot, scores. Allen then steps back on step to half court line and waits for Katz to retrieve the ball)* Ball. *(Katz turns, walks to ball, picks it up, tosses it to Allen, who tosses it straight back, wordlessly. Katz, in turn, tosses it back to Allen, who drives straight past Katz and scores again)*

ALLEN: Twenty-fifteen.

KATZ: Let's go . . . *(Allen and Katz face each other, as Katz fights for the ball. He succeeds in stopping Allen's drive, but Allen turns suddenly and shoots a smooth hook shot, bouncing the ball not near the basket, but instead violently off the backboard proper, causing the ball to bounce straight back to Allen, who turns quickly around, catches the ball and shoots an easy one-hand push shot. A startled Katz watches, mouth dropped open, eyes wide)*

ALLEN: Sixteen. *(Allen retrieves ball, jogs back to halfcourt line, smiles. He tosses ball to Katz, who touches it with a slap and tosses it back to Allen)*

KATZ: Go!

ALLEN: Nervous?

KATZ: Yuh. Sure. You bet. Let's go, okay?

ALLEN: Yuh. Sure. You bet. Okay . . . *(Allen dribbles ball out, slowly. Katz moves in front of him, cautiously. Katz suddenly lunges and steals the ball. Allen rolls between Katz and the basket. Katz leaps to make a jump shot. Allen leaps to guard the shot. Katz does not shoot, but instead holds the ball, committing a "traveling" penalty. Wordlessly, Katz tosses the ball back to Allen and play resumes. Allen moves back to the halfcourt line, tosses the ball to Katz, who touches same and tosses it back to Allen, who nods and begins his move forward again, toward the basket. Katz tries the identical lunge and fake that worked before. This time, Allen lifts the ball, Katz stumbles through and Allen rolls to his left, drives in to the basket, shoots: scores)*

KATZ: *DAMMIT!*

ALLEN: *(Smiles)* Nice try.

KATZ: Thanks.

ALLEN: Good move.

KATZ: Right. Thanks.

ALLEN: Just shouldn't try it twice in a row . .

KATZ: Yuh. Right.

ALLEN: Seventeen. Four to go . . . *(Tossess ball to Katz)* Touch. *(Katz returns ball)* Thanks. *(Allen nods, steps forward, shoots, scores, nods, tosses ball to Katz)* Touch. *(Katz bows his head, weeps. Allen looks at him)* You want to stop?

KATZ: *God damn you! God . . . damn . . . you!!!*

ALLEN: You didn't answer me, Katz. Do you want to stop?

KATZ: What for?

ALLEN: Call it a draw?

KATZ: *(Throws ball violently to Allen)* Eighteen, you: twenty, me. Play!

ALLEN: Okay . . . *(He steps forward and shoots an easy long one-hand push shot that swishes in for a score)* Nineteen. Ball, please? *(Katz turns and retrieves ball. He bounces it to Allen)*

KATZ: You ever play with your son?

ALLEN: With Bobby? *(Pauses)* Not too much, no.

KATZ: He's not too much, sportswise, is he?

ALLEN: I don't know. I haven't seen him much . . . He was smoking cigarettes, I guess. Drugs, probably . . . *(Pauses)* Naw, he's not too much, sportswise. I guess that's true . . .

KATZ: Kinda' strange, isn't it? His father being who he is: you . . . all that . . . you'd figure he'd be more than he is . . . sportswise.

ALLEN: Maybe that's the way it is, with fathers and sons . . . Maybe that's just natural.

KATZ: What did *your* father do? For a living, I mean . . .

ALLEN: Yuh. I see what you mean.

KATZ: Huh?

ALLEN: I said I see what you mean.

KATZ: You didn't answer me.

ALLEN: What he did?

KATZ: Yuh.

ALLEN: I figured you knew.

KATZ: Why would I ask then?

ALLEN: He coached junior high basketball.

KATZ: Yuh. You were right. I knew.

ALLEN: He wasn't *my* coach.

KATZ: How come?

ALLEN: He wasn't alive . . . when I started playing . seriously.

KATZ: How'd he die?

ALLEN: You know something, Irving? The relationship of father and son isn't exactly *planned*. I mean, I didn't *pick* Bobby. He was what *came along*.

KATZ: You believe that?

ALLEN: Yuh, I believe that. I know guys I've played with . . . pro players . . . their sons are decent . . . some of them play ball . . . some of them don't . . . But they're not all ashamed of their fathers, ya' know. And plenty of them are divorced, too!

KATZ: The sons? Divorced? Early isn't it? Little kids getting divorced? Sounds strange. Weird.

ALLEN: I always heard Jews had the brains . . .

KATZ: Yuh. You got it. Brains, money and big noses: that s what we've got . . .

ALLEN: I've never met a kid as smart as you are. That's a fact.

KATZ: How's my game?

ALLEN: Pro-level potential.

KATZ: How do I rate against *you* at age fourteen?

ALLEN: Even.

KATZ: I'll have to work harder . . .

ALLEN: It must have been something for you, huh? When your father . . . died. It must really taken the wind out of your sails.

KATZ: I don't have sails.

ALLEN: Three years now, right?

KATZ: Four years, four months, six days . . *(Looks at watch)* . . . six hours. *(Looks at Allen)* I don't think about it much. What the hell, right? The worms crawl in, the worms crawl out. What's to think about?

ALLEN: What's your mother like?

KATZ: Nice. What's your's like? *(Pauses)* You lookin' to set up a trade or somethin'?

ALLEN: Were you real close with your father?

KATZ: You gonna' play, or you losing your nerve?

ALLEN: Were you?

KATZ: What's goin' on here, huh? Is this a game, or what?

ALLEN: Where you?

KATZ: He was thirty-eight; fat; never even watched sports on television, let alone play them. He went to work at seven in the morning and he came home around ten at night. I'd wait up every night just to hear him say "What's'a matter with you, Irving? It's ten'a'clock and you got school t'morrow? You wanna' end up sellin' black bean soup like your father? You wanna' end up cryin' day and night like your mother?" *(Looks at Allen, smiles)* My mother has emotional problems. She cries a lot. Since my father got shot in the neck, she only cries from seven in the morning 'til ten at night. She use'ta go 'round the clock. She's getting better. *(Pauses)* I don't wanna' end up with the black bean soup and I don't wanna' end up cryin' round the clock . . . and I don't wanna' end up like you. I don't like any of the choices here . . . *(Pauses)* I use'ta' wanna' end up like you. That's a fact.

ALLEN: You're your own man, Irving.

KATZ: *(Interrupting sharply)* I'm my own birdturd, Irving! *OOOOooooo!!!* How come you turned out ta' be such a nothing, huh? How come you turned out ta' be such a *whining nothin'! OOOOOoooooo-Ooooooo!!!* You got all the yah-tah-duh yah-tah-duh *sincere* crap look in your eyes, like I'm s'pose'ta' feel *sorry for you!* Bad break, huh? Your game just sort'a fell to nothin', right? I'm s'pose'ta feel sorry for that! Your lunatic son empties a gun into my father's neck and gets to walk around the neighborhood like he's a hero and I'm some sorta' jerk for havin' no father and *you* want *me* to feel sorry that *it hurts you!* *(Screams)* I'M SORRYYYYYYYeeeeeee!!! *(Softer)* You bet your ass Jews are smarter. I just wish we were *taller,* that's the truth. Then we'd have it all! *ALL! (There is a short silence during which the two men look at one another. Katz breaks the silence, softly)*

KATZ: *(Attitude changes)* I wanna' finish this game now, okay? *(Throws ball to Allen)* Your move. *(Allen nods. He starts out with the ball, fades to his left and intentionally knocks ball toward Katz, who catches it and tosses it back to Allen, fiercely)* Don't you ever—*ever*—boot a ball in my direction, pal. I got my points on you *straight* and I'm gonna' beat you straight. *You . . . hear . . . me?* Shoot! *(Allen pauses, aims, shoots, hits)*

ALLEN: Even up.

KATZ: *(Softly)* Yuh.

ALLEN: You wanna' throw fingers ta' see who takes it out? *(Pauses)* Counta' it's tied and my height advantage and all . . .

KATZ: *(Softly)* I wouldn't mind.

ALLEN: Throw two out ta' three?

KATZ: *(Nods)* Call it.

ALLEN: Odds.

KATZ: Once, twice, three, shoot! *(They do)* Mine. Once, twice, three, shoot! *(They do)* I'll take it out. *(Katz dribbles the ball to the halfcourt line. He offers the ball to Allen)* Touch.

ALLEN: Ready. *(Allen tosses the ball back to Katz, one bounce. Katz holds the ball in one hand, wipes his other hand on his pantleg; then switches hands and wipes the other hand; then his brow. Then he places his hair behind his ears; he nods. Katz dribbles the ball out and fakes left. Allen rolls with him. Katz rolls quickly right: Allen drifts off-balance. Katz charges around and straight to a point underneath the basket. He could easily sink a basket, but he doesn't. Instead, he faces Allen)*

KATZ: *(He tosses the ball to Allen, starts to exit. Stops)* I changed my mind. I don't wanna' win this way. I wanna' win it straight. I don't want you spottin' me no fifteen points . . . no five, or nothin', really. I wanna' win it straight . . . start it even. *(Pause)* I'll give you a rematch exactly ten years from now, okay? *(Pauses)* I'll be taller. *(Allen tosses the ball to him. He tosses it straight back at Allen)* Keep it. Practice. The more you practice, the better you get. Two steps backwards, closer to exit) I'll be twenty-four. Right here. June 5th [*N.B. insert date of performance here in place of June 5th, except on June 5th.*] . . . 2 o'clock . . . *(Pauses)* You ought to wear better shoes. You won't slip so much . . . *(Two more steps backwards: edge of stage)* You won't forget, okay? *(Allen stares at Katz)* You'll be here, right? *(Allen nods agreement)* You got it.

(Katz turns and exits. Allen bows his head a moment. Silence. Allen looks at basketball in his hands. He moves to a position under the net. He tosses in a lay-up. He looks at the ball in his hands. He tosses in another lay-up, catches the ball as it passes out of the net, and tosses in another lay-up. Slowly, at first: the rhythm of Allen's hops, shots, catches and hops increases until it is machinelike: perfect. He moans a long low moan, softly at first, growing increasingly sonorous. All sound stops: the shots continue. He hops, lays the ball in the basket—one bounce off the backboard each time—catches the ball as it passes through the net, hops; starts it all again. Except for the sound of the ball against the backboard and its passing through the hoop and net, and the sound of Allen's movement and breathing, there is silence all around. The lights fade out.)